# SUSANNA:

## *The Mother of the Wesleys.*

# SUSANNA:

## The Mother

### of the

### Wesleys

By the Reverend John Kirk

LONDON:

HENRY JAMES TRESIDDER, AVE MARIA LANE.

1864.

# Contents

# PREFACE

MORE than a hundred and twenty years have passed away since Susanna Wesley entered into rest. Her name has been everywhere received with respect; and by a large and influential Christian Community it has been cherished with strongest affection. Her success in the education of her children has been the theme of universal admiration; and no one has yet ventured to hazard even a conjecture as to how much the cause of religion and the well-being of the human race are indebted, under the Divine blessing, to her steady piety and extraordinary talents. The numerous biographies of her sons; all the histories of Methodism; and a number of periodicals have contained brief, and in some instances very able sketches of her character. But up to this hour, no volume worthy to be called a memorial of her has issued from the press.

The following pages are an attempt to supply, in some small degree, this remarkable deficiency. The plan upon which they are written aims to make Mrs Wesley the central figure, around which the persons and incidents associated with the narrative may be appropriately grouped. The chronological order of arrangement has, therefore, been entirely disregarded, except where it could be rendered subservient to the main design. But in order to guide the reader to the time to which the leading facts should be referred, the proper dates have generally been inserted in connexion with the most important events.

Had I been disposed to dwell upon the various historical facts comprehended in the period of the narrative, the work would have been largely increased in size. I have, therefore, contented myself with an occasional glance at the side-lights of general history, and that only when it was absolutely necessary. If, however, it should be thought that, here and there, "like a purple beech among the greens," there is an occasional paragraph, which, at first sight, "looks out of place," I should not be at all surprised. My only hope is, that the irrelevant passages may, in themselves, be worthy of the reader's attention.

In the preparation of the volume I have sought information from every available source, as far as it has been known to me. The valuable documents contained in Clarke's "Wesley Family;" the parish Registers in the different places where the persons connected with the narrative resided; the contemporary literature of the period; and various denominational Magazines, have all been freely laid under contribution. Had I wished to crowd the foot of every page with references to authorities, I have had ample opportunities for so doing. But as they would have been disregarded by the great majority of readers whom I had chiefly in view, such references have been introduced but sparingly. I have not, however, made any statement of facts without a careful comparison of authorities; and if necessary, they can easily be produced. I have also had the advantage of making free use of two valuable collections of unpublished documents connected with the Wesley Family. By this means a new light has been thrown upon several important incidents connected with family-life at Epworth. To George Morley, Esq., of Leeds, and Mr John Wesley of London, I tender my most hearty thanks for the generous manner in which they allowed me access to these deeply interesting documents. My warmest acknowledgments are also due to the Rev. William B. Pope, and another friend whose name I must not mention, for very valuable aid in the revision of the sheets as they passed through the press, to the Rev. William M. . Punshon, A.M., for placing in my hands the manuscript of his eloquent Lecture on "Wesley and his Times;" to the Rev. William Beal for much important information; and to the Revs. John P. Lockwood, John Mason, Richard Smailes, and several other friends who have, in various ways, supplied me with kindly counsel and help. I must now bid farewell to a task, which has afforded many hours of pleasant and profitable study. Whether this humble memorial of Susanna Wesley shall meet with a favourable reception from the Christian Community or not, I feel that in its preparation I have received the reward of my toil.

The words of Doctor Clarke, to whose volumes all subsequent writers on these topics must be deeply indebted, most appropriately express my own emotions:—"I have traced her life with much pleasure, and received from it much instruction; and when I have seen her repeatedly grappling with gigantic adversities, I have adored the grace of God that was in her, and have not been able to repress my tears."

—LONDON, February 1864.

## PREFACE TO THE SECOND EDITION.

I CANNOT refrain from expressing my gratitude for the favourable manner in which the following pages were received on their first publication. A large edition, comprising more than two thousand copies, was disposed of in six months. This far surpassed any expectations of success, which I had ever allowed myself to indulge. It is, also, a great satisfaction to know that the statements and conclusions of the book, though sometimes differing from those of previous writers, have been generally accepted as correct. In the present edition, one paragraph in the last chapter, the result of more definite information, has been substituted for another, and a few slight corrections have been made in other places. With these exceptions, this second edition is substantially a reprint of the first.

_____

## SIGNIFICANT DATES IN THE LIFE OF SUSANNA WESLEY

| 20 January 1669 | Birth | London. |
|---|---|---|
| 1681 | Conversion | |
| 12 Nov. 1688 | Marriage to Samuel Wesley. | |
| | Samuel is curate at St. Botolph, Aldersgate, London (about a year.) | |
| 1689 | Samuel is chaplain on a British ship for about six months. | |

7

| | |
|---|---|
| 10 Feb. 1690 | Samuel, first child, born at Annesley home in London. |
| 1690 | Samuel is curate at Newington Butts, Surrey, for nearly a year. |
| Summer 1691 | Samuel is rector at South Ormsby, Lincolnshire. |
| 17 June 1703 | Birth of John, later founder of Methodism. |
| 1705 | Samuel jailed in Lincolncastle, superficially for debt, intensified by a political grudge. |
| 9 Feb. 1708/9 | Fire destroys Epworth rectory; family saved, but all possessions (including her father's literary remains, lost. |
| 1711/12 | Susanna holds controversial Sunday evening services in the rebuilt rectory while Samuel attends convocation in London. |
| Dec. 1716 | |
| Jan. 1717 | Poltergeist incident in the Epworth rectory. |
| Circa 1724 | Nearby parish of Wroot given to Samuel Sr.; family occasionally lives there. |
| 28 Apr. 1735 | Death of Samuel Wesley, Sr. forces Susanna to vacate rectory. |
| By Nov. 1735 | Moves to nearby Gainsborough with daughter Emilia. |
| Sep. 1736 | Moves to Tiverton, Devon, with Samuel Jr. |
| Jul. 1737 | Moves to Wooton, Wiltshire, near Marlborough And afterward to Fisherton, near Salisbury, with the Halls (daughter Martha and son-in-law Westley. |
| Apr. 1739 | Moves with the Halls to London. |
| Late 1739 | Moves to the Foundery, son John's newly acquired Methodist headquarters. |
| 30 Jul. 1742 | Death at the Foundery, London. |
| 1 Aug. 1742 | Burial, Bunhill Fields, City Road, London. |

NOTE: The names of the Wesley daughters may be a bit confusing, considering they often had nicknames.

Emilia was often called "Emily." Susanna is referred to as "Sukey." Mary was called "Molly." Mehetabel was "Hetty." Anne was called "Nancy." Martha was "Patty" or "Pat." And finally, Kezzia was called "Kezzy."

# I. PARENTAGE.

Children's children are the crown of old men;
And the glory of children are their fathers.
—PROVERBS OF SOLOMON.

"MONICA is better known by the branch of her issue than the root of her parentage." This characteristic saying of Fuller applies with far greater force to Susanna Wesley than to the mother of Augustine. Like that "branch of the Lord" under whose fostering shade it sprang up and flourished, the branch of her issue is, indeed, "beautiful and glorious." It has become so lofty and widespread in its spiritual renown as to overshadow completely the root of her illustrious parentage. Her ancestry may be traced up to an early period of our country's history. Some of them, it is believed, could boast patrician blood, and occasionally filled important stations in the Commonwealth; while others rejoiced in a nobility far higher than that of birth, or wealth, or station, —the nobility of personal godliness and filial relation to Him who is "Lord of all."

Her Father, according to the old Baptismal Register, A. still preserved, was (sic) "Samuell the sonne of John Anslye, and Judith his wife." Warwickshire, renowned for its undaunted earls; the home of Perkins and Byfield among our divines, of Drayton and Shakespeare among our poets, was the shire of his nativity. There is, however, considerable difference among the authorities as to the precise locality of his birth. Williams, who preached his funeral sermon, says he was born at Killingworth; and he is followed by Whitehead and Moore; but as there is no such place in the county, this must be a mistake. Another of his biographers fixes upon Kenilworth; but there is no evidence in favour of the supposition that he first saw the light in that romantic spot, so crowded with historical associations, and immortalised by Walter Scott in his fascinating romance.

9

Clarke, in his "Wesley Family," says he was born at Haxeley; and this is a little nearer the truth, at least in sound. Four miles north-west of Warwick there is a small village called Haseley, comprising about forty houses, and two hundred and fifty inhabitants. In the days of William the Conqueror, the manor was certified to contain "three hides and half a virgate of land; a church, and a mill; and the ancient woods belonging thereto, extending a mile in length and two furlongs in breadth." Here, in the ancient church, dedicated to Saint Mary, and still standing, young Annesley was baptized on March 27, 1620. He was, therefore, in all likelihood, born within the limits of this parish, if not in the village itself Numbering among his relatives some who "feared the Lord and thought upon His name," many and fervent prayers were offered on his behalf, even before he was born. His aged grandmother, who passed to her reward shortly before his birth, desired as her last request that, if his mother should bring forth a man-child, his name should be called Samuel; because "she had asked him of the Lord." The only son of his mother, and his father dying when he was about four years old, he was reared with tender and godly solicitude. The most careful attention was paid to his early religious training. His opening mind soon indicated seriousness beyond his years. His anxiety to prepare himself for some useful service, forcibly reminds us of Milton's beautiful description of the "Holy Child Jesus:"—

> "When I was yet a child, no childish play
> To me was pleasing; all my mind was set
> Seriously to learn and know, and thence to do,
> What might be public good."

From the moment of his birth, his parents, in solemn vows and prayers, had consecrated him to the Lord "for the work of the ministry." The thought of this "high calling," as the momentous destiny of his life, early took full possession of his own breast. While yet young, and when most boys would be quietly plodding through the mere elements of secular learning, he was ardently reading twenty chapters a-day out of the Holy Book,—a practice continued to the end of life, -that he might

10

equip himself, as quickly and well as possible, for the faithful ministration of the everlasting Gospel. With him, this preparation was no boyish pastime, no Sabbath amusement in the interval of worship; but a sacred resolve in the fear of God, from which he never swerved in after life. Dreams of discouragement, and even of martyrdom for "the Word of God and the Testimony of Jesus," sometimes haunted his night visions; but they failed to shake his noble purpose. Daniel De Foe, who knew him well, sat under his ministry, and held him in highest regard, summarises these facts of his early history in an elaborate elegy:—

"His parents dedicated him by vow
To serve the Church, and early taught him how.
As Hannah, when she for her Samuel prayed,
The welcome loan with thankfulness repaid;
So they, foreseeing 'twould not be in vain,
Asked him of God and vowed him back again:
And he again as early did prepare
To list a willing soldier in the sacred war.

His pious course with childhood he began,
And was his Maker's sooner than his own.
As if designed by instinct to be great,
His judgment seemed to antedate his wit:
His soul outgrew the natural rate of years,
And full-grown wit and half-grown youth appears;
Early the vigorous combat he began,
And was an older Christian than a man.
The sacred study all his thoughts confined,—
A sign what secret Hand prepared his mind,—
The Heavenly Book he made his only school,
In Youth his study and in Age his rule."

During his college course at Oxford,—remarkable for temperance and hard-working industry, rather than peculiar aptitude for learning, or distinguished success, -the conviction of his call to the ministry continued in unabated force. In due time he realised the dearest wish of his heart; and towards the

11

close of 1643, or the beginning of 1644, he was solemnly ordained to the sacred office, probably according to the Presbyterian form.

[The dates here appear to be in great confusion. Calamy gives a certificate of ordination, signed by seven ministers, and dated December 18, 1644. It states that Annesley was ordained to act as chaplain on board the Globe. This is a month after his first signature appears in the Register as rector of Cliffe. Calamy immediately goes on to say that he went to sea in 1648. Still he was at Cliffe in 1650, according to the Register. Was he at sea with the Earl of Warwick from August to December 1648, according to Calamy, while he still held the living of Cliffe?]

Some assert that immediately after ordination "he began to cast his net, as a fisher of men," in the exercise of a chaplaincy on board a man-of-war; but of this we fail to discover satisfactory evidence. In November 1644, we find his signature in the parish Register of Cliffe, in Kent, into which valuable living he had recently been "intruded;" and this was probably his first settled charge." Here he had to encounter the most violent opposition. If we may trust the account in his funeral sermon, the parishioners, accustomed to a jovial parson, "who greatly delighted them by his company at their dancing, drinking, and merriments on the Lord's Day," and most likely chafed at his removal by the hand of authority, were not prepared to welcome peacefully a minister who would set his face as a flint against all this "rioting and drunkenness." They hailed him to his new parish with "spits, forks, and stones," and many times threatened his life. This was a rough beginning for a young divine "not much above twenty." But his moral courage quailed not before the howling tempest. His dauntless answer to these rude greetings was truly noble and heroic. "Use me as you will, I am resolved to continue with you until God has fitted you, by my ministry, to entertain a better, who shall succeed me. Then, when you are so prepared, I will leave you." By his holy life, kindliness of heart, and ministerial fidelity, the storm of opposition was soon hushed. The enmity of these furious spirits "was changed into a passionate kindness." The moral wilderness, so arid and noxious when he commenced his labours of spiritual husbandry, "rejoiced and blossomed as the

12

rose." The beauties of the spiritual landscape, "as a field which the Lord had blessed," blended in exquisite harmony with the surrounding loveliness of "the Garden of England." When Annesley came upon the stage of public life, the national quarrel between Royalist and Parliamentarian was rapidly reaching its height. It was almost impossible for any public man, or any prominent minister of religion, to hold a neutral position in relation to the two great parties striving for the mastery. While he held the living of Cliffe, he was called, in due form, to preach before the House of Commons, in 1648. The nation was in a frenzy of excitement. The King was a prisoner in the Isle of Wight. The Lower House had predominant sway. The custom of the times all but imperatively demanded that these official discourses should make allusion to the leading questions of the day, and Annesley followed the ordinary course. His sermon, as published by order of the House of Commons, contains a very unfortunate passage in relation to the King. Speaking of the conduct of the Israelites in demanding a monarch as their ruler, he says,—"The people are now, as then, 'We will have a King!" He hearkens to the people, and sets the king upon his throne. They shout out "*Vivat* " Surely they are now happy! He reigns over them one year well; two years indifferent. What then? You see the Scripture veils. I waive it. What he did in the business of Amalek, Gibeon, David, Abimelech; what wars, famine, cruelty Israel lay under, I would rather you should read than I speak. God give the King a spirit of grace and government! 'Woe unto thee, O land, when thy King is a child!' is rather meant of a child in manners, than in years." This passage, so acceptable to the Parliamentary party, was intensely offensive to the Royalists, who regarded it as a reflection upon the King. Even some of Annesley's biographers have accepted it as full proof that he "went all the lengths of the Presbyterian party." The passage is mischievous in its very vagueness, apparently hinting at far more than it expresses. But, while it clearly indicates his disapproval of some parts of the King's conduct, it by no means proves that the writer held republican principles, or abetted and approved the measures which brought the unfortunate monarch to the scaffold. If his own testimony in later life is to be relied upon, he publicly

13

disapproved that deed of blood; and his maturer principles were far nearer allied to those of the Royalists, than of the men of the Commonwealth. In a petition, addressed to Charles the Second immediately after the Restoration, and still preserved in the State Paper Office, he alleges that he "publicly detested the horrid murder" of the late King: that he "refused the engagement," and persuaded others against it; that he "peremptorily refused to send out a horse against" His Majesty at Worcester; that he sent "a man all night above forty miles to seize upon the keys of the church, and prevent one that would, against his consent, have kept the Day of Thanksgiving for their success at Worcester;" that he had several times said "to some of note in the army, that God would discover Cromwell to be the worst hypocrite that ever the Church of Christ was pestered with, for he would pull down others only to make his own way to the throne." He declares that, "upon these and other expressions of disliking the Powers then uppermost, to whom complaint was made," he was "necessitated to quit a parsonage worth between two and three hundred pounds per annum, and get into the least parish in London, without any other title besides the choice of the people." Now, unless we are prepared to impeach Annesley's sincerity and truthfulness, and to regard him, as he regarded Cromwell, as one of the "arrantest hypocrites that ever the Church of God was pestered with," we must accept this as a frank and honest statement of his views and conduct in relation to the events to which it refers. This petition also enables us to trace one or two matters in the Doctor's personal history, which hitherto have not been very clear. Calamy and others say that he left Cliffe in consequence of his pledge to remove as soon as the inhabitants were prepared for the ministry of a worthier man than himself. But he declares that he was "necessitated" to remove as the result of his disapproval of the "horrid murder" of Charles, and other manifestations of royalist views in opposition to the dominant will. This probably explains the "remarkable providence" which "led him to London," so significantly alluded to, but not stated by his biographers. These facts disclose additional reasons why his parishioners were so deeply afflicted at his departure. Not only had he been a priceless blessing to their souls, and won

14

their strongest affection; but the tender relation was severed by a rude necessity laid upon him by the hand of authority. Amid "many tears and cries," and a thousand other tokens of heart-felt love, he walked forth from among his beloved flock, probably not knowing what might befall him. The "smallest parish in London," mentioned in the petition, was probably that of Saint John the Evangelist, clustering around the ancient edifice in Friday Street, Cheapside, where he zealously laboured six or seven years.

In July 1657 Cromwell, who, according to the petition already quoted, had twice refused to present him to a valuable living of four hundred a-year, when nominated by the proper patron, sent for Annesley, and, "to cover his base injustice," gave him the Lord's Day evening Lecture at Saint Paul's, with "a salary of a hundred and twenty pounds per annum, out of the four hundred pounds per annum formerly settled by Parliament for that and a week-day Lecture." This emolument he was afraid of losing at the Restoration, and therefore petitioned Charles for its continuance. The first answer, July 21, 1660, declared "His Majesty's pleasure" that the "petitioner might continue in the said Lecture; but for the salary, His Majesty knows nothing of it, nor is obliged to pay it." Soon after, an additional answer discharged him from his duty, on the ground, that "the said pretended Lecture" was incumbent upon the Dean and Chapter, who were commanded to "take charge thereof as heretofore." On the twentieth of October, 1658, by the favour of Richard Cromwell, "Cripplegate was made glad by his settlement therein." This gladness, however, was not universal. After the Restoration, some of the parishioners forwarded a petition for his removal. They allege that Charles the First had "conferred the said vicarage on Doctor Bruno Ryves, Dean of Chichester;" but "by reason of the late troubles, the said Doctor Ryves could not enjoy the benefit of His Majesty's gracious favour," nor they "the benefit of his labours, to the great grief and sorrow of their hearts. So at present one Doctor Annesley doth possess the said vicarage, contrary to the votes and desires of most of the inhabitants, . . . . pretending to be settled upon us by a grant from the late Tyrant, or his son." They therefore prayed his removal and the appointment of Doctor Ryves, "that so numerous a people may not any longer be left destitute of an orthodox and godly divine, to instruct them in all the ways of godliness and loyalty." We are not disposed to attach more importance to these representations, as against Annesley, than they are really worth. In charging him, by implication, with heterodoxy, and lack of godliness and loyalty, they do him a serious and unmerited wrong. If there be any truth in the petition, he suffered himself to be imposed upon the parish by Richard Cromwell in spite of the opposition of some of the inhabitants. The oppositionists did not gain their end. Annesley was confirmed in the living, and continued his useful labours until August 1662. Now came a memorable epoch in the history of the Church of England, and a terrible crisis in the families of two thousand of her most godly ministers. The Act of Uniformity, requiring every clergyman to declare, among other things, his "unfeigned assent to all and everything contained and prescribed in " the Book of Common Prayer, on pain of losing all his emoluments, and being prohibited preaching or lecturing in any place, passed the legislature early in 1662. Then began "great searchings of heart" among the men against whom it was notoriously levelled. Who can imagine the struggle between the varied and tender influences pleading on the side of compliance, and the stern convictions of conscience, which prompted to a stout resistance? Happy social intercourse; the village home; the rural walk, so full of pleasant memories; the venerable church, hallowed by the recollection of its blessed services; and, above all, the beloved flocks, whose thought these Pastors had educated, whose moral and spiritual sensibilities they had quickened and matured, must all be given up. It was a sad wrench from all they held dear, except the priceless blessing of "a good conscience." Then loomed up before them the prospect of silent Sabbaths; public reproach; years of homelessness; and life passing away with little of that fruit which, in the estimation of such men, alone endues it with the greatest sweetness and value." VAUGHAN'S Memorial Volume.

On August 17, "nearly two thousand" of these noble men addressed their congregations for the last time within the walls of National Churches. Among the holiest and best of this large band of confessors, was Samuel Annesley. His relative, Lord

Anglesea, then in high favour with the ruling powers, used efforts to induce him to conform, and probably offered him high preferment if he remained in the Establishment. But he would not yield; and at no small cost of feeling and money, "he went out, not knowing whither he went." During the ten following years we have no traces of his dwelling-place, except the vague statement that he remained in London. The common informer sometimes tracked his steps with keen and malignant eye; but he escaped being hauled before the judge and cast into prison. "His Nonconformity created him many outward troubles, but no inward uneasiness. God often remarkably appeared for him;" and one magistrate was suddenly struck dead while signing the warrant for his apprehension. Happier days, however, were about to dawn. Early in 1672, the King issued the famous Declaration of Indulgence, proclaiming the suspension of "all manner of penal laws in matters ecclesiastical, against whatever sect of Nonconformists or recusants." Annesley licensed a "Meeting House" in Little Saint Helen's, Bishopsgate Street. He soon gathered a large congregation and a flourishing church. Loving his flock and loved by them in return, during the next quarter of a century he was one of the most attractive, laborious, and useful preachers of his day. His personal appearance was noble and commanding. "Fine figure;" "dignified mien;" "highly expressive and amiable countenance," are the phrases used by his contemporaries. Hardy in constitution and almost insensible to cold, hat, gloves, and top-coat were no necessities to him, even in the depth of winter. The days of "hoare frost" and chilling winds found him in his study, at the top of the house, with open window and empty fire-grate. Temperate in all things, he needed no stimulants, and from his infancy hardly ever drank anything but water. He could endure any amount of active exercise and toil, preaching twice or thrice every day of the week without any sense of weariness. Until the time that the Divine Voice said unto him, "Get thee up and die," his "eye was not dim, nor his natural force abated." While he never swerved from his principles as a Nonconformist, he never offensively obtruded them as matters of noisy contention. When the ablest of Presbyterians, Independents, and Prelatists gathered up their strength and girded on their armour to

17

champion the church-principles of their respective denominations; when Baxter, Bates, and even the "seraphic Howe," left the higher themes of celestial contemplation to mingle in the wordy strife, not one controversial pamphlet issued from Annesley's pen. He was a man of marked prominence among his sect; a very prince in the tribe to which he belonged. He possessed an intellect capable of grasping the leading points of the discussions going on around him. His judgment was apparently clear and serene. The weight of his moral character was beyond all price to his party. He could not be indifferent to his principles, for he had sacrificed seven hundred a year rather than abjure them. How was it, then, that he stood aloof from the all-absorbing strife? There were other themes more congenial to his thoughts, and in the contemplation and enforcement of which he probably believed he could more glorify God, and better serve the spiritual interests of his community. He could walk about Zion, telling the towers thereof, marking well her bulwarks, and considering her palaces; but he felt that his calling was not to labour upon these outer-works of the City of God. The temple and the altar were the place of his ministry. Catching the holy light streaming from the Heavenly Shekinah, keeping the fire of a living love ever burning upon the altar, he bade the worshipping throngs "draw nigh unto God," while he offered "incense and a pure offering."

"How we may attain to love God with all our hearts:" How "we may give Christ a satisfactory account why we attend upon the ministry of the word:" how to "understand the Covenant of Grace:" and how we may enjoy "communion with God,"—these were the sacred casuistries which he was most anxious to discuss and settle for himself and his people. His preaching, consisting largely in what was then called "the solution of cases," was lively, simple, and attractive. De Foe, who speaks of "his taking aspect" and his "charming tongue," gives the following description of his pulpit style —

"The Sacred Bow he so Divinely drew,
That every shaft both hit and overthrew.
His native candour and familiar style,

18

Which did so oft his hearers' hours beguile,
Charmed us with godliness; and while he spake
We loved the doctrine for the teacher's sake.
While he informed us what those doctrines meant,
By dint of practice more than argument,
Strange were the charms of his sincerity,
Which made his action and his words agree."

His liberality was only bounded by the extent of his means. He consecrated a tenth of all his own substance unto the Lord; and was a faithful almoner of many. "The sick, the widows, the orphans were innumerable whom he relieved and settled." The poor looked up to him as a common father. He spent much in the relief of needy ministers, in the education of candidates for holy orders, and in the circulation of Bibles, Catechisms, and profitable books. "O, how many places had sat in darkness," exclaims Williams in his funeral sermon; "how many ministers had been starved, if Doctor Annesley had died thirty-four years since!

The Gospel he even forced into several ignorant places, and was the chief Every day he prayed twice in his family,–and domestic worship was a more extensive service in those days, than now,-and three or four times in his closet. Every extraordinary occurrence in his household was celebrated by a religious fast. Every affliction, "before he would speak of it, or pitch upon any means to redress it," was spread before God in prayer. His supplications "were mighty," and the returns were remarkable and frequent. Though a sensitive and most affectionate husband, grace enabled him calmly to bear the tidings of his wife's death. "The Lord gave, and the Lord hath taken away; blessed be the name of the Lord," was his saintly utterance. Consecrated to God in infancy, he declared he "never knew the time when he was not converted." Need we wonder that the ministry of such a man was greatly honoured of God? Living in the unclouded light of the Divine countenance, and holding unbroken communion with Heaven, his doctrine dropped as the rain, his speech distilled as the dew; "as the small rain upon the tender herb, and as the showers upon the grass." He had "great success. Many called him father, as the

19

instrument of their conversion; and many called him comforter."

Such was Doctor Annesley, the Father of Susanna Wesley. Reserving the description of his last hours for a subsequent chapter, we proceed to consider another inquiry,–Who was Mrs Wesley's Mother? This question has cost us no inconsiderable amount of perplexity and trouble. None of Annesley's biographers even hint at his marriage. With the exception of the venerable William Beal, in a recent edition of his "Wesley Fathers," no writer makes the remotest allusion to the subject of our present inquiry. The omission greatly surprised us; and long was our search in order to supply it. From a careful examination of the Registers at Cliffe, we found that Annesley was married at the time he held that important living. The Baptismal records for 1645, inform us that "Samuel, son of Samuel Annesley, Chief Minister of this Parish of Cliffe, was baptized the thirtieth day of November." There is, also, the entry of his burial in 1650. And in the records of 1646, we read, "Mary, wife of Samuel Annesley, Rector of this Parish, was buried the second day of December: she was buried in the Chancell, at the East end of the great tomb, on the South side." It is clear, however, that this wife of Annesley's youth, and mother of his first-born son, could not be the mother of his daughter Susanna. We next pondered John Wesley's statement, that "her father and grandfather were preachers of righteousness." But this furnished no clue which could lead to any satisfactory results. The promise of success seemed to rise up before us, when we accidentally came upon the following sentence, in a letter of Wesley to his brother Charles — "You know that Mr White, sometime Chairman of the Assembly of Divines, was my grandmother's father." This was the Rev. John White, so long known as "the Patriarch of Dorchester;" "a grave man, yet without moroseness;" "a constant preacher, so that in the course of his ministry he expounded the Scriptures all over, and half over again; " who "absolutely commanded his own passions, and the purses of his parishioners, whom he could wind up to what height he pleased on important occasions." FULLER'S "Worthies of England." But, alas, further search proved that the grandmother to whom Wesley alludes as the daughter of this

20

good man, was the wife of John Westley of Whitchurch, and mother of the rector of Epworth; and not the consort of Samuel Annesley, or the mother of his daughter Susanna. Foiled at every step, and about to give up all further effort, a friend directed our attention to a curious old folio, entitled, "A Complete History of the Most Remarkable Providences, both of Judgment and Mercy, which have happened in this present age." There, in the middle of a chapter of curious epitaphs, we read,— "The following Epitaph was written upon the tombstone of John White, Esquire; a member of the House of Commons in the year 1640, and Father of Doctor Annesley's wife, lately deceased,—

'Here lies a John, a burning, shining light,
Whose Name, Life, Actions all alike were WHITE.'"

The book was published by Dunton, Annesley's son-in-law; and the statement may, therefore, be relied upon, as he was a careful collector of facts, and, from his close connexion with the family, had every means of knowing the truth. According to Clarendon, this John White was "a grave lawyer, and made a considerable figure in his profession." The borough of Southwark elected him as their representative to the Long Parliament, in 1640. A Puritan from his youth, he was very decided in his religious principles, and took an active part in the ecclesiastical controversies of the times. He was an active member of the Assembly of Divines; Chairman of the "Committee for Plundered Ministers;" and, of course, a strong witness against Archbishop Laud on his important trial. He published the "Century of Scandalous Malignant Priests;" and, in the opinion of Whitelock, "was an honest, learned, and faithful servant of the public, though somewhat severe at the Committee for Plundered Ministers." He died in January 1644, and was buried in the Temple Church with great ceremony, the members of the House of Commons attending his funeral. The reader will not fail to observe the somewhat remarkable coincidences here disclosed between the great-grandfathers of the Founder of Methodism. They bore the same Christian and surname. They were both eminent in their respective

21

professions; the one in the Gospel, the other in the Law. Both were members of the far-famed Westminster Assembly of Divines; both held high positions, the one in the Church, the other in the State; and both were thoroughly attached to their religious principles. If, therefore, there be anything in an ancestry which combines learning, respectability and godliness on both sides, John Wesley may certainly claim a true nobleness of descent. The daughter of John White, the "grave lawyer" and earnest and respectable Puritan, was probably married to Samuel Annesley about the time of his removal to London, in 1652. The few dim intimations concerning her which have turned up in the course of our researches, impress us with the idea that she was a woman of superior understanding, and earnest and consistent piety. She was deeply loved by her husband, who cherished a passionate desire to be buried in her grave. She spared no labour in endeavouring to promote the religious welfare of her numerous children. Her daughter Elizabeth "acknowledges in her papers, found after her death, the good Providence of God in giving her religious parents, that, with united endeavours, took a mighty care of her education." After a somewhat careful study, we have failed to discover any great similarity in the intellectual qualities and predominant character of Susanna Wesley and those of her father. His temperament was sprightly and social; hers thoughtful and reflective. His intellect was ready, rather than profound; hers strong and penetrating. His judgment was somewhat given to waver; hers, when once formed, no earthly influence could shake. Perhaps, if we had the advantage of clearer light, we should find that, unknown as is the mother of Susanna Wesley to the world, from her were inherited those grand qualities of character so much admired in her daughter; and it might possibly be further revealed, that the godly ordering of the family in the Epworth rectory was only a beautiful and blessed imitation of that which prevailed in the house of the Nonconformist minister, under the care of Susanna Wesley's own mother.

# II. GIRLHOOD.

Lady, that in the prime of earliest youth

Wisely hast shunned the broad way and the green,

And with those few art eminently seen,

That labour up the hill of heavenly truth,

The better part with Mary and with Ruth

Chosen thou hast. –MILTON.

"BORN in London!" This, unless you can tell number, street, and nearest main thoroughfare, is the vaguest way in which the birth-place of a mortal can be announced. A rustic hamlet of twenty houses; a solitary homestead on a bleak hill-side, or in the very heart of some heather-purpled moor-land, is a thousand times more preferable as a place of entrance into life, than the widespread wilderness of the British Metropolis. If from some retired spot, you happen to rise in the world of wealth, or weave for yourself a fair wreath of literary renown, or are "had in reputation" for your solid Christian worth in the Church of God, men of after-times will point to your parent home and say, "This man was born there!" But however lofty your subsequent fame, you can add nothing to the glory of the great city, by the fact that you were born within her borders. Thousands have gone on pilgrimage to the house where "the sweet Swan of Avon" entered the world; but who ever saw even a hero-worshipper searching for the home where the Bard of Paradise gave the first signs of life? Are the admirers of Shakespeare more numerous or enthusiastic than the admirers of Milton? The explanation lies in the simple fact, that the one was born in a pretty provincial town; the other was doomed to face the world from a most unpoetic locality called Bread Street,

23

Cheapside. Between Bishopsgate Street and Spital Square lies a short, narrow, obscure yard, which we never pass without a momentary pause and a few pleasurable reflections. The neighbourhood, like many others in the Metropolis, is "very much decayed." But two hundred years ago, the houses, now so strangely altered though not improved by the changes through which they have passed, were the abodes of wealthy and respectable citizens. This is Spital Yard, where Doctor Annesley lived during the time of his pastorate over Little Saint Helens. At the top of one of these houses, probably that which blocks up the lower end of the yard, he had his oratory, where he devoutly read twenty chapters a-day in the Holy Book; in some of these rooms he held conferences with grave divines about the state and prospects of their churches; from one of these door-ways, the mortal remains of himself and his beloved wife passed to their final earthly resting-place. And if the Mother of the Wesleys were not born in one of these very houses, on January 20, 1669, it is certain that here she spent her girlhood and enjoyed her childish pastimes; here the fine qualities of her noble mind were first called into play; here she studied church-controversies, and decided for herself, while yet of tender age; and from hence, accompanied by "the virgins her companions," she went forth out of her chamber, decked in bridal attire, "on the day of her espousals." "How many children has Doctor Annesley?" said a friend to Thomas Manton, who had just consecrated one more to the Lord in the Holy Sacrament of Baptism. "I believe it is two dozen, or a quarter of a hundred," was the startling reply. "This reckoning children by dozens," sagely remarks the eccentric John Dunton, "is a singular circumstance; an honour to which few persons ever arrive." Is it possible to catch a glimpse of this "quarter of a hundred" children of one family, and form some definite idea of the home circle in which Susanna Wesley passed her earliest years? Records largely fail us, and the task can be only partially performed. Many of them, probably, were but "sons of a night," and, like early spring flowers, withered away the moment life's morning sunbeams began to beat upon their head. Others bloomed into youthful beauty; and a few developed into mature life. Besides SAMUEL, the first-born, buried at Cliffe, there was

24

a second son of the same name. Trained for merchandise, he left home, and friends, and wife, for a lucrative situation in far-distant India. There he amassed wealth, made promises to some of his poorer relatives which he never fulfilled; died among strangers; and over the manner of his death, —whether by accident, disease, or violence,—hangs a still unlifted veil of uncertainty. JUDITH, who bears her grandmother's name, is represented as a "virgin of eminent piety;" finding her "sweetest entertainment in good books;" keeping "constant watch over the frame of her soul and the course of her actions, by daily and strict examination of both;" and, finally, rejecting a wealthy lover, whose passion she warmly reciprocated, because she discovered that he was "given to much wine." ANNE was "a wit for certain; than whom art never feigned, nor nature formed a finer woman." Wealth, acquired by marriage, only made her more humble and condescending. Her life was "one continued act of tenderness, wit, and piety."

ELIZABETH, the devout and affectionate wife of Dunton, was "pleasant, witty, and virtuous; mistress of all those graces that can be desired to make a complete woman;" fearing God from her youth, and closing a life of holiness with a death of triumph. When the vital flame began to burn a little dim, she said, "Heaven will make amends for all ! It is but a little while before I shall be happy. I have good ground to hope that when I die, through Christ, I shall be blessed; for I dedicated myself to God from my youth. O what a mercy it is to be dedicated to God betimes!" In carefully examining Dunton's pages, we also catch a glimpse of SARAH, whose name alone survives, and of three other daughters who grew up and entered into the marriage state. And, finally, there is that "grateful and most ingenuous youth" BENJAMIN, the youngest son, and executor to his father's will.

As we have no record of more than three sons, the first of whom died very young, it is probable that the "two dozen, or a quarter of a hundred" children of Doctor Annesley, consisted mainly of the gentler sex. Of this goodly number of fair

25

daughters, Susanna was the youngest. The incidents of her childhood are, for the most part, beyond recall. "Preservation from ill accidents, and once from a violent death," she records among the many loving-kindnesses and tender mercies, which crowned her girlish years. Not the remotest hint of the place and mode of her education has come down to us. Was she sent to school, or placed under tutors at home? Did an elder sister conduct the school-training of the younger ones? Did the good mother, as we are disposed to think, like Susanna herself in later times, make this the chief business of her life? To these questions there is no satisfactory answer. All we positively know is, that she received in early life a thoroughly good education.

It is generally admitted that she had a respectable knowledge of French, and probably read some devotional works in that fashionable tongue, though I have discovered no positive proof of this conjecture. The English language she had thoroughly mastered, and wrote it with marvellous neatness and grammatical accuracy. For clearness, strength, and well-constructed sentences, her writings, though not prepared for the public eye, compare favourably with the most classic English of her times. Logic and metaphysics are commonly supposed to have entered largely into her intellectual training; and her letters and treatises are not without indications that her mind was early familiarised with these abstruse and "unlady-like" studies. We know not whether she excelled in music; whether harp or piano gave forth their dulcet notes in response to her delicate and skilful touch; but there is ample proof that she was not without the accomplishment of song, which she taught to her children and practised in her family. Not content, however, with regarding her as thoroughly educated in the learning and accomplishments considered essential for young ladies of similar station in her times, it has been the favourite idea of all her previous biographers, that she extended her studies to the classics, and was well acquainted with Greek and Latin. But is there not some mistake here? In addition to the antecedent improbabilities of the case, I have diligently searched her writings without discovering a solitary

26

Greek or Latin word, or the remotest hint that she was familiar with these languages, either in earlier or later life. This presumptive argument cannot be set aside by the Supposition, that her own good sense would not allow her to parade her learning in her correspondence. They who knew classics in those times sprinkled their correspondence with learned words and phrases, as well as employed them in conversation. Mrs Wesley was constantly corresponding with sons who had a good knowledge of both Greek and Latin. Her letters related to subjects of a scholastic and theological character, where learned references and quotations would have been perfectly in place. In writing to their father, these young scholars freely interlaid their epistles with Latin and Greek, and sometimes composed them entirely in the former language. But when writing to their Mother, good English is alone employed. This difference seems unaccountable on the supposition that Mrs Wesley possessed the classical attainments so commonly ascribed to her. There is, also, an important passage in one of her husband's letters, unnoticed by previous writers, but which has an important bearing upon the question. When encouraging Samuel, who had just left home for Westminster School, to write very freely about his secret thoughts and temptations, his father says, "I will promise you so much secrecy that even your Mother shall know nothing but what you have a mind she should; for which reason it may be convenient you should write to me still in Latin." What need we any further witness? The advice to write in Latin in order that his Mother, if the letter accidentally fell into her hands, should not be able to understand its meaning, clearly shews that she was ignorant of that ancient language. But do we detract from the just fame of this remarkable woman by supposing she was "no classic?" Certainly not. Make the abatement to the full, and her acknowledged attainments amply prove that, in the best sense of the phrase, she was a well-educated woman. Amidst all this intellectual culture, her domestic training was not overlooked. Many young ladies in our own day are "highly educated;" "thoroughly accomplished." Music, dancing, and song are quite in ballroom and the amenities of elegant society; and this is their sole education. While they are regarded only as

27

"accomplished daughters," these attractive attainments may do very well. But how fares it when they pass from a mother's care to become the head of a domestic establishment, having servants under them? What know they about "those vulgar things" called household matters? Are they not looked upon as a burden and "a bore?" Under their management, instead of a well-ordered house, confusion soon asserts her sway and rules supreme in all domestic matters. This was not the training received by Susanna Annesley. She was as well instructed in the affairs of the kitchen and the servants, as in those of the drawing room and the visitors. As we trace, in subsequent chapters, her consummate management of a large household on very inadequate means, and with often only one servant, the conviction will irresistibly force itself upon us that, in early life, she did not disdain to study and understand every part of woman's domestic duty. She left her father's house thoroughly accomplished in everything necessary for a young lady to know in any household where she might become a wife, a mistress, and a mother. We do not desire the abatement of one jot or tittle in the intellectual education of young ladies; or even in what are commonly known as accomplishments. But we do plead that mothers and daughters should combine the useful with the ornamental; a thorough domestic training with the highest culture of mind and manners their means will allow, and their contemplated station in society require. Then, and only then, will our English homes become such as all right-hearted Englishmen will respect and love,—scenes of order, comfort, and peace. Then will the wife, like Susanna Wesley at Epworth, take her proper place, and reign as queen in her own house. The sceptre of her influence will exert its quiet sway over every department. "The heart of her husband will safely trust in her," because "she looketh well to the ways of her household, and eateth not the bread of idleness." He that findeth such a wife "findeth a good thing," and will declare, "her price is above rubies." It will readily be inferred, that the intellectual powers of Susanna Wesley were of no common order. Her strong and penetrating mind,—perhaps a little too self-confident in these early years,—feared no difficulty. In search of truth, she looked the most formidable objections full in the face. Her attention

28

once aroused to the consideration of a given subject, all its perplexities must be canvassed, and honest conclusions attained on the sole ground of its own merits. Happily her first intellectual efforts were stimulated by good thoughts, and strengthened by wholesome reading. Her mind was no hot-bed of speculative notions and romantic sentimentalisms, forced into unnatural growths by the heated influence of fiction. The three-volume novel, after which young ladies now so deeply sigh, and which they so earnestly devour, is a creation of later times. But had it been in existence, this girl would not have sated her mental appetite with such light and frothy food. She recognises "good books" among the early mercies of her childhood; but we are left to divine what books they were. No doubt they mainly related to experimental and practical religion. The writings of Bunyan, Jeremy Taylor, and many of those precious and godly treatises, which, in that prolific age of theological literature, streamed from the ready pens of the early Puritans, were most likely among her chosen and instructive book-companions. But her mental movements were not limited by this usual circle of female reading. She plunged fearlessly into the troubled stream of theologic controversy, and well-nigh made shipwreck of her faith. Arianism and Socinianism were not uncommon in those times; and her active intellect girded itself for the perilous investigation. This boldness of speculation, in one so young, and on subjects the most sacred and difficult, is not to be commended. It ministers to self-confidence, and often leads to the entire overthrow of belief in Divine Revelation. Mrs Wesley's faith in the leading verities of the Gospel was shaken, and her mind drawn away from the truth. Her wanderings in the terrible wilderness of this deadly heresy were probably not long. Happily, the clue to guide her out of its dangerous labyrinths was found and followed. Samuel Wesley,— most likely at that time her affianced husband,—was a master in this particular controversy, even in early life. While a student in a Dissenting academy, he was employed to translate some of the writings of John Biddle, the father of English Socinianism, "and was promised a considerable gratuity for doing it." But when he discovered the true character of his author, he refused to prosecute the allotted task. This indicates a clear and strong conviction on the important doctrines in dispute; and it was his joy to be the means of Susanna Annesley's rescue. In one of her private meditations, she mentions it among her greatest mercies, that she was "married to a religious orthodox man; by him first drawn off from the Socinian heresy, and afterwards confirmed and strengthened by B. B.,"—most likely Bishop Bull, whose able defences of the evangelical faith were published in the days of her youth. By these means her theological views became thoroughly established. Many passages in her writings contain clear expositions and admirable defences of the great truths concerning the Holy Trinity, the Godhead and atonement of the Lord Jesus, and the Divine Personality and work of the Eternal Spirit. This same independent thinking manifested itself also in relation to another much-disputed question. In her times ecclesiastical controversies lifted up their voice and clamoured for attention. Discussions on forms of church-government ran high. Conformity and Nonconformity were pitted against each other, and courageously championed by the most vigorous of their sons. Such controversies generally make little impression upon the girlish minds of any age. Content to pay becoming attention to "the weightier matters of the law," they are mostly ready to pass by the "mint, and anise, and cummin," and leave purely ecclesiastical questions to the judgment of the other sex. But in this, as in many other respects, Susanna Wesley was an exception to the general rule. The din of the wordy controversy naturally invaded her father's house, and the mind of the quick and thoughtful girl was set in motion. She began to thread her way through the principal parts of this thorny disputation before she was "full thirteen." The result was that, renouncing the ecclesiastical creed of her father, she attached herself henceforth to the communion and services of the Established Church. This act indicates strength of will, as well as strength of thought. If, as Clarke and others represent, she had "examined the whole controversy between the Established Church and the Dissenters," she must have been one of the most industrious readers and precocious logicians the world ever saw. We doubt, however, if her own words, written about her fortieth year, will sustain this representation. Speaking of a

30

treatise she had prepared for her children, and which was unfortunately consumed with the Epworth parsonage, she says, "And because I was educated among the Dissenters, and there was something remarkable in my leaving them at so early an age, not being full thirteen, I had drawn up an account of the whole transaction, under which I had included the main of the controversy between them and the Established Church, as far as it had come to my knowledge." We fail to find in this passage anything to sustain the statement, that she had mastered the whole of this difficult question in her thirteenth year. The reference is to what she had accomplished in the written treatise, rather than to the studies of her youthful days.

The fact remains that, when a mere child, she changed her views on grounds satisfactory to her own mind, and no hindrance was placed in the way of her acting according to her convictions. As we reflect upon this remarkable incident, the question naturally arises, Were there any special circumstances which would explain this singular conduct when everything around her would seem to lead in a different direction ? As her mother and sisters appear to have remained true to the community of her father, there could be no influence from that quarter tending to such a result. Under her parental roof many leading Nonconformist ministers frequently gathered. Discussions on church government no doubt arose; probably "lamentations were sometimes heard concerning the feeble and faithless condition of their churches." To an intelligent and inquisitive child, in a home where religion prevailed, all this might suggest serious inquiry concerning the cause of these lamented evils. Thus stimulated, the girl thought for herself, and the result was a complete change of views."

There is some plausibility in this attempt at a solution. But were there not deeper and tenderer influences at work? Annesley's house was not only the resort of grave and old-established divines, but of young and lively students from the Dissenting academy at Stepney.

Among them was Samuel Wesley, a sprightly intelligent youth, whose after-life became closely linked with that of Susanna Annesley. His attention was directed to this very controversy, and with precisely the same results. He renounced Nonconformity for the forms and ministry of the Establishment. His act of renunciation occurred in 1683, when the subject of our memoir was only a little more than thirteen. The change was, therefore, going on in both minds at the same time, and their conversions were all but contemporaneous. Were these young people on such intimate terms that Samuel confided his doubts to Susanna? In another, and far more important matter, we have seen that young Wesley's influence led her to abandon her dangerous leanings to heretical principles in doctrine. Why might not that same influence work with equal potency in a question of church economy? It is certain that they were well acquainted; that Wesley was a visitor at the house when the change took place; and that their early friendship, never broken off, ripened into love, and led to their happy marriage in half-a-dozen years. Is this the cause, hitherto hidden, which led to this decisive change at so early a period? If not, the real influences operating to produce these results will probably remain in secret. We must now direct attention to a different topic, and look for a moment at the casket in which the precious gems of this clear intellect and noble heart were enshrined. The Annesley daughters are generally reputed to have possessed fair claims to be called beautiful. When Dunton strolled into the Meeting-House in Little Saint Helen's one Sabbath morning, he says:—"Instead of engaging my attention to what the Doctor said, I suffered both my mind and my eyes to run at random. I soon singled out a young lady that almost charmed me mad." This was one of Annesley's daughters. She happened, however, to be "pre-engaged." But the smitten lover found his new-born affection easily transferable, and successfully wooed her eldest sister. He has left us a minute description of his "fair Iris," and as the only pen-and-ink sketch of any of the Annesley family we possess, it is worth inserting, "Iris is tall; of good aspect; her hair of a light chestnut colour; dark eyes, her eyebrows dark and even; her mouth little and sufficiently sweet; her air something melancholy, sweet, and agreeable; her neck long and

32

graceful; white hands; a well-shaped body; her complexion very fair. But to hasten to that which I think most deserves commendation, I mean her piety, which, considering her youth, can scarce be paralleled. Her wit is solid. She has enough of that quick wit, so much in fashion, to render her conversation very desirable. She is severely modest, and has all kinds of virtues. She never yet, I dare venture to say, gave anyone an ill word when absent; never when present commends them. Her humour is good to a miracle. She is an agreeable acquaintance; a trusty friend. And, to conclude, she is pleasant, witty, and virtuous; and is mistress of all those graces that can be desired to make a complete woman." If we regard this tender portraiture as life-like, Elizabeth Annesley was indeed fair, beautiful, accomplished, and good; qualities which have all been claimed, and with some show of reason, for her youngest sister. "She was not only graceful, but beautiful in person," says Clarke. "Her sister Judith, painted by Sir Peter Lely, is represented as a very beautiful woman. One who well knew both said, 'Beautiful as Miss Annesley appears, she was far from being so beautiful as Mrs Wesley.'" This description of the admiring Doctor has been far outdone by a transatlantic historian, who writes after the following fashion —"A portrait of Susanna Wesley, taken at a later date than her marriage, but evidently while she was still young, affords us a picture of the refined, and even elegant, lady of the times. The features are slight, but almost classical in their regularity. They are thoroughly Wesleyan, affording proof that John Wesley inherited from his Mother not only his best moral and intellectual traits, but those also of his physiognomy. Her dress and coiffure are in the simplest style of her day, and the entire picture is marked by chaste gracefulness. It lacks not, also, an air of that high-bred aristocracy from which she was descended." This is certainly very definite and glowing. The historian has minutely studied the portrait on which he gazed with so much emotion. We allow that it is "a picture of the refined, and even elegant, lady of the times." But, alas, the fascinating illusion must be dispelled! The portrait, upon which this description is so carefully written, is no more the likeness of Susanna Wesley than Susanna of the Apocryphal story.

33

Intended to represent a titled lady, it may not lack "an air of highbred aristocracy." But as to the "thoroughly Wesleyan features," a microscope would fail to disclose a single line of the calm intellectual face of the Epworth family. There are two portraits of Mrs Wesley just now claiming to be genuine: the one taken in comparatively early life, and which is not satisfactorily authenticated; the other in extreme old age, a copy of which accompanies the present volume. But neither of them conveys the idea of what are commonly styled very beautiful features. Our impression is that, while Susanna Wesley excelled her sisters in strength of mind and extent of solid attainments, she was probably not their equal in the graces of personal attraction. We believe she lacked also their well-known hilarity and wit; and was more grave and thoughtful than the rest of the Annesley daughters. Her figure was probably slight; her stature about the average female height; her features good rather than beautiful; bearing more vividly traces of deep thought and grave contemplation, than of vivacity or sparkling wit. The Wesley face seems to us to be truly Wesleyan, derived, in its leading features, far more from the Father than the Mother. But enough of these speculations. "Favour is deceitful, and beauty is vain; but a woman that feareth the Lord she shall be praised." And this supreme excellency Susanna Wesley richly possessed. The religious households of those times were indeed schools of piety and nurseries of the church. The whole domestic life was often, in an eminent degree, imbued and regulated by a devout and earnest godliness. How beautiful is the following description of the family life of Sir Thomas Abney in the noble old mansion where Isaac Watts so long found a home, and dear to our own memory as the place where, for a considerable time, we studied to prepare ourselves for the office and work of the ministry ! "The Lord's-day he strictly observed and sanctified. God was solemnly sought and worshipped, both before and after the family's attendance on public ordinances. The repetition of sermons, the reading of good books, the instruction of the household, and the singing of the Divine praises together, were much of the several employments of the Holy-day; variety and brevity making the whole not burdensome, but pleasant, leaving at the same time room for the devotions of the closet, as well as for intervening works of necessity and mercy. Persons coming into such a family with a serious tincture of mind, might well cry out, 'This is none other than the house of God! This is the gate of heaven | Besides the ordinary and stated services of religion, occasional calls and seasons for worship were much regarded. In signal family mercies and afflictions; in going journeys; in undertaking and accomplishing matters of great moment, God was especially owned by prayer and thanksgiving, the assistance of ministers being often called in on such occasions. Through the whole course of his life, he was priest of his own family, except when a minister happened to be present." A similar refuge of religion and domestic happiness was the house of Susanna Wesley's childhood. "I can look back with joy," said her eldest sister as she neared the grave, "on some of the early years that I sweetly spent in my father's house, and how I comfortably lived there. O what a mercy is it to be dedicated to God betimes!" And Susanna herself fails not to tell us, that she was "early initiated and instructed in the first principles of the Christian religion;" and had a "good example in parents, and in several of the family." These privileges she duly improved for her spiritual welfare. In childhood, she "received from the heart the form of doctrine" delivered from her saintly father's lips. The bright domestic examples, she loved to imitate; and while yet young, she consecrated her service unto the Lord. From the first, hers was a religion of enlightened principle, rather than transient emotion. Rigid indeed was the care she exercised over herself, lest she should become absorbed in childish sports, or mere worldly pastimes. "I will tell you," she writes to her son, "what rule I observed in the same case when I was young, and too much addicted to childish diversions, which was this, —never to spend more time in any matter of mere recreation in one day, than I spent in private religious duties." Precious rule ! Who among the young observe it now? This one passage foreshadows the grand principles upon which this devout woman "fashioned" her entire life. This is the history of Susanna Wesley's early years, as far as they can be traced. These are our impressions of her as she appeared in her father's house:—

"Grace was in all her steps, heaven in her eye,

In every gesture dignity and love."

Her religious life will form the subject of a later chapter. But as we now contemplate her, she stands forth, at the age of nineteen, with attractive features and graceful form; an intellect keen and penetrating; a highly-disciplined and well-stored mind; a judgment calm and clear; a heart strong, though not demonstrative, in its affections, or peculiarly intense in its emotions; a "zealous Church-woman, yet rich in a dowry of Nonconforming virtues;" and over all, as her brightest adorning, "the beauties of holiness" clothing her "with salvation as with a garment."

"Not perfect,-nay, —but full of tender wants;

No angel, but a dearer being, all dipt

In angel instincts, breathing Paradise;

Who look'd all native to her place, and yet

On tip-toe seem'd to touch upon a sphere

Too great to tread."

Surely she is a maiden worthy the most princely spirit that may woo her hand and win her heart! And such a meet companion Providence had in store for her in the noble-hearted and intelligent Samuel Wesley. We are not wishful to interlay our narrative with a series of sermonic addresses. But we cannot finish the present chapter without a few words to one particular class of readers. Are these pages passing under the eye of any fair and accomplished young lady not decidedly religious; whose heart has not yet yielded to the claims of Christ; whose life is not a life of holy obedience to the Divine will? Allow me, my dear young friend, to press immediate decision on this vital matter upon your attention. Ponder, I beseech you, your solemn duties and responsibilities. Meditate upon the pattern of womanly excellence which these pages exhibit for your example and encouragement in well-doing. The Gospel is the only religion in the world which exalts and adorns the female character; which places woman in her proper position as the friend and companion of man, as an heir of the same destiny; one with him in the common Saviour, and equally interested in the great blessings of redemption and salvation. All these collateral and secondary benefits of the Gospel you richly share and highly prize. But, oh, you are living without the more glorious and essential privileges which that Gospel offers. It calls you to repentance, faith, and holiness. It offers you the enjoyment of conscious forgiveness, and elevated fellowship with God. It holds out to you a preparation for heaven; a happy and triumphant death; "an abundant entrance into the everlasting kingdom of our Lord and Saviour Jesus Christ." Yet, these things you are disregarding. You are living "without God," and have no hope of heaven. Oh, "acquaint now thyself with Him and be at peace; and thereby good shall come unto thee." "How long halt ye between two opinions?" Your time for decision is now, and not at a future day. Compared with the claims, privileges, and duties of personal godliness, everything is trifling and insignificant. Graceful form, beauty, rank, domestic pleasure, all "fade as a leaf." They vanish as the mist before the morning sun. Religion only abideth forever. Trust not, then, in vanity. Pursue shadows no longer. Be not satisfied until the graces which naturally adorn your sex are, in your case, found in beautiful combination with the "grace" which "bringeth salvation." O seek after this "hid treasure;" secure this "one thing needful;" secure it now. By a hearty repentance and true faith in the merit of your Saviour's atonement, accept the offered gift of pardon and holiness. Why should you longer delay? "Behold, now is the accepted time. Behold, now is the day of salvation." Yield now to your convictions of conscience, and the gentle strivings of the Holy Spirit which you have so long endeavoured to resist and silence. Draw near to Him who now draws near to you. "Hearken, O daughter, and consider, and incline thine ear; forget also thine own people and thy

37

father's house; so shall the King greatly desire thy beauty; for He is thy Lord; and worship thou Him." From the depth of your penitent and yielding heart, offer this one solemn prayer,

"O never in these veils of shame,

Sad fruits of sin, my glorying be :

Clothe with salvation, through Thy name,

My soul, and let me put on Thee!

Be living faith my costly dress,

And my best robe, Thy righteousness!


"Send down Thy likeness from above,

And let this my adorning be;

Clothe me with wisdom, patience, love,

With lowliness, and purity,

Than gold and pearls more precious far,

And brighter than the morning star!"

# III. FUTURE HUSBAND.

He was a faithful man, and feared God above many.
—BOOK OF NEHEMIAH.

THE Wesley Family is commonly supposed to have been ancient and respectable. The later members of it believed that their progenitors came from Saxony, and that slips of the paternal tree were planted almost simultaneously in England and Ireland. Clarke, with his usual love of tracing everything to an Oriental origin, finds the etymon of the name in an Arabic word that signifies "union or conjunction;" and favours the idea that the Wesleys came from Spain, "where multitudes of Arab families were long settled." He also supposes that some of them were among the fiery Crusaders, or had been on pilgrimage to Palestine, because they "bore the escallop shell in their arms." We have no wish to conduct our readers through all these labyrinths of conjecture, as no satisfactory results could be gained. From whatever quarter the Wesley Family originally came, whether descended from Asiatic, Spanish, or Saxon ancestry, or whether, as we are disposed to believe, they belonged to our own favoured Isle,— deriving their name from some local scene or circumstance,—it is clear that the branch of the family with which we have to do was long settled in Dorsetshire. They were eminent for their learning, piety, and self-sacrificing adherence to what they believed to be the true doctrines and principles of Christianity. The first in the direct ancestral line of whom we have any knowledge, is BARTHOLOMEW WESLEY, great grandfather of the Founder of Methodism. Born, probably, in the last year of the sixteenth century, and educated at Oxford, where, like many other men of his time, he studied medicine as well as divinity, he came upon the stage of public life just when violent ecclesiastical tempests were lowering over the churches of this country. As the vicar of Charmouth and Catherston, villages in the Southwestern extremity of Dorset, he discharged his sacred duties with becoming diligence and fidelity, using a "peculiar plainness of speech which hindered his being an acceptable popular preacher." Driven from his living immediately after the Restoration, he practised medicine for a livelihood; preaching whenever a safe opportunity presented itself; and honoured for his blameless character, sincere piety, and many domestic virtues. The place of his birth; the character of his boyhood; the home and changing scenes of his declining years; the spot where he found a grave to hide him from the fiery trials through which he had passed, are buried in oblivion. "He lived several years after he was silenced," says Calamy; "but the death of his son,"—the only member of his family of whom we have any account,—"made a sensible alteration in him; so that he afterward declined apace, and did not long survive him." The son, whose death so deeply affected his father's heart, rises before us as one of the loveliest characters of those remarkable times. The circumstances and sufferings of his life justly entitle him to a foremost place among the worthiest confessors of early Nonconformity. Educated with the greatest religious care, he had "a very humbling sense of sin and a serious concern for salvation," even while a schoolboy. When at Oxford, where Thomas Goodwin had formed "a Gathered Church'" among the collegians, he was distinguished for his piety. This is no common praise, when we remember that he was surrounded by such students as Howe, Charnock, and others of no small note. His proficiency in learning, especially in the Oriental tongues, attracted the attention and won the esteem of John Owen, then Vice Chancellor of the University. Returning to his native neighbourhood, he joined the "Gathered Church" at Melcombe, and began to preach, exercising his gifts among his own people, the villagers of Radipole, and the hardy sailors along the shore. Recommended to the work of the ministry by his own church, after much fasting and prayer, and approved by the ecclesiastical examiners, he received the living of Winterbourn Whitchurch in 1658, worth about thirty pounds a year. Having married a daughter of John White, "sometime Chairman of the Assembly of Divines," he was "necessitated to set up a school, that he might be able to maintain his growing family." He exercised a rigid supervision over his own soul. His Diary,

40

would it had been preserved —"not only recorded the remarkable events of Providence, which affected his outward man, but, more especially, the methods of the Spirit of grace in His dealings with his soul; the frame of his heart in his attendance on the ordinances of the Gospel; and how he found himself affected under the various methods of Divine Providence, whether merciful or afflictive." The dark clouds now gathered over this devout and hard-working pastor. A succession of storms discharged their violence upon his head. Base informers brought false and scandalous accusations against him, and secured his imprisonment for six months, without a trial. An unbending Independent in his ecclesiastical principles, his refusal to read the Book of Common Prayer led to new troubles. There was a long interview with his diocesan, in which he displayed a scholarship, logic, and Christian temper which we cannot fail to admire. Then came the Act of Uniformity, and on the memorable seventeenth of August, 1662, he preached an impressive farewell sermon "to a weeping audience" from that most appropriate of all texts, "And now, brethren, I commend you to God, and to the word of His grace, which is able to build you up, and to give you an inheritance among them that are sanctified." After lingering a few months in his old parish, during which time his son Samuel was born, and baptized in the church from which his father had so recently been "thrust out," he retired to Weymouth. The land lady who gave him shelter, was fined twenty pounds for the offence; while he was commanded to pay five shillings a week, "to be levied by distress." He wandered to Bridgewater and Taunton, where "he met with great kindness and friendship from all three denominations of Dissenters, who were afterwards very kind to him and his numerous family." Then "a gentleman who had a very good house at Preston, two or three miles from Melcombe, gave him free liberty to live in it without paying any rent." He accepted this unlooked-for kindness as a marked interposition of Providence, wondering how it came to pass, "that he who had forfeited all the mercies of life should have any habitation at all, when other precious saints were destitute;" and that he should have "such an house of abode while others had only poor mean cottages." Then came terrible temptations about fulfilling his

41

call to preach the Gospel. Silenced at home, he meditated a "removal beyond sea, either to Maryland or Surinam. After much consideration and advice, he determined to abide in the land of his nativity, and there take his lot." Preaching only in private, he kept himself longer out of the hands of his enemies than many of his brethren. But, "notwithstanding all his prudence in managing his meetings, he was often disturbed; several times apprehended; and four times cast into prison." In his "many straits and difficulties," he was "wonderfully supported and comforted, and many times surprisingly relieved and delivered." Finally, he was "called by a number of serious Christians at Poole to be their pastor; and in that relation he continued to the day of his death, administering all ordinances to them as opportunity offered."

His manifold and heavy trials,—all the result of his unflinching adherence to the testimony which he held,— soon prepared him for an early grave. "The removal of many eminent Christians into another world, who were his intimate acquaintance and kind friends; the great decay of serious religion among many that made a profession; and the increasing rage of the enemies of real godliness, manifestly seized and sunk his spirits. And having filled up his part of what is behind of the afflictions of Christ in the flesh, for His body's sake, which is the Church, and finished the work given him to do, he was taken out of this vale of tears, to that world where the wicked cease from troubling, and the weary are at rest, when he had not been much longer an inhabitant here below than his blessed Master, whom he served with his whole heart, according to the best light he had." Denied sepulture within the walls of the sacred edifice, his remains lie undistinguished among the common graves of the churchyard. In that day when the "many that sleep in the dust of the earth shall awake," John Westley shall "come forth unto everlasting life;" while many of his persecutors shall arise to "shame and everlasting contempt."

Of this saintly man's "numerous family," the greater part probably died young. The names of four only have been preserved,—Timothy, Elizabeth, Samuel, and Matthew; and of these there are only two of whom we have any account.

MATTHEW was educated for the medical profession, and rose to considerable eminence in his calling. He settled in London, where he obtained a very extensive and lucrative practice. When admitted into Dunton's Athenian Society, he was announced as "a civilian, Doctor of physic" a "learned, good, and ingenious man, and so generous" that he could never be persuaded to receive any remuneration for his contributions to the famous "Athenian Gazette." Clever, witty, and somewhat cynical, he occasionally made himself merry with matters which ought always to be treated with soberness. When his nephew Charles was dining with him one day, "he bestowed abundance of wit" upon John Wesley's "apostolical project," declaring that when the French found "any remarkably dull fellow among them, they sent him to convert the Indians." Charles checked his raillery, by repeating,

"To distant lands the Apostles need not roam,
     Darkness, alas! and heathens are at home,"

and heard no more about his "brother's apostleship." In 1731, he visited the Wesley family at Epworth. The arrival of a wealthy relative from London at the poverty-stricken parsonage was a wonderful event, and excited great curiosity among the rustic parishioners. "It was odd," says Mrs Wesley, "to observe how all the town took the alarm and were upon the gaze, as if some great prince had been about to make an entry." The first two days the visitor was very stately and reserved, narrowly watching the conduct of the children, and scrutinising the general condition of things around him.

Then he began to thaw; chatted freely with the girls, "who told him everything,"—as girls usually do; and held frequent conversations with Mrs Wesley. Toward his brother he was very courteous, but equally shy. The wealthy physician looked with amazement upon the miserable furniture, and the mean attire of the poor country parson's daughters. Having only one child of his own,—and he, alas, turned out a most dissipated man, and a disgrace to his noble family name, -he could not understand how his brother, with a "numerous offspring" and a stinted income, happened to be in such straits as not to provide better

43

for his household, and lay up something for his children after his decease! Full of these thoughts, he returned to London and penned a letter, abounding in stinging reflections and sweeping censures. He declared that the rector had long enjoyed "a plentiful estate," and "great and generous benefactions," without providing for those of his own house. "This," writes the man of wealth, "I think a black account. I hope Providence has restored you again to give you time to settle this balance, which shocks me to think of To this end I must advise you to be frequent in your perusal of Father Beveridge on Repentance, and Doctor Tillotson on Restitution; for it is not saying, 'Lord! Lord!' will bring us to the kingdom of heaven, but doing justice to all our fellow creatures; and not a poetical imagination that we do so." This solitary outburst of irritation, however, did not prevent the full play of his strong natural affection. He took two or three of his nieces to reside with him when they were young; educated them at his own expense; and provided them with suitable marriage portions. Hetty was a special favourite.

> Hetty, beautiful and accomplished, eloped [with a man thought to have been Will Atkinson, a dishonest lawyer] and slept one night with him, thinking they would be married the next day. He had no intentions of marriage. As a result, she became pregnant, and had to face denunciation from her father. Five months pregnant, she married an unrefined plumber, William Wright, who later became a drunkard and a wife abuser. Her father never forgave her.

He watched over her delicate health with tenderest care; made her his chosen companion during his weeks of leisure and recreation; and did much to develop the beautiful qualities of her mind. Hear her own sweet testimony:—

"'Twas owing to his friendly care I breathed at ease the rural air, Her ample bounds where Reading spreads, Where Kennet winds along the meads, ... Where Thompson the retreat approves, By streams refresh'd and gloom'd with groves, Where, from Cadogan's lofty seat, Our view surrounding landscapes meet. 'Twas there he made my leisure blest, There waked the muse within my breast." Some of his relatives supposed him to be sceptically inclined on the subject of religion. There is, however, good reason to believe that he never cast off his Christian profession, but continued a strict Nonconformist to the end of his days. During his visit to Epworth, "he always behaved himself very decently at family prayers," writes Mrs Wesley; "and in your father's absence, said grace for us before and after meat. Nor did he ever interrupt our privacy; but went into his own chamber when we went into ours." "He was exemplarily moral in his words and actions, esteeming religion, but never talking of its mysteries." After a long illness, his nephew Charles found him dying, in June 1737. "He pressed my hand; shewed much natural affection; and bade me give his love to his sister." He met the last enemy with great calmness. All fear was taken away, and, with his head reclining on the bosom of his favourite and affectionate niece, he breathed his last.

The best part of the unfortunate Hetty's life was with her uncle. Matthew Wesley introduced her to the literary talents of London and here she was appreciated, and her talent for poetry recognized.

Hetty mourned his loss in strains of great tenderness and beauty:—

"How can the muse attempt the string,
    Forsaken by her guardian power?
Ah me! that she survives to sing

Her friend and patron, now no more!

Yet private grief she might suppress,
Since Clio bears no selfish mind;
But, oh! she mourns to wild excess
The friend and patron of mankind.
Alas! the sovereign, healing art,
Which rescued thousands from the grave,
Unaided left the gentlest heart,
Nor could its skilful master save.
Who shall the helpless sex sustain

45

Now Varro's lenient hand is gone,
Which knew so well to soften pain,
And ward all danger but its own?
His darling muse, his Clio dear,
Whom first his favour raised to fame;
His gentle voice vouchsafed to cheer, -
His art upheld her tender frame:
Pale envy durst not shew her teeth;
Above contempt she gaily shone
Chief favourite, till the hand of death
Endanger'd both by striking one.
Perceiving well, devoid of fear,
His latest fatal conflict nigh;
Reclined on her he held most dear,
Whose breast received his parting sigh.
With every art and grace adorn'd,
By man admired, by heaven approved,
Good Varro died—applauded, mourn'd,
And honour'd by the muse he loved."

Concerning SAMUEL WESLEY, the other son of the persecuted vicar of Whitchurch, and the future husband of Susanna Annesley, our information is more ample, and our sketch must be more minute and extended. Without discussing the conflicting statements about the time and place of his birth, we regard the entry of the baptism of "Samuel, son of John Westley," on the seventeenth of December 1662, still preserved in the parish Register of Whitchurch, as decisive that he was born in that town in the preceding November, a few months after his father was ejected from the living. His father dying while Samuel was receiving his grammar learning at the Dorchester Free School, "and nearly ready for the University," some Dissenting friends, without his "mother's application or charges," sent the youth to London to be entered at one of their private academies as a candidate for the Nonconformist ministry. Reaching town on 8 March 1678, he found that Doctor G—, who "had the care of one of the most considerable of those seminaries," and who had promised him his tuition free of charge, had recently died. He went for a time to a grammar school, the master of which provided for him a handsome subsistence at the University, and urged him to graduate there. But the Dissenters offering his relations greater advantages in the provision of thirty pounds a year, he was sent to the Stepney academy, then under the care of the Rev. Edward Veal,—"a learned, orthodox minister, of a sober, pious, and peaceable conversation," and "eminently useful for the instruction of youth." Deprived of his fellowship in Trinity College, Dublin, "for Nonconformity to the ceremonies imposed in the Church, and for joining with other ministers in their endeavours for a reformation," he settled at Wapping, where he "had several pupils to whom he read University learning." While prosecuting his studies in this neighbourhood, Wesley had the privilege of listening to many of the most able Nonconformist ministers, whose sermons he was accustomed carefully to write out. He was a frequent hearer of the great and good Stephen Charnock; and once he listened to the inimitable allegorist, whom he playfully designates "Friend Bunyan." The feeling against the Church of England fostered among these Dissenting students at Stepney, was exceedingly strong; and young Wesley, smart, clever, and selfreliant, was an apt pupil in this, as in most other things. With some pretensions to poetic power, he soon became "a dabbler in rhyme and faction;" and was unwisely employed by his superiors to write sarcastic pieces upon Church and State. Some of the gravest and most learned ministers sent for him, suggested subjects, furnished matter, and occasionally encouraged him with something more tangible than words, in his "silly lampoons." Some of them even transcribed his writings, "and several of them revised and corrected them before they were printed." Prosecuted by the neighbouring justices, Veal was obliged to "break up his house" and relinquish his tutorial duties. Wesley, who had been with him two years, was then recommended to a similar establishment at Newington Green, conducted by the Rev. Charles Morton,-"an ingenious and universally learned man, but his chiefest excellency lay in mathematics." During his four years' academic career, Wesley made great proficiency in learning, and lived a life of strict uprightness and morality. But there was an entire lack of everything like deep experimental religion. His temper was irritable; his disposition unforgiving, or, in his own words, "too keen and revengeful,"—a spirit utterly alien to that which ought to animate the breast of a youth preparing himself for the Christian ministry. Surrounding circumstances probably had something to do with this unamiable temper. He became more and more dissatisfied with his position, and resolved to renounce it. "Being a young man of spirit," writes his son John, "he was pitched upon to answer some severe invectives" recently published against the Dissenters. During the preparation for this assigned task, he saw reason to change his opinions, and instead of writing the proposed answer, he "renounced the Dissenters and attached himself to the Established Church." His own account differs slightly from this, yet may be perfectly compatible with it. When he had been two years at Newington Green, he began to make closer observations upon things around him. The more he reflected on the political principles and conversation prevalent among his fellow students, the more he disliked them, and doubted whether he "was in the right." He was also intimate with "two reverend and worthy" relatives. One of these visited him at Morton's seminary, and "gave him such arguments against that schism with which he was then embarked, as added weight to his reflections when he began to think of leaving it." The arrangements for his education for the Dissenting ministry were made for him when quite a youth, and probably without any consideration or consent on his part. He had been twice hindered from going to the University, for which he had evidently a strong inclination. And when all these circumstances are fairly considered, we need not be surprised at the change. The Dissenters had been kind and generous to him as a poor fatherless boy, dependent upon a widowed mother in straitened circumstances; and though in the heat of controversy, he afterwards spoke of his old friends with too much asperity, he did not leave them in any dishonourable way. Out of a legacy, which just then came into his hands, he paid the principal of the academy his just due, and discharged every farthing of the few unimportant debts he had contracted among his associates. Living at the time with his mother and an aged aunt, both too strongly wedded to Dissenting principles to bear with patience the disclosure of his intentions, he rose betimes one August morning in 1683, walked all the way to Oxford, and entered himself as "a servitor of Exeter College." With only forty-five shillings in his pocket and no hope of any supplies from home, his financial prospects were not the most promising. But he nobly braced himself for his task. By rendering help to others, and by the efforts of his pen, for which Dunton "gave him as much as he could afford," he closed his University career with a purse five times heavier than he carried with him to this ancient and honourable seat of learning. We have only a solitary, but most refreshing glimpse of his extra-college movements at Oxford. He was not insensible to the obligations resting upon him to do good; and the first ray of Christian activity which he sent forth shone upon them who "satin darkness and in the shadow of death." Calling up reminiscences of his own early efforts for the spiritual welfare of the prisoners, he writes to his sons, who, in after years, pursued the same benevolent course;—"Go on, in God's name, in the path your Saviour has directed you, and that track wherein your father has gone before you; for when I was an undergraduate at Oxford, I visited them in the castle there, and reflect on it with great satisfaction to this day." As we look at him in these holy toils, the words of quaint old Fuller rise to the mind:—"Thus was the prison his first parish; his own charity, his patron presenting him to it; and his work was all his wages." Returning to London, he was "initiated in deacon's orders by the Bishop of Rochester, at his palace of Bromley, August the seventeenth, 1688; and on the twenty-sixth of February following, was ordained priest in Saint Andrew's Church, Holborn." It is generally allowed that, by the party with whom he had allied himself, both in secular and ecclesiastical politics, Wesley was regarded as a young man of superior merit, whose active co-operation it was desirable to secure in the furtherance of their measures. His biographers, with a solitary exception, and all the historians of Methodism record with evident delight, that the court party solicited him to preach in favour of James' celebrated Declaration, and seconded their request with promises of speedy and high preferment. But the young minister, proof against this seductive influence, "rose in bold resistance to the daring aggression on Gospel liberty which the schemes of the Court involved." Surrounded by a congregation of soldiers courtesans, and noble families not a few, all-eager to hear his arguments in favour of the King's proceedings, he read out for his text;—"If it be so, our God whom we serve is able to deliver us from the fiery furnace, and He will deliver us out of thy

49

hand, O King ! But if not, be it known unto thee, O King, that we will not serve thy gods, nor worship the golden image which thou hast set up." He not only refused to read the Declaration, but delivered a bold and masterly discourse against it. The effect was most remarkable:

"Resistless truth damp'd all the audience round,
The base informer sicken'd at the sound;
Attentive courtiers, conscious, stood amazed,
And soldiers, silent, trembled as they gazed,
No smallest murmur of distaste arose;
Abash'd and vanquish'd seem'd the Church's foes."

More than once have we heard the incident eloquently described in popular lectures, and hailed with loud and repeated cheers. Even Macaulay, with all his marvellous accuracy, has recorded it as a fact. We are sorry to dissipate so pleasant an illusion; but in relation to Samuel Wesley, the story is entirely without foundation. It rests solely on the authority of the poem we have just quoted. Written by the younger Wesley, and beginning,
"Accept, dear Sire, this humble tribute paid, This small memorial, to a Parent's shade," it has been concluded that it refers to the poet's own father. The poem describes a scene of domestic plenty and hospitality strangely foreign to all we read of the discomforts of the Epworth rectory. It was written "upon a clergyman lately deceased"—the Rev. John Berry, the poet's father-in-law,-and published four years before the death of Samuel Wesley. It could, therefore, have no reference to him. Besides, the Declaration of James was ordered to be read in the churches in May, 1688; and as Wesley was not ordained until August of that year, he was not in holy orders at the time, and could not, therefore, preach against the measures of the King. But from all we know of his fearless opposition to every movement in favour of Popery, we can easily believe that, had Wesley been placed in the circumstances referred to, he would not have hesitated to pursue a course like that which the poem describes. He was no supporter of the policy of James the Second. While a student at Oxford, he had divined the King's character, and resolved on his own course. James visited the University and

50

called the master and fellows of Magdalen College to account for not electing his nominee as their president. When they appeared before him, he lectured them after a most un-Kingly fashion:— "You have not dealt with me like gentlemen. You have been unmannerly as well as undutiful. Is this your Church-of-England loyalty? I could not have believed that so many clergymen of the Church of England would have been concerned in such a business. Go home ! Get you gone ! I am King; I will be obeyed. Go to your chapel this instant; and admit the Bishop of Oxford. Let those who refuse look to it. They shall feel the whole weight of my hand. They shall know what it is to incur the displeasure of their Sovereign." They offered him their petition. He angrily flung it down. "Get you gone, I tell you. I will receive nothing from you till you have admitted the Bishop."

Young Wesley witnessed this unseemly exhibition, and years afterwards, he wrote; —"When I heard him say to the master and fellows of Magdalen College, lifting up his lean arm, "If you refuse to obey me, you shall feel the weight of a King's right hand, I saw he was a tyrant. And though I was not inclined to take an active part against him, I was resolved from that time to give him no kind of support." Of course, Wesley hailed the Revolution as a grand deliverance from tyranny and Popery; and it is a fact worth recording, that "This Briton's pen first pleaded William's cause, And pleaded strongly for our faith and laws." He "wrote and printed the first thing that appeared in defence of the government, after the accession" of William and Mary. Besides this work, probably a pamphlet, in "answer to a speech without doors," he "wrote a great many little pieces more, both in prose and verse, with the same view." These services did not meet with any magnificent returns from the royal hand. But although Mary, "according to her true judgment, did by no means think it fit" to confer upon him an Irish Bishopric, when recommended by the Marquis of Normanby, she cherished for him a kindly regard; accepted the dedication of his "Life of Christ; " and had she not soon after been taken away, he would have received some more substantial favour at her hands. When this young High-Church clergyman had served a London curacy for one year, he was made chaplain to a man-of-war. During his cruise "in Old Ierne's angry seas," he commenced his curious poem on "The Life of our blessed

51

Lord and Saviour, Jesus Christ." This elaborate heroic,-extending to nearly eleven thousand lines, with preface, notes, and "sixty copper-plates,"—was evidently a favourite project. He not only gave to it all his leisure-time, but tells us that, "ere dappled morn had dressed the skies," he rose to ply his attractive task. And if industry and perseverance were alone necessary to success, his poem would have been far more worthy of public attention than it now is. After twelve months spent in this pleasurable employment, he returned to London; and the current of his after history naturally blends with that of his devoted wife.

# IV. MARRIAGE.

Marriage is not like the hill Olympus, wholly clear, without clouds. Yea expect both wind and storms sometimes, which, when blown over, the air is the clearer and more wholesome for it. Make account of certain cares and troubles that will attend thee. —THOMAS FULLER.

AN earlier page has intimated that Doctor Annesley's house was frequently visited by leading Nonconforming pastors of London and the neighbourhood. But the Doctor's deep interest in the rising ministry of his Denomination, made his home readily accessible also to young students passing through their academic courses, and equipping themselves for their solemn calling. In this way, rather than through the introduction of any mutual friend, as is commonly supposed, Samuel Wesley was welcomed within the circle of this interesting family. He was present at Dunton's marriage with Elizabeth Annesley, in 1682. The humorous bridegroom tells us that "as soon as dinner was ended, an ingenious gentleman, at that time a student in the Rev. Mr Veal's house," called the happy couple out from the company, and presented them with an "Epithalamium." The juvenile composition is sufficiently wild and ardent, liberally sprinkled with the customary phrases about "little Cupids," "golden Hymen," "charming bride," "envious swains," and "marble-hearted virgins," without any trace of religious sentiment or aspiration. A few years afterward, when death had stricken down the happy bride of that morning, the sorrowing widower pressed his early friend to write an appropriate epitaph. Wesley, who was evidently aware of Dunton's weak side, playfully observes in reply, "If you please to accept this epitaph, it is at your service, and I hope it will come before you need another epithalamium." It is clear, then, that the acquaintance of Wesley and Susanna Annesley was formed when they were both very young. How it ripened into the strong and tender passion of mutual love; when the actual courtship commenced, and how it was carried on; whether there were an

53

unbroken correspondence during his absence at Oxford, and an immediate renewal of personal intercourse on his return to London; at what church the marriage took place and by whom the ceremony was performed, are matters on which we have not been able to gain the least information. Sometime, probably late in 1689, or early in 1690, the auspicious day arrived, and they were solemnly united in holy matrimony, according to the rites and ceremonies of the Church of England. Dunton tells us that before his marriage with Elizabeth Annesley, the good Doctor preached a preparatory sermon on, "This is a great mystery." He shewed that "the duties of the married state must be performed, if the comforts of it be expected; that "the comforts of marriage have their whole dependence upon the performance of the duties;" that "the espousals of Christ with His Church are a great mystery;" and that "Christ espousing the Church is the best pattern of all Christian marriages." The application "was particular, and came home to the present case." They were "largely attended to church," where the Doctor gave away his daughter, which, says Dunton, "I took as a peculiar favour from himself, it being more than some of his sons-in-law could obtain. When the public ceremony was over, we returned to my Reverend father-in-law's, where the entertainment was plentiful enough, and yet gravely suited to the occasion and circumstance." And such, in all probability, were the ceremonies and festivities, so grave and becoming, which attended the marriage of Susanna Annesley. Her husband was now a curate on only thirty pounds a year. They "boarded" in London and the neighbourhood, "without going into debt," until the autumn of 1690, when Wesley received his first preferment in the Church. About ten miles from Horncastle, there is the neat little village of South Ormsby, wearing that pleasant aspect common to most Lincolnshire villages, skirting the parks and woodlands surrounding some noble family's country mansion. The ancient church, resting on a small eminence, overlooks the comparatively modern rectory, built on the lower ground adjoining the church-yard. The outward aspect is attractive and genial enough; and the living now has its temporal comforts in a good degree: but in the days of Samuel Wesley the income was that of a common porter. As to the "rectory," and the noble spirit of its chief inhabitant, some idea may be formed from the worthy man's own description:—

"In a mean cot, composed of reeds and clay,
  Wasting in sighs the uncomfortable day:
  Near where the inhospitable Humber roars,
  Devouring by degrees the neighbouring shores.
  Let earth go where it will, I'll not repine,
  Nor can unhappy be, while Heaven is mine."

Here, in this miserable den, there were fifty pounds a year to live upon, "and one child additional per annum." Yet there was no complaining. With true parental affection, each new comer was welcomed as a gift from God; and noble were the struggles to provide bread for the increasing household. While the thrifty wife did her best to make things go as far as possible, the rector plied his pen with unceasing diligence. His "Life of Christ," which he published while here; his treatise on the Hebrew points; and his contributions to Dunton's Athenian Oracle, one-third of which he wrote with his own hand, helped to keep the wolf from the door for seven long years.

The living had been obtained for him, without any solicitation on his own part, by the Marquis of Normanby. This nobleman, John Wesley tells us, had a house in the neighbourhood of the parish, where a woman whom he kept generally resided. The disreputable "lady" insisted on being very friendly, and on visiting terms with the rector's wife. Such intercourse was very distasteful to Mrs Wesley; but all ordinary methods failed to free her from the nuisance. Coming in one day and finding this unwelcome visitor sitting with his wife, the clergyman unceremoniously walked up to her, and fairly handed her out of the house. "The nobleman resented the affront so outrageously as to make it necessary for my father to resign the living." We have no reason to dispute the chief statements in this incident. It is just what we might expect a man of Samuel Wesley's principles and temperament to do; and what a noble marquis, in such circumstances, would be very likely to resent. But when we find this very nobleman continuing Wesley in office as his chaplain, and giving handsome donations in after years towards rescuing him from pecuniary embarrassment, we can hardly think that the resentment was so intense and active as to oblige Wesley to leave his living. As there appears to have been no appreciable interval between the resignation of South Ormsby and the removal to Epworth, it is most likely that the grant of Epworth was the only reason for leaving his first village charge. The death of her father, which took place at this particular juncture, deeply affected Mrs Wesley. During a severe and long-continued affliction, he was perfectly resigned to the Divine will. He charged those around him not to entertain hard thoughts of God because he suffered so much in his last end. "Blessed be God," he exclaimed, "I have been faithful in the work of the ministry above fifty-five years!" Having enjoyed "uninterrupted peace and assurance of God's love for above thirty years last past," the holy calm of soul was not broken when the waves and billows of death went over his head. "I have no doubt, nor shadow of doubt! All is clear between God and my soul. He chains up Satan; he cannot trouble me." His mind had so long been filled with thoughts of God and heaven, that, even in moments of mental wandering, "he still breathed the same spirit, and spake of Divine matters most consistently. His head was not free of those projects for God, which in health it was ever full of." "Come, dear Jesus! The nearer the more precious, and the more welcome," was a sentence often falling from his lips. Then the flood of holy joy so inundated his soul that he exclaimed, "I cannot contain it! What manner of love is this to a poor worm! I cannot express a thousandth part of what praise is due to Thee! We know not what we do when we aim at praising God for His mercies! It is but little I can give; but, Lord, help me to give Thee my all! I will die praising Thee, and rejoice that there are others that can praise Thee better. I shall be satisfied with Thy likeness!—Satisfied —Satisfied O, my dearest Jesus, I come!" "In him," says Williams, in closing his funeral sermon, "the world have lost a blessing; the Church have lost a pillar; the nation have lost a wrestler with God; the poor have lost a benefactor; you, his people, have lost a faithful pastor; you, his children, a tender father; we in the ministry, an exemplary fellow-labourer." He desired that his remains should rest with those of his beloved wife, and in the old register of Saint Leonard's, Shoreditch, for December, 1696, we read, "Samuel Annesley was buried the seventh day, from Spittle-Yard." He sleeps within the walls of that grand old edifice, but no slab or monument marks his precise resting-place. The Omniscient Eye observes his dust. His flesh resteth in hope; and could we give it voice it would speak in the words of the ancient man of Uz, "Thou shalt call, and I will answer Thee; Thou wilt have a desire to the work of Thine hands!" And when that time of the consummation of all things shall arrive, then shall his dying utterance be realised: "As for me, I will behold Thy face in righteousness; I shall be satisfied, when I awake, with Thy likeness." Mrs Wesley's affection for this honoured parent was intense and constant. She cherished his memory and meditated upon his saintly character to her latest hour. Sometimes she felt a peculiar nearness to him, as though she held converse with his ascended spirit. Her son John heard her say that she was frequently as fully persuaded that her father was with her, as if she had seen him with her bodily eyes. She left her statement without any explanation; but her real views may probably be elicited from her writings. When speaking of the mysterious noises in the Epworth parsonage, described at large in our next chapter, she observes, "I am rather inclined to think there would be frequent intercourse between good spirits and us, did not our deep lapse into sensuality prevent it." The following remarkable passage in her beautiful and masterly exposition of the Apostles' Creed, still more fully explains her meaning:—"What knowledge the saints in heaven have of things or persons in this world, we cannot determine; nor after what manner we hold communion with them, it is not, at present, easy to conceive. That we are all members of the same Mystical Body, Christ, we are very sure; and do all partake of the same vital influence from the same Head; and so we are united together. And though we are not actually possessed of the same happiness which they enjoy; yet, we have the same Holy Spirit given unto us as an earnest of our eternal felicity with them hereafter. And though their faith is consummated by vision, and

57

their hope by present possession; yet the bond of Christian charity still remains. And as we have great joy and complacency in their felicity, so, no doubt, they desire and pray for us." Though not prepared to explain the manner in which the intercourse is carried on, Mrs Wesley clearly held the doctrine of spiritual communion with departed saints. This theory, so enchanting and soothing to those whose friends have departed hence in the Lord, has been received by many devout and able divines. There are unmistakable indications that it was regarded with considerable favour by Mrs Wesley's gifted sons. After Charles has sung his noble hymns of triumph over the exodus of some of his saintly friends, he is not slow to tell us, that in his public services, and private meditations, he felt communion with them. It was John Wesley's constant custom to preach on All-Saints'-Day, one of his most favourite Church festivals, on communion with the heavenly multitude. He declares also that he many times realised such a sudden and lively apprehension of deceased friends, that he has turned round to look if they were not actually and visibly present at his side; and "an uncommon affection for them" sprung up in his heart. In his dreams of the night, he sometimes held "exceeding lively conversations with them," and doubted not that "they were very near." There is a striking illustration of one of these "exceeding lively conversations" in the following passage from the "Life of Mrs Fletcher:"—"Last night I had a powerful sense, in my sleep, of the presence of my dear husband I felt such sweet communion with his spirit as gave me much peaceful feeling. I had for some days thought that I was called to resist, more than I did, that strong and lively remembrance of various scenes, both of his last sickness and many other circumstances, which frequently occurred with much pain. This thought being present to my mind, I looked on him. He said, with a sweet smile, 'It is better to forget." "What, said I, 'my dear love, to forget one another?" He replied, with an inexpressible sweetness, 'It is better to forget. It will not be long. We shall not be parted long; we shall soon meet again." He then signified, though not in words, that all weights should be laid aside." This is, probably, more or less, the experience of all good people who have loved ones "on the other side of the flood." But, however we may account for the feeling, we fail to find in the Holy Scriptures any satisfactory recognition of this alleged communion of saints on earth with saints in heaven. We have an utter abhorrence of the blasphemies, so common in our own day, which profess to carry on this intercourse by the action of "mediums" and unmeaning sounds. Solemn mysteries are to be reverently regarded, rather than rudely explored. We are probably encompassed by multitudes of spiritual existences, both angelic and human. However light and thin the curtain that screens them from mortal vision, it is not transparent; and we will not attempt either to pierce or lift it. "We walk by faith, not by sight." If nothing conscious can pass between us and the glorified; if all interchange of thought and feeling be closed; if our mutual sensibilities find no point of contact or medium of expression,-we are, in some sense or other, "come unto the spirits of just men made perfect," as well as unto "an innumerable company of angels." If intercourse be closed, meditation is free and active. The contemplation of their virtues in this mortal life, and of their happiness in heaven, exerts an influence over our minds which prompts to a cheerful emulation of their spirit, that we may finally share their blessedness. "Wherefore, seeing we also are compassed about with so great a cloud of witnesses, let us lay aside every weight, and the sin which doth so easily beset us, and let us run with patience the race that is set before us, looking unto Jesus, the Author and Finisher of our faith; who, for the joy that was set before Him, endured the cross, despising the shame, and is set down at the right hand of the throne of God." Beautiful and cheering indeed are the words of Winter Hamilton, in one of his sweetest and most eloquent discourses —"When we seem to descry among the nations of the saved, those whom we have cherished; when there stands forth from them, father, mother, brother, sister, the partners and children of our desolate households,-we feel a moral complacency in them that destroys not tenderness but which refines and sanctifies it; that awakens awe, but which also softens and endures it. The love which once held us is strengthened; but it is woven of more solemn ties than before. We hail that cloud of witnesses. We go up and salute the Church triumphant. We exercise not, however, an unreciprocated love. We know that we did possess it. We forget not our parting with them,-how their eye glazed as it rested fondly on us; how their trembling breath whispered still their undying attachment; how their hand grew cold and nerveless in our grasp! Have affections which death could not chill, turned suddenly indifferent and unheeding? Are they weaned from us? Are we forgotten? Is all sympathy withdrawn? Hearts grow not selfish in heaven. It is the world of love. Friendships are treasured there. The saints dwelling in it are alive to all the interests of the Church on earth. They take their part in the importunities for its avengement, and in the acclamations of its triumphs. They look forward to 'the coming of our Lord Jesus Christ with all His saints, and to "our gathering together unto Him." Spirits made perfect can abandon no love that it was ever their right to form, their duty to cherish, their benefit to exercise. Their perfection is the pledge that each holy attachment is raised to that perfection." Who can contemplate these glowing truths and not feel the overwhelming force of the apostolic exhortation:—"Where fore the rather, brethren, give diligence to make your calling and election sure; for if ye do these things, ye shall never fall: for so an entrance shall be ministered unto you abundantly into the everlasting kingdom of our Lord and Saviour Jesus Christ."

At the close of the passage extracted from her exposition of the Creed, Mrs Wesley suggests that our glorified friends may possibly desire "good things" on our behalf, and even "pray for us" in the heavenly sanctuary. This opinion has the merit of having been held by some of the most eminent divines in the seventeenth century, and probably in much earlier times. The lively and eloquent Thomas Adams, speaking of the militant and triumphant parts of the one universal Church, observes:— "They sing hosannas for us, and we hallelujahs for them. They pray to God for us, and we praise God for them, for the excellent graces they had on earth, and for their present glory in heaven." And the sober Anthony Farindon, whose pulpit was regarded as the theological chair of England, offers the same view. "The blessed saints departed, though we may not pray for them, yet may pray for us, though we hear it not."

60

This opinion will most likely be regarded as unscriptural and dangerous. The common creed of our times is, that heaven is a place

"Where faith in sight is swallow'd up,
    And prayer in endless praise."

Prayer, it is argued, is an expression of want, and as in the world of perfect blessedness the glorified will feel no needs, they will not require any prayer to express them.

But is there not something more in prayer than the expression of wants, and the supplication of supplies? Is there no lofty communion with God, so sweet and refreshing to the devout heart? And may not prayer in this sublime sense form part of that endless service which the heavenly congregation render day and night in the upper sanctuary? In their celestial ministries, the elders of the glorified Church not only "sing as it were a new song." They "fall down before the Lamb, having every one of them harps, and golden vials full of odours, which are the prayers of saints." And while the kingdom of God remains unfinished on the earth, may they not, like the Great Intercessor Himself, pray for the world's conversion? Has that prayer which they so fervently and often poured forth on earth, become unsuited to their present position and service? "Thy kingdom come! Thy will be done in earth as it is in heaven !" The disembodied spirits of the "noble army of martyrs" cry from beneath the altar with a loud voice, "How long, O Lord, Holy and True, dost Thou not judge and avenge our blood on them that dwell on the earth !" Is it inconsistent with the laws of that higher sphere in which they live, or with their nearness to the throne, that the sainted dead should so remember friends still on the earth as to desire and pray for us? For the full solution of these and many other questions relating to heavenly employments, we must wait until we "enter in through the gates into the city."

# V. EPWORTH

Thou sufferedst men to ride over our heads:
We went through fire and water.
—Psalm of David.

CLOSE bordering on the winding Trent, in one of the most fertile parts of Lincolnshire, are the parish and manor of Epworth. The surrounding country forms the Isle of Axholme, containing nearly fifty thousand acres of land and fourteen thousand inhabitants. The Idle, Torn, and Don flow around its southern and western side ; the Trent bounds it on the East; and the ancient Bykers dyke, running from the Idle to the Trent, completes the circuit, and converts it into a river-islet. Were we writing its history, we should have to recount many a fierce sally of wild Britons from its neighbouring forests upon the sturdy Roman invader, as he marched on in his career of northern conquest. Situated at the extremity of two ancient Saxon kingdoms, the princes of Mercia and North-Humbria made it the scene of many deadly conflicts: while its contiguity to the Trent and the Humber rendered it of easy access to the barbarous hordes of Danish marauders, in their frequent expeditions to our eastern shores. Christianity found a lodgment within its limits early in the Saxon period; but the inhabitants remained in a condition of semi-barbarism long after other parts of the country had been reformed and civilised. The "men of the Isle" enjoyed many peculiar privileges above their surrounding neighbours; but they were a savage and brutal race. Lawless violence prevailed; and for more than a hundred years, litigious quarrels, arising out of disputes about the rights of land, frequently agitated the whole neighbourhood. Meanwhile, the "low levels" of the Isle which, from time immemorial, had been subject to almost constant submersion from the river, were little better than a swamp, where lurking ague found a constant home. When the overflows took place they "broke the banks, and drowned the country for a vast many miles round about." Flocks and herds had to be "boated to the hills," or left to perish in their folds; and many human lives were frequently lost. A "woeful spectator of the lamentable destruction of my native soil and country," says, "I and my company have been confined to an upper chamber, and seen no dry land for the space of these seven days. I did see the mothers, Pyrrha-like, trudging middle-deep in water with theire infants hanginge upon theire breastes; and the fathers, Deucalion-like, bearinge theire children upon theire shoulders, to seek higher ground for theire succour. All sorts of people in pitifull distress; some to save theire lives, some theire goods and cattle, some to get food for theire hungrie bodies." (sic)

The value of these "low levels," however, soon became apparent in the eyes both of natives and foreigners. In the time of the Stuarts, a charter for draining the whole country-side was given to Cornelius Vermuyden, a Danish money-lender who had frequently accommodated the First Charles in his pecuniary straits. After immense expenditure, disputations, frays, and toils, the work was finished. A considerable part of "the King's chase" was rescued from the dominion of the lawless waters. The arable and pastureland of the neighbourhood was increased by many thousand acres of "a fine, rich brown loam, than which there is none more fertile in England."

In the centre of this remarkable district stands a small market town, irregularly built, but pleasantly situated on the slope of a gentle hill. It is the recognised "Metropolis of the Isle," containing about two thousand inhabitants, and rejoicing in the appropriate name of Epworth, —from Heapeurde, "the Hill Farm," or "the farm on the rising ground." The church, resting on a considerable eminence on the north side of the town, commands an extensive prospect. It is dedicated to Saint Andrew, and is of rather ancient date. It consists of nave, aisles, chancel, and tower; and like many other Lincolnshire churches, has the appearance of having been built at different times. The town has become a place of deepest interest to two religious Denominations. There the Founder of Methodism and the planter of its earliest offshoot were born; and in the old parish church they were both dedicated to God in the Holy Sacrament of Baptism.

At the close of 1696, or the beginning of 1697, the rectorship of this parish, still in the gift of the Crown, was conferred upon Samuel Wesley, in accordance probably with some wish or promise of Queen Mary before her departure." Wesley's own words are:—"He wrote a book, which he dedicated to Queen Mary, who for that reason gave him a living in the country, valued at two hundred pounds per annum, where he remained for nearly forty years." stall, or scite of the parsonage, situate and lyenge betweene the field on the East, and Lancaster-Lane on the West, and abuttinge upon the High-Street on the South, and of John Maw,-sonne of Thomas,—his tenement, and a croft on the North," contained, "by estimation, three acres."

Mary died in December 1694; and the Epworth living was not entered upon by Wesley until two years afterwards. Either, therefore, she must have conferred upon him "the next presentation,"— supposing that to be possible,—or expressed some desire in accordance with which the living was so bestowed.

He had rendered some service to her cause by writing in favour of the Revolution, which placed her husband on the throne. Three years before, he had dedicated to her a metrical and illustrated "Life of our Lord Jesus Christ," which she highly approved; and at her death he had the honour of "scattering a few verses, and more tears, over her grave." The living was "proffered and given without his having solicited any person; without his ever expecting, or even once thinking of such a favour." But it is not unlikely that his former services, as well as the dedication of his "Heroic Poem" to the Queen, were remembered at Court. Epworth was four times the value of any of his former appointments; and, with an increasing family to provide for, he joyfully accepted the offer.

The necessary arrangements completed, the broad seal duly affixed to his title, and the requisite fees discharged, Wesley with his noble wife, young Samuel, Emilia, [or Emily] Sukey, and Mary, then an infant in arms, crossed over to the "other side of the county," and took possession of the new home. The "upper classes" of the parishioners were small landowners, dreadfully careful of their cash, and living chiefly on bread, buttermilk, "ash heap-cakes," eggs, and flour puddings. The "ladies," in many instances, wore the very gowns and cloaks which had so well served their mothers before them. The memory of the "oldest inhabitant" could not remember ever seeing a farmer arrayed, at any one time, in a complete suit of new clothes. The first-class maidservant rejoiced in forty shillings a year wages. She got up at three in the morning to ply the spinning wheel for a while before she went to milk the lowing kine. She clad herself in "linsey woolsey" garments, blessedly ignorant of gay ribbons and artificial flowers, crinoline, mantelette, and Victoria boots, which feed the pride and ruin the pockets of so many of her class in our own times. The broad acres were largely covered with hemp and flax, in the dressing of which most of the population were employed; and the manufacture of canvass, sacking, wool sheets, and heavy linen goods, was profitable to the entire neighbourhood. The parsonage, evidently no stately mansion, consisted of "five baies, built all of timber and plaister, and covered all with straw thache, the whole building being contrived into three stories, and disposed into seven cheife rooms, namely,–a kitchinge, a hall, a parlour, a butterie, and three large upper rooms; besydes some others of common use; and also a little garden impailed, betweene the stone wall and the South."

There "was one barn of six baies, built all of timber and clay walls, and covered with straw thache; and out-shotts about it, and free house therebye." Then came "one dove-coate of timber and plaister," covered with the usual "straw thache;" and, finally, "one hempkiln, that hath been usealeie occupied for the parsonage ground, adjoyning upon the South." This house, humble as it was, being larger than the Wesleys "had on the other side of the county," and their family increasing, new furniture was necessary.

For this purpose, as well as "for setting up a little husbandry when he took the tithes into his own hands," the rector was obliged to "take up fifty pounds more" in addition to moneys already borrowed. In process of time, the glebe was stocked and cultivated. There were cows in the meadows and swine in the stye. The flax and the barley waved in the field. The "two-eyed-nag," and "Bounce," and "Mettle," were employed in tilling the ground, or carting home the produce; while the "filly" and the "nag" afforded to the rector and his wife pleasant and healthy equestrian exercise. The milkmaid warbled her song with the carol of the lark; and the patient hind went "forth unto his work, and to his labour, until the evening." Had not Wesley been entirely dependent upon borrowed capital, for which, in some cases, heavy interest had to be paid, he might now have obtained some relief from the cares that had hitherto oppressed him. This "interest money" was a heavy millstone about his neck, and, combined with some severe losses, made the Epworth parsonage a place of poverty and temporal distress. The "one barn of six baies" was an unsubstantial structure, and fell down when it had been in his possession only twelve months. Then, during the dry summer of 1702, some sparks fell upon the thatch of the house, which speedily ignited, and a third of the miserable hut was burnt to the ground. Mrs Wesley and the children were in the study when the fire broke out. The mother, taking two of the little ones in her arms, rushed through the smoke and flame. One child, however, was left behind. Happily, the neighbours heard her cries for help, and rescued her from the impending death. The library was saved, and "not many of the goods" were missed.

The calamity was, nevertheless, very severe. The family had to be crowded for many months into the few remaining rooms, and the expense of restoration, especially to a man already oppressed with debt, was no light thing.

When the rector, who was at the other end of the town visiting the sick, heard of the salvation of his household, he wrote, "For which God be praised, as well as for what He has taken I find 'tis some happiness to have been miserable; for my mind has been so blunted with former misfortunes that this scarce made any impression upon me."

One would almost imagine that devouring fire was Samuel Wesley's adverse element; for he certainly suffered from it more frequently than most men. Within twelve months after this partial destruction of the parsonage, his entire growth of flax, on which he relied to satisfy some of his hungry creditors, was consumed in the field; and in 1709, the rectory, with all its contents, was destroyed by fire. Near midnight, on 9 February the sprightly little Hetty, frightened by a burning sensation at her feet, looked up and saw pieces of lighted wood falling from the roof of the room. The rector was roused by the loud cry of "Fire! fire!" in the street.

He "started up, and, opening his door, found the fire was in his own house." Bidding his wife and eldest daughter "rise quickly and shift for themselves," he rushed to the nursery, where the servant and five children were sleeping. When they got into the hall, and were completely surrounded by the flames, it was found that the keys of the lower doors had been left up-stairs. It was a perilous moment, and an awful death seemed inevitable. Happily, the keys were obtained "a minute before the stair-case took fire." "When we opened the street door," says Mrs Wesley, "the strong north-east wind drove the flames in with such violence that none could stand against them. But some of our children got out through the windows; the rest through a little door into the garden. I was not in a condition to climb up to the windows, neither could I get to the garden door. I endeavoured three times to force my passage through the street door, but was as often driven back by the fury of the flames. In this distress I besought our blessed Saviour for help, and then waded through the fire, naked as I was, which did me no further harm than a little scorching my hands and my face." When the tenants of the nursery were aroused, the maid caught up the youngest child, and told the others to follow her; but a lovely boy, six years old, lay sleeping on and taking his rest, unconscious of danger. When all the others were safe, he was missed. His father, thinking he heard him crying in the nursery, strove to stem the torrent of flame for his rescue. Thrice was he driven back, and the burning staircase began to crash and fall beneath his tread. Finding he could render him no help, he knelt in the hall, and in an agony of prayer, solemnly commended his soul to God. Meanwhile the child awoke, and seeing the room full of light, he thought it was day, and called the servant to take him up. As no one answered, he put his head out of the curtains, and saw "streaks of fire" running along the top of the room. He arose and ran to the door, but all he saw was a roaring sea of flame. Climbing on a chest near the window, he was seen from the yard below. "I will run and fetch a ladder," said one of the people. "There will not be time," answered another. "Here; I have thought of a shorter way. I will fix myself against the wall; lift a light man and set him on my shoulder." The house being low, the expedient succeeded, and the child was thus delivered from a terrible death. Another moment and he must

68

have perished beneath the fall of the burning roof. All the world is familiar with the fact that the child thus miraculously saved was none other than John Wesley, the Founder of Methodism. He remembered this providential deliverance through his entire after-life with the deepest gratitude. He commemorated it by an engraving, under one of his portraits, of a house in flames, beneath which is the impressive motto, "Is not this a brand plucked cut of the burning?" When they took him into the house where his father was, he cried out, "Come, neighbours, let us kneel down; let us give thanks to God! He has given me all my eight children. Let the house go: I am rich enough!" The next day, as the rector pensively paced the garden, surveying the blackened ruins of the house, he picked up a leaf of his cherished and expensive Polyglott Bible, on which just one solitary sentence was legible: Wade; vende omnia quae habes, et attolle crucem, et sequere Me;—"Go; sell all that thou hast; and take up thy cross, and follow Me." This was indeed a sore calamity: the destruction was complete. "I lost," says the rector, "all my books and manuscripts; a considerable sum of money; all our linen, wearing apparel, and household stuff, except a little old iron; my wife and I being scorched by the flames, and all of us very narrowly escaping with our lives." Very little of the old materials was left; and as for furniture, he declares, "We had now very little more than what Adam and Eve had when they first set up house-keeping." But there were other things quite as grievous as these material losses. There was no house in which they could live as a complete family; and for a long time they had to be scattered in the houses of friends and others. All domestic discipline was at an end; all regular studies interrupted. This was the sorest trial to Mrs Wesley. Those fine, intelligent, well-trained children, who had been so carefully shepherded in the fold of the rectory, were scattered in a wilderness. They came in contact with rough natures, and learned many habits which it cost their Mother much time and labour to reform and cure. "For some years," she says, "we went on very well. Never were children in better order. Never were children better disposed to piety, or in more subjection to their parents; till that fatal dispersion of them, after the fire, into several families. In those they were left at full liberty to converse with servants, which before they had always been

69

restrained from ; and to run abroad, and play with any children, good or bad. They soon learned to neglect a strict observation of the Sabbath, and got knowledge of several songs and bad things, which before they had no notion of That civil behaviour which made them admired, when at home, by all which saw them, was, in great measure, lost; and a clownish accent and many rude ways were learned, which were not reformed without some difficulty." How true are the words of Inspiration, "Evil communications corrupt good manners:"

Was this terrible conflagration, involving the all but irreparable temporal ruin of a large and respectable family, the result of accident or design? Both sides of the question have had their supporters; but we are fully persuaded it was the act of some malignant incendiary. The fire did not occur in the "dry time" of summer, when a few sparks would ignite the thatch; but in the depth of winter, when the inflammable roof-covering was in the worst possible condition to be lighted by accident. It did not commence in the daytime, when the grates were filled with crackling wood, or glowing coals, or sparkling peat; but at the dead of night, when all fires had been extinguished for hours. It did not break out in any lower room; but in the thatch of the roof, and must, therefore, have been lighted from without. And who in his senses would insinuate that it was "arson," when the character of every member of the family forbids the suspicion, and there was no insurance from which compensation could be obtained? The only fair conclusion is, that the house was fired by some malicious person or persons unknown. It must be remembered that such desperate doings were no strange thing to "the men of the Isle." Both before and after the conflagration of the parsonage, those who had sinned against the popular will were made to feel the people's wrath in a similar way. Their crops were destroyed, their farm-buildings pulled down, and the torch deliberately applied to their dwelling-house. And not long before this crowning act of their wickedness, they had shewn their animus against the Wesley family. by a series of most dastardly and inhuman outrages. They had assembled under the windows and "complimented" them all night long "with drums and guns." Three cows, the main support of the household, were stabbed in one night, though none of them "was killed outright." The report

70

was maliciously circulated that they had "accidentally run against a scythe," or that "the brawn had done it." To the innocent children they said, "O, ye devils! We will come and turn ye all out of doors a-begging shortly." They "twined off the iron latch of the house door." They "hacked the wood" in order to shoot back the lock; and what could this be for but robbery, or even a still fouler crime? The poor housedog, "who made a huge noise within-doors, was sufficiently punished for his want of politics and moderation," by having his "leg almost chopped off by an unknown hand." The rector not unnaturally concluded that it "was this foul beast" of an imbruted populace, this "worse than Erymanthean boar, In Greek mythology, the Erymanthean Boar (Greek: ὁ Ἐρυμάνθιος κάπρος) is remembered in connection with *The Twelve Labours*, in which Heracles, the (reconciled) enemy of Hera, visited in turn "all the other sites of the Goddess throughout the world, to conquer every conceivable 'monster' of nature and rededicate the primordial world to its new master, his Olympian father," Zeus. who fired his flax by rubbing his tusks against the wall." And if the flax, why not the parsonage? The reason frequently assigned for this deadly hatred of some of his parishioners, leading to such melancholy results, is the rector's uncompromising pulpit fidelity and strict pastoral discipline. We are not disposed, however, to attach much weight to this particular view. He had exercised his calling among these very people several years before this enmity assumed any hostile form: and the outrages we have described all took place after he had given great umbrage by his conduct in a great political crisis. The general election of 1705 was one of the most violent this country has ever known. From the Land's-End to Berwick-on-Tweed the people were roused to the conflict by the party-cry, "The Church is in danger!" According to Burnet, the press teemed with pamphlets declaring that "the Church was to be given up; that the Bishops were betraying it; that the Court would sell it to the Dissenters." Many High-Church clergymen echoed the rallying cry from their pulpits, and, as in later times, aspirants for senatorial honours industriously laboured to make political capital out of an ecclesiastical excitement. The contest for the county of Lincoln was exceedingly bitter and severe. The old members, Sir John Thorold and "Champion" Dymoke, offered themselves for reelection. The new candidates for parliamentary fame were Colonel Whichcott and a gentleman named Bertie. The lands of Axholme being divided among a greater number of owners than

71

any other part of the county, the freehold voters were consequently numerous. In a contested election, therefore, this insignificant corner of the shire became the chief battleground of the contending parties. Whoever could carry "the Isle," with its seven or eight hundred "free and independent electors," was sure of the victory. Wesley, as the leading clergyman of the neighbourhood, was early and zealously canvassed by both parties. He promised Thorold that he would not vote against him; but he positively refused to support "the Champion." Whichcott was a neighbouring gentleman with whom he was on friendly terms; and to him the rector pledged his "vote and interest." When, however, he returned from a short visit to London on private business, he found the position of affairs greatly altered. The party-cry had reached the Isle, and the contest had assumed a most violent form. Thorold and "the Champion" were "true blue," stanch for Royalty and the Church; while Whichcott and Bertie, both professedly Churchmen, had thrown themselves into the hands of the Dissenters, and had become the representatives of revolutionary measures in the Establishment. The Church, the clergy, and "the memory of the Martyr were openly scandalised;" while the character and doings of Cromwell were highly exalted. These changes, after he had promised Whichcott his vote, placed Wesley in very peculiar and trying circumstances. To assail the Church he so much loved was to touch the apple of his eye. When he found a combination to endanger her interests, he naturally took alarm. And when he saw that the man to whom he had pledged his vote on the understanding that he was a friend of the Church, had become the avowed representative of an extreme party, who desired and predicted her overthrow, he considered himself absolved from his promise. Though "equally against his inclination and his interest," he resolved to "drop both when honour and conscience were concerned," and vote for "the friends of the Church."* And who shall condemn him for so doing? Had he known that Whichcott would take the course he did, and become the champion of those whom he regarded as enemies of the Establishment, Wesley would never have promised him his vote: and to have voted for him after he openly avowed the Dissenting opinion which he felt it convenient to profess in order to gain the election, would have been a public renunciation of principles

72

which Wesley had long and sacredly held, and for which he had sacrificed much. We have no positive information as to the active part the Epworth rector took in this exciting contest. He declares, "I concerned myself only in the election of my own county, which I thought I had as much right to do as any other freeholder."" The probability is that, with his strong and sincere ecclesiastical opinions—and the question with him was a Church question without any reference to secular politics—he threw himself thoroughly into the election strife. Under the given circumstances, he was not the man to remain inactive, or to satisfy himself by simply recording his vote. He most likely followed out the full convictions of his duty; and the consequences to himself and family were humiliating and afflictive. The opposite party loaded him with every kind of insult and persecution within their power. On the steps of his own church he was called "rascal and scoundrel." Having covenanted in an unholy alliance to destroy his life, they lay in wait for him and his servant many hours; but being forewarned, he returned home another way and escaped. While visiting Lincoln to record his vote, the infuriated "Isle people" wreaked their malice upon his afflicted wife and unoffending children. Nearly a whole night, they "kept drumming, shouting, and firing off pistols and guns" under the window of the room where Mrs Wesley lay, feeble and exhausted from a recent confinement. The new-born infant had been committed to the care of a nurse just opposite the parsonage. The noise kept her awake "till one or two in the morning." Then, heavy with sleep, she "overlaid the child," and became the unconscious instrument of its death. When she awoke and found her precious charge crushed and suffocated beneath her own person, she ran to the rectory almost distracted, and threw the child into the hands of the servant. The maid ran to Mrs Wesley's room and, ere the Mother was well awake, the infant, "cold and dead," was placed in her arms. "She composed herself as well as she could," says her husband, "and that day got it buried." These, however, were but the beginning of sorrows. Nothing short of his utter ruin would glut the vindictive malice of his enemies. They used their influence in high places so successfully as to deprive him of the chaplaincy of a regiment, which he had obtained from the Duke of Marlborough "with so much expense and trouble." Unfortunately, he also numbered some of them among his minor creditors; and no sooner was the election contest over than they made him feel that he was in their power. Coming out of his church from a baptismal service, he was arrested for a paltry debt of less than thirty pounds, owing to an unfeeling creditor called Pinder, a relative and violent supporter of Colonel Whichcott. A few hours' delay would have enabled the rector to meet the demand. "My adversary was sent to, when I was on the road," he writes, "to meet me, that I might make some proposals to him. But all his answer was that I must immediately pay the whole sum, or go to prison." There was furniture in the house and stock on the farm; but Wesley's ruin, and not the payment of the debt, was the austere creditor's immediate object. He was, therefore, hurried away to Lincoln Castle, before any of his friends could come to his rescue. He left home "with no great concern for himself;" but his heart was riven at the thought of leaving his "poor lambs in the midst of so many wolves." No sooner was he within the walls of the prison than he exclaimed, "Now I am at rest, for I am come to the haven where I've long expected to be . . . . A jail is a paradise in comparison of the life I led before I came hither!" He was not insensible to his real position; but, like a man who has long struggled under the apprehension of some fearful calamity, he felt that the actual crisis was more endurable than the agonising suspense. The "worst," which he had so bravely, but vainly struggled to ward off, had come, and the next step must be one of rescue and advance. "I hope to rise again, as I have always done when at the lowest," he writes; "and I think I cannot be much lower now." Although plunged into a debtor's cell, where many in his profession would have hidden themselves as far as possible from the gaze of their fellow-prisoners, Samuel Wesley did not forget his high calling as a minister of the Lord Jesus. He saw around him men who deeply needed the Gospel, and seized upon his imprisonment as an opportunity of usefulness. Only two days after his arrival he writes, "I don't despair of doing some good here,—and so long I shan't quite lose the end of living, and it may be do more in this new parish than in my old one: for I have leave to read prayers every morning and afternoon here in the prison; and to preach once a Sunday, which I choose to do in the afternoon, when there is no service at the minster. I am getting

74

acquainted with my brother jail-birds as fast as I can; and shall write to London next post, to the Society for Propagating Christian Knowledge, who, I hope, will send me some books to distribute among them." To his noble and heroic wife, this incarceration of the rector must have been the severest possible trial. Left "as sheep in the midst of wolves," subject to gross insults and threatenings, the family life in the parsonage was one of perpetual struggle and apprehension. Yet she bore it with all the fortitude and generous patience which became her position, "and which," says her husband, "I expected from her." Tis not everyone could bear these things; but, I bless God, my wife is less concerned with suffering them, than I am in the writing. She is not what she is represented, any more than me." Entirely dependent upon the produce of the dairy for the subsistence of the family, and absolutely destitute of money, her anxieties would certainly have crushed a woman of inferior spirit, and less confidence in the God of her life. She felt deeply lest her husband should be in greater straits for necessary food than herself and children. What little jewellery she possessed, including "the token and pledge" of her marriage covenant, she sent for his relief. It was instantly returned, "and God soon provided for him." His arrest had been occasioned by unflinching adherence to the Church of his choice, and sincere, yet perhaps over-zealous, efforts to keep out of the legislature men opposed to her interests. The clergy, with good Archbishop Sharp at their head, felt that he deserved their generous sympathy. He made a full and candid statement of his liabilities, amounting to "about three hundred pounds;" and in a short time more than half his debts were paid, and arrangements made for their complete liquidation. After three weary months in the grim old Castle, during which his spirit never failed him, preaching to his fellow-prisoners, writing his "Answer to Palmer," "tempted to print his case in his own vindication," and rejoicing that he would "sometime have a more equal Judge than any in this world," he returned to his family and his parish without fear of any man seizing him by the throat and saying, "Pay me that thou owest!" Most of his friends advised him to leave Epworth, and seek a more congenial sphere of labour, free from those deep prejudices and deadly hostilities manifested by "the men of the Isle." But he resolutely disregarded their counsel. "I confess I am not of that mind," he writes to the Archbishop of York, "because I may yet do some good there; and 'tis like a coward to desert my post because the enemy fire thick upon me. They have only wounded me yet, and, I believe, can't kill me." Among these enemies, Robert Darwin, one of his richest parishioners, gained a bad pre-eminence for outrageous conduct. "He was," says Mrs Wesley, in writing to her son, "one of the most implacable enemies your father had among his parishioners: one that insulted him most basely in his troubles: one that was ready to do him all the mischief he could, not to mention his affronts to me and the children, and how heartily he wished to see our ruin, which God permitted him not to see." This violent persecutor met with a most awful death. Returning from Bawtry Fair in a state of senseless intoxication, he fell from his horse and disjointed his neck. His companions "immediately pulled it in again, and he lived till next day; but he never spoke more. His face was torn all to pieces; one of his eyes beat out; his under lip cut off; his nose broken down; and, in short, he was one of the dreadfullest examples of the severe justice of God that I have known. This man and one more," adds Mrs Wesley, "have been now cut off in the midst of their sins since your father's confinement." And who can wonder that she saw in events like these, the avenging hand of Him who hath said, "Touch not Mine anointed, and do My prophets no harm?" The prejudices of his parishioners were by no means smoothed away after the rector's return to his parish. The hostilities continued to increase until they culminated in the dastard deed, which burnt his house to the ground. Then a truce ensued: a better feeling sprang up; and the family fairly entered upon a life of quietness and hope. Preparations were made for the erection of a new parsonage, more substantial and fireproof than its predecessor. The old foundations were dug up; bricks were substituted for wood and plaster, and a commodious dwelling gradually rose to completion. Compared with the hovel, which it superseded, the house was a roomy and convenient mansion. We read of kitchen, parlour, and dining room; study and nursery; best chamber, matted chamber, and painted chamber; and, over all, the wide and ghostly garret. As if he endorsed the sentiment of Bacon, that "gardening is the purest of all human pleasures," the rector commenced laying out the beds and casting in the seeds. The "two fronts" of the house he planted with wall-fruit. Mulberry-trees, cherry-trees, and pear trees, he set in the garden, and walnuts "in the adjoining croft." This pleasant task he undertook, that he "might do what became him, and leave the living better than he found it." The family again gathered under one roof. The necessary reforms were rigidly enforced; domestic discipline was restored; and the painstaking processes of education were vigorously resumed. The former house has its legends of wonders, and is celebrated throughout the world as the place from which the Founder of Methodism was so marvellously rescued: and the latter house is renowned as the scene of events concerning which no satisfactory explanation has yet been given, but without a brief sketch of which our narrative would be incomplete.

## OLD JEFFERY, POLTERGEIST OR PRANK?

The legendary literature of the world teems with wonderful stories of haunted houses, where invisible spirits were believed to utter mysterious sounds, to perform extraordinary pranks, and sometimes communicate revelations of the future, or disclose the dread secrets of the hidden world. These beliefs, though strongest and most prevalent where the Gospel is unknown or least influential, are not peculiar to generations "of old time," or to any particular nation under heaven. And one of the most remarkable and best authenticated tales of this description, in comparatively modern times, is connected with the Epworth parsonage.

On 1 December 1716, when night had mantled the rectory with her shadow, the maid heard a "terrible and astonishing noise," like "the dismal groans of one in extremes, at the point to die." Strange knockings, commonly three-times-three,—the rector's own peculiar rap at the door, and too "loud and hollow" to be imitated, were soon heard by the whole family. The signal of approach was as "the swift revolution of a windmill, when the wind changes;" or the "quick winding up of a jack, just like the running of the wheels and creaking of the iron-work." Then followed rumblings in the lower rooms and in the garret; rapid footsteps, as of a man "walking up-stairs in jack-boots," trailing a nightgown after him; gobbling like a turkey-cock; and dancing in

77

an empty room, whose door was locked. Casements clattered. Warming-pans and every vessel of brass and iron rang out a discord of strange sounds. Latches moved up and down with uncommon swiftness. Without the touch of human hand, doors flew open, banged, and violently pushed against those who sought to pass from one room to another. Lumps of coal seemed dashed upon hard floors, and shivered into a thousand pieces; or the bright pewter service to leap from its resting-place on the shelves. Boots and shoes appeared to whirl and move without any visible cause. Hoards of silver coin fell jingling on the floor, which made Samuel ask, "Have you dug in the place where the money seemed poured out at your feet?" The house shook from top to bottom. The sleeping children began to moan and sweat. The wind rose, whistled, and howled in dismal cadences. The mastiff whined and trembled, hurrying to some human presence for protection. The rector's trencher once danced upon the table at the Sunday dinner, "without anybody touching it; when, lo! an adventurous wretch took it up and spoiled the sport, for it remained still ever afterwards." Three different times was the minister himself jostled by this invisible power. The bed on which Nancy sat was "lifted up several times to a considerable height." She leaped off, exclaiming, "Surely Old Jeffery will not run away with me!" While Sukey was writing her last letter to Mr S., "it made a great noise all round the room; and the night after she left for London, it knocked till morning, with scarce any intermission." The prayers for the King and the Prince of Wales were specially obnoxious to it. The loud demonstrations against His Majesty brought it under the suspicion of being a Jacobite, and a great enemy of "our Sovereign Lord, the King." This provoked the loyal rector to offer three prayers for the Royal Family instead of two; and Samuel declared that if he were King he would "rather Old Nick were his enemy than his friend." When Nancy swept the rooms, Jeffery followed her, like a second person doing it over again, she thinking, meanwhile, it might as well have done it in reality and saved her the trouble. The corn-mill whirled round for a time with great velocity, and Robin declared had it been full instead of empty, Old Jeffery might have "ground his heart out before he would have stopped him." Though heard by all, the references to Jeffery's visible manifestation are not so conclusive. Sitting moodily by the back kitchen fire in a fit of illness, Robin thought he saw "something like a small rabbit coming out of the copper-hole, its ears flat upon its neck, and its little scut straight up." It "turned round five times very swiftly." Robin ran after it with the tongs; but the mysterious creature vanished away, and the valiant plough-boy "ran to the maid in the parlour." Mrs Wesley supposed she saw under the bed "something like a badger without a head," run quickly away: and Robin thought he caught a glimpse of the same creature sitting by the drawing-room fire; but when he approached, it rushed past him and disappeared. If these statements fail to prove the visible appearance of this disturber of the Wesley family, they in no degree, as Southey justly observes, "invalidate the other parts of the story, which rest upon the concurrent testimony of many intelligent witnesses." If attributed to any other than supernatural causes, the noises became perfectly outrageous. Though often adjured to tell the purpose of its coming, Jeffery maintained a perfect silence. The study remained free from intrusion until the rector called it "a deaf and dumb devil," and bade it come to him if it had anything to say, and not frighten young and helpless children. Jeffery immediately announced his acceptance of the challenge by imitating Wesley's peculiar knock at the gate, with a violence, which threatened to shiver the boards in pieces. Henceforth it visited the study as freely as the garret or the nursery, and thought no more of disturbing the clergyman in his meditations, than the children in their sleep. These annoyances continued eight or nine weeks. When first heard, they were supposed to portend or announce the death of some member of the family. Several days passed away before they were perceived by the rector; and as such sounds, according to vulgar opinion, were not audible to the person whose evil they foreboded, they refrained from telling him, lest he should think it betokened his own departure. But when the disturbances became so loud and frequent that none of the family durst be alone, Mrs Wesley informed him of the entire circumstances, and intimated her belief in their supernatural character. "Sukey," said he, in a somewhat wrathful manner, "I am ashamed of you. These boys and girls frighten one another; but you are a woman of sense and should know better. Let me hear of it no more." The answer rather vexed the young ladies, who devoutly wished he might now hear it himself—a wish speedily gratified. The very next night he was roused from his slumbers by nine loud and distinct knocks, as from a heavy staff upon a chest. He rose and prosecuted a strict search from room to room, where the noises were heard, and was fully convinced that they could only be produced by supernatural causes. All fears for the rector's life being dispersed, the family began to dread that the eldest son in London had met with a violent death. The thought became so painful that it could be endured no longer, and the afflicted father resolved to seek some favourable moment to interrogate Jeffery on the subject. He went into Nancy's room and adjured it to speak; but "there was no voice, neither any to answer." "These spirits love darkness," he exclaimed; "put out the candle and perhaps it will speak." Still there was only the usual knocking, and, to Nancy's great joy, no articulate sound. Thinking that "two Christians were an overmatch for the Devil," he ordered all down-stairs, hoping it would have "courage to speak when he was alone." Failing to get a positive answer, he resolved to solicit a negative one;—"If thou art the spirit of my son Samuel, I pray thee knock three knocks, and no more!" Immediately all was silent, and remained so during the night. Mrs Wesley earnestly prayed that the noises might not be heard in her own room, during her hour of devotion, from five to six in the evening. Her prayer was answered, and she was never troubled while so engaged. The family soon became so accustomed to these ghostly proceedings that all dread passed away, and they were a source of amusement to the younger inhabitants of the parsonage. When the gentle tapping at the bed's head began, they would say, "Old Jeffery is coming; it is time to go to sleep!" When the noises were heard in the daytime, little Kezzy chased the sounds from room to room, desiring no better amusement than to hear the mysterious answers to the stamp of her own foot. The tidings of these wonders spread abroad; others beside the Wesleys sat up and listened to them; and they became the absorbing topic of discourse in the whole neighbourhood. "Send me some news," writes Sukey to her brother; "for we are excluded from the sight, or hearing, of any versal thing, except Jeffery." "Any author," says Southey, "who in this age relates such a story, and treats it as not utterly incredible and absurd must expect to be ridiculed. But the testimony on which it rests is far too strong to be set aside, because of the strangeness of the relation." For any such ridicule, we are prepared. We have threaded together the leading facts and circumstances from a careful examination of all available documents, and the story, as told by the Wesley family, we most assuredly believe. But where and what is the most likely solution of the difficulties which it presents? To this question divers answers have been given. Rats were regarded, in the first instance, as the cause of these mysterious sounds; and a horn was vigorously blown about the house for nearly a whole day. But as the noises continued, and many of them being such as no irrational creatures could imitate, this notion was soon abandoned. One of the family firmly believed it to be witchcraft, because the rector "had for several Sundays before its coming preached warmly against consulting cunning men," a habit very common among his parishioners. Then came the conclusion that the whole was the result of trickery practised by the servants, aided by some of the neighbours. But all the means employed to discover any such deception utterly failed; and no man who carefully studies the minute accounts of the whole affair will adopt this solution. John Wesley believed it was a messenger of Satan, sent to buffet his father for his rash vow to leave his family in consequence of his wife refusing to say amen to the prayer for the King. Had the noises been heard immediately after the event to which reference is made, there might have been some show of reason in this solution. But what these noises had to do with circumstances said to have occurred sixteen years before, it is hard to divine. Clarke throws out a hint that the house was probably haunted, and tells a story about the murder of a burglar while attempting to break into the parsonage. But this would only cut the knot; and the tale of murder, as he acknowledges, rests on mere rumour. Coleridge is very positive, and says, "This, indeed, I take to be the true and only solution,—a contagious nervous disease; catalepsy." There is no answering this dogmatic settling of the matter. But we feel that, in view of all the circumstances of the case, it makes a greater demand upon our faith than even a miracle itself. Stevens, the American historian of Methodism, has suggested, that the noises in the parsonage "were strikingly similar to marvels which, in our own times, have suddenly spread over most of the civilised world, perplexing the learned, deluding

81

the ignorant, producing a 'spiritualistic' literature of hundreds of volumes and periodicals, and resulting in extensive church organisations." We willingly disclaim all pretensions to learning in the lore of this modern spiritualism. But if, as competent authorities assert, there are subtle forces in nature which, under certain conditions, can be brought into play and so controlled as to produce these particular sounds, there is a ready solution of these much-vaunted mysteries. We do not deny that, in many respects, the noises at Epworth and those common to what are called spirit-rapping, are strikingly similar. But in many of their leading features, they are wide as the poles asunder. In the parsonage, there was no darkened room, no careful preparation, no "medium" in whom these mystic forces are said to inhere, and at whose will they are ready to rush forth into active operation. The full explanation of Jeffery's movements, we are persuaded, cannot be found here."

The English editor of Stevens's work thinks it "not at all unlikely that, at first, the wind shook the rickety old building about, and, whistling through unknown crevices, produced sounds which none could, at the time, explain." This excited fears, which, in turn, brought in the supernatural element to account for the noises. Without discussing this ready solution, we may just remind the writer, that what he calls "the rickety old building," was the substantial parsonage standing at this day, and which had not been built more than six or seven years when the noises were heard!

There have been solutions of a more ambitious character. Isaac Taylor, deeply versed in philosophic speculations, and for whose transcendent talents and eminent services to true Christianity we have the profoundest respect, has dealt with Old Jeffery after a fashion of his own. "Once in a century, or not so often," he writes, "on a summer's evening, a stray Arabian locust —a genuine son of the desert,—tempest-borne, we know not how, has alighted in Hyde-Park, or elsewhere. This rare occurrence, and which it is so difficult to explain, is indeed out of the course of nature; but it is not supernatural; certainly it is not a religious event. Nor to judge of them by their apparent characteristics, are many other occurrences, similar to the Epworth rectory noises and disturbances, to be thought of as touching any religious question. In truth, there is nothing in these facts of a celestial complexion; nor are they grave enough to be reputed infernal. We can incur no risk of committing sacrilege when we deal with occult folk, such as 'Jeffery,' huffingly and disrespectfully. Almost, while intent upon these quaint performances, one seems to catch a glimpse of a creature,—half-intelligent, or idiotic, whose pranks are like one that, using a brief opportunity given it by chance, is going to the extent of its tether in freaks of bootless mischief . Why may not this be thought? Around us, as most believe, are beings of a high order, whether good or evil, and yet not cognizable by the senses of man. But the analogies of the visible world favour the supposition that, besides these, there are orders, or species, of all grades, and some, perhaps, not more intelligent than apes or than pigs. That these species have no liberty, ordinarily, to infringe upon the solid world is manifest; nevertheless, chances or mischances, may, in long cycles of time, throw some—like the Arabian locust—over his boundary, and give him an hour's leave to disport himself among things palpable." This is, indeed, speculative philosophy; but is it in jest or in earnest? We venture to believe that the amiable author would find some difficulty in reconciling its principles in this case, with the principles of his Christianity. "The mistake," he tells us, "is, when such occurrences are not of a kind that can be rejected as tricks or fictions, immediately to attribute to them a religious meaning, or to see in them the Hand of Heaven." Admitting his theory, that there are round about us orders of all grades, "and some, perhaps, not more intelligent than apes or than pigs;" and that, "in long cycles of time," one of these may be "thrown over his boundary," and obtain "an hour's leave to disport himself among things palpable;" still we ask, Are not all things—whether in the heavens above, or in the earth beneath, or in the waters under the earth–subject to Divine control? Are not the bounds of their habitation fixed by Divine appointment? And can any one of them, from the least even unto the greatest, be thrown over his boundary and "disport himself among things palpable" by mere "chance or mischance?" Supposing such an event to occur, would it be any "mistake" to see in it "the Hand of Heaven?" And even in so

83

apparently trivial a circumstance as an Arabian locust, "tempest-borne, we know not how," alighting in Hyde Park, "once in a century, or not so often," would there be any "mistake" if we saw the wise disposal of Him in whose hand is the breath of every living thing? "Are not two sparrows sold for a farthing? — and one of them shall not fall on the ground without your Father." Mr Taylor's reasoning is certainly curious, and probably original; but as a solution of the difficulty in question, it is most unsatisfactory, and leaves us just where it found us.

Southey did himself honour by the way in which he treated this most perplexing subject. Priestly, who first collected and published the family letters in relation to it, observed that it was "perhaps the best authenticated and best told story of the kind extant." But he argued, that where no good end was to be answered, we may safely conclude that no miracle was wrought. "It may safely be asserted," replied Southey, "that many of the circumstances cannot be explained by any such supposition," as a trick of the servants; "nor by any legerdemain; nor by ventriloquism; nor by any secret of acoustics. The former argument would be valid, if the term miracle were applicable to the case. But by miracle Doctor Priestly evidently intends a manifestation of Divine power; and in the present instance no such manifestation is supposed, any more than in the appearance of a departed spirit. Such things may be preternatural, and yet not miraculous. They may be not in the ordinary course of nature, and yet imply no alteration of its laws. And with regard to the good end which they may be supposed to answer, it would be end sufficient if sometimes one of those unhappy persons, who, looking through the dim glass of infidelity, see nothing beyond this life, and the narrow sphere of mortal existence, from the well-established truth of one such story, –trifling and objectless as it might otherwise appear,—be led to a conclusion, that there are more things in heaven and earth than are dreamt of in their philosophy."

And were none of those keen and inquiring minds in the Epworth rectory in danger of looking through the dim glass of infidelity and seeing nothing beyond this life? Let the following passage from a letter of Emilia Wesley, whose temptations to unbelief were unusually strong, be carefully pondered in this connexion. "I am so far from being superstitious, that I was too much inclined to infidelity; so that I heartily rejoice at having such an opportunity of convincing myself, past doubt or scruple, of the existence of some beings besides those we see. A whole month was sufficient to convince anybody of the reality of the thing, and to try all ways of discovering any trick, had it been possible for any such to have been used." After all, my own opinion about Jeffery and his mysterious movements is very much like that of young Samuel Wesley, expressed at the time. "My Mother," he wrote, "sends to me to know my thoughts of it, and I cannot think at all of any interpretation. Wit, I fancy, might find many, but wisdom none."

NOTE: Other writers have recorded that the Reverend Samuel Wesley confronted the "ghost" to cease frightening the family and meet him in his study man to man. The door to the study was then slammed shut with a potent force. However, after the Wesley family became used to their intruder and were no longer frightened, the disturbances at Epworth ceased as abruptly as they had begun.— Editor.

Stephen Tomkins in *John Wesley: A Biography*, says, "What are we to make of "Old Jeffery?" The story is said to be one of the best-authenticated stories of its kind ever by people who study them. Enough educated people witnessed the manifestations to give it unusual credibility. Certainly, much of the story could be explained as hoax, much of the remainder as suggestibility and auto-suggestion and another part as being the tale growing in the telling. Nevertheless, even this still seems to leave us with something genuinely inexplicable." (19, 20).

# VI. THE RECTOR IN HIS PARISH.

THE last chapter has shown us how wild, and even malignant against all that was good, the generality of the Epworth parishioners were during the earlier years of Wesley's ministry among them. Though professedly members of the Established Church, with only "one Presbyterian, and one Papist," like a solitary Canaanite in the land, "to balance him," the Sabbath congregations were exceedingly small. The communicants at the Holy Sacrament of the Supper seldom numbered twenty. The baptism of children was either totally neglected, or so long delayed that the "monsters of men-children brought to the font," made the minister's arms ache with their weight, while their "manful voices disturbed and alarmed the whole congregation." Many of the Islanders had also gained a bad pre-eminence in various gross immoralities, and keenly resented any attempt for their reformation. With his eminent abilities and scholarly attainments, an intelligent city congregation would have been a far more congenial sphere for Samuel Wesley's labours than this rudest corner of Lincolnshire; while humbler talents and less refinement would probably have been more acceptable and useful to this rural flock. But, notwithstanding these heavy discouragements, he gave himself to his work with all the energy of a man of God, and all the ardour of an ambassador for Christ. And in order to a correct and comprehensive view of the connexion of the Wesleys with Epworth, it is necessary to glance at the rector among his flock, and endeavour to ascertain the result of his thirty-nine years' parochial toil in the moral wilderness of Axholme. The first thing which arrests our attention is, the zealous and systematic way in which he discharged the important duty of pastoral visitation. He was no recluse in his parish. From the very strong and general impression about his extensive learning, studious habits, and marvellous propensity for "rhyming," he has been too commonly regarded as a mere hard-working student, passing his time between the pulpit and the study; occupying his position as a parish priest for the purposes of "learned leisure," rather than the "cure of souls;" never moving among his people, or mixing in their society. This is an entire mistake. He cultivated toward his flock, what he happily calls, a "well-ordered familiarity." There was not a parishioner whom he did not know by name, and for whom he had not a kindly greeting whenever he crossed his path. In addition to the most sedulous attention to the sick, and that general intercourse which every clergyman must necessarily have with the people of his charge, Samuel Wesley compelled himself to a more systematic, searching, solemn visitation of his parish at different and distant intervals. And on these occasions he went from house to house, until his whole allotted sphere of labour, which was nearly three miles long, had been compassed. This was not a visitation for mere pastoral gossip, making himself agreeable in trifles, attempting to compensate by bland intercourse for the lack of faithful duty. It was a real shepherding of the flock; a downright dealing with the heart and conscience. "Who can read? who can say their prayers and Catechisms? who have been confirmed? who have received the Communion, or are of age to do it? and who have prayers in their families?" — these were the solemn inquiries which he pressed home upon his people. Moving among them as a minister of God, charged to give a good account of the souls committed to his care, "he sifted their creed, and permitted none of them to be corrupt in their opinions or practice without instruction or reproof." In this special manner he had gone three times through his parish, carefully noting down the results, and was prosecuting his fourth visitation when overtaken by his last affliction. When trembling with age and manifold infirmities, he reports to his Diocesan, "Looking a little among my people, I found there were two strangers come hither, both of whom I have discovered to be Papists, though they come to church; and I have hopes of making one or both of them good members of the Church of England." All this was a beautiful illustration of the apostolic advice: "Be instant in season, out of season; reprove, rebuke, exhort with all long-suffering and doctrine." Two or three instances of the manner in which he used to reprove sin are well worth quoting. None of them come under the class of ordinary reproof; and we record them less as examples to be followed, than as illustrations of character. They shew clearly that Samuel Wesley was not afraid to risk something when he thought his duty required him to lift up his voice in rebuking evil. To one of his respectable parishioners he administered a reproof after a fashion of his own, and not without a touch of that stern humour which he so greatly relished. Taking advantage of his well-known leniency, many of his unprincipled hearers defrauded him of the "tithes and offerings," to which he had an unquestionable right. At one time there was a combination among them to give him as much trouble as possible, by paying their dues only "in kind;" and even then they did not hesitate to lay dishonest hands on his appointed "tenth." Going one day into the field where the tithe-corn was laid out for removal, he found a farmer deliberately cutting off the ears of wheat and putting them into a bag with intent to appropriate them to his own use. Without saying a word, the rector took the delinquent by the arm and walked with him into the market-place. Seizing the bag, he turned out the corn before all the people and told them what the culprit had been doing. He then left him with his pilfered spoils to the judgment of his neighbours, and quietly walked home. This clearly was not all that the sacrilegious thief deserved: but the moral influence of such a reproof upon the offender himself and the parishioners generally, as well as upon the minister's own position and character in the eyes of his rude flock, was no doubt far more wholesome than a magisterial committal, and a month's hard labour at the treadmill. Another illustration of his mode of reproof savours more of the playful and the humorous. At Temple Belwood, not far from Epworth, lived a poor miserly wretch, who was hardly ever known to dine a friend, or relieve a case of distress. Coming under a momentary impulse of another kind, he invited Wesley and a select circle of friends to dinner. As soon as the repast was ended, the clergyman, being requested to return thanks, delivered the following impromptu grace:—

"Thanks for this feast ! for 'tis no less

Than eating manna in the wilderness.
Here meagre famine bears controlless sway,
And ever drives each fainting wretch away;
Yet here, —O how beyond a saint's belief!—
We've seen the glories of a chine of beef;
Here chimneys smoke which never smoked before,
And we have dined where we shall dine no more!"

However much we may admire the cleverness and wit of a reproof like this, we cannot sympathise with the way in which the sarcastic, the playful, and the religious are mingled in an act of devotion. Wesley probably thought the strange compound of oddity and avarice, at whose expense he had just dined was insensible to any reproof of an ordinary kind, and therefore adopted this remarkable course in hope that it might make an impression, which would produce better thoughts. If so, he was disappointed. It is said that immediately after the last line— "And we have dined where we shall dine no more!"— had fallen from his lips, the old man exclaimed in unmistakable tones, "No, gentlemen; for it is sadly too expensive 1° How true are the words of Inspiration: "Though thou shouldest bray a fool in a mortar among wheat with a pestle, yet will not his foolishness depart from him." You "may separate the straw and the chaff by thrashing: you may take off the husk by rubbing and trituration; you may turn the grain to meal or flour by grinding; but to drive folly from the human heart is more than man can do." The following illustration of Wesley's fertile invention and fearlessness in the discharge of this difficult duty, exhibits a happier and more successful result. Dining one day at a London coffee-house, he saw a small company of gentlemen at the other end of the room. One of them, an officer in the Guards, kept pouring forth a succession of profane oaths. Knowing he could not speak to him directly without great difficulty, he ordered the waiter to bring a glass of water, and said, loud enough to be heard, "Carry it to that gentleman in the red coat; and desire him to wash his mouth after his oaths l" The officer rose in a fury; but his companions restrained him, saying, "Nay, Colonel you gave the first offence. You see the gentleman is a clergyman. You know it is an offence to swear in his presence." Many years afterwards, while walking in Saint James' Park, he met a gentleman who inquired if he had ever seen him before. All recollection of him had passed from Wesley's mind. The stranger then adverted to the scene in the coffeehouse, and said, "Since that time, sir, I thank God, I have feared an oath, and everything that is offensive to the Divine Majesty; and as I have a perfect recollection of you, I rejoiced at seeing you, and could not refrain from expressing my gratitude to God and you." "Blessed are they that sow beside all waters!" Many of these words of the wise shall be as "bread cast upon the waters, found after many days." Oh, how would vice be restrained and religion promoted if all the Lord's people obeyed that ancient precept, —"Thou shalt in anywise rebuke thy neighbour, and shalt not suffer sin upon him!'" Samuel Wesley took a deep, though by no means a meddling, interest in all parochial business wherein he was concerned as the minister of the parish. During Rogation-Week, he headed the annual procession of the authorities and the rising generation, waving the orthodox willow wand, in "beating the boundary." The practice, he thought, "might have prevented a great deal of loss to the parish and the minister if it had been constantly done formerly." He was most conscientious in the administration of all public charities, and took a kindly interest in the welfare of the deserving poor. The Sacramental collections, to "which he always gave something himself, for example more than any conceived obligation," he disposed of according to a definite regulation. Three parts were given to the funds of the charity school, and "the fourth reserved in bank for such poor sick people as had no constant relief from the parish, and who came to the Sacrament." This was clearly an arrangement made of his own free will, and not forced upon him by external pressure. The afflicted, "whether in mind, body, or estate," had in him an ever-ready and sympathising friend. Often did he contribute of his own scant income, and exert his influence with his well-to-do neighbours, to rescue some honest, but unfortunate parishioner from pecuniary embarrassment, or save him from a debtor's prison, and his family from beggary and ruin. His administration of discipline was exceedingly strict and impartial. Though never going beyond the treatment or penalty prescribed by the ecclesiastical laws, it was nevertheless sometimes harsh and severe. One crime, which we need not more particularly indicate, was very prevalent among his rude and ignorant flock; and he resolved to employ every appliance that the laws of the Church placed in his hands to arrest its progress, and make the guilty ones ashamed of their criminal courses. When the offenders were, what he quaintly calls, "lean couples," he undertook "to see the court charges defrayed, which," he adds, "I hope will be as moderate as possible, because most of it is like to come out of my own pocket." There were, however, many "fat couples," guarded "with impenetrable brass." Against these, in consequence of the free use of this formidable means of defence, it was no small matter to bring home the charges, so as to secure a conviction. But he resolved to do his duty, and, as far as possible, carry out the provisions of Church discipline irrespective of the station or quality of the offender. "I ever thought it my duty," he writes, "since I have been the minister of any parish, to present those persons who were obnoxious to it, if the churchwardens neglected it, unless where the criminal was so sturdy and so wealthy, as that I was morally certain I could not do it without my own inconvenience or ruin: in which case God does not require it of me." Conscientiously acting upon these principles, it was sometimes his painful duty to withhold "the cup of the Lord" from the "sturdy offender" who had outraged morality, and refused to make some amends by submitting to the demands of discipline. And sometimes another form of punishment, far more severe and shameful, was adopted. The criminal was seen standing for three successive Sabbaths, on the damp mud floor in the centre of the church, without shoes or stockings; bareheaded; covered with a white sheet; and shivering with cold. This was "doing penance;" and the offender publicly stood forth as a warning to others, that they might not follow his pernicious ways. We know not whether these severities recovered any out of the snare of the Devil, or prevented others being led captive at his will; but we certainly rejoice that these public "spectacles" in our churches, however common in earlier times, are now numbered with the things which are passing away, and not likely to be

92

revived. Having traced his movements among his parishioners, let us enter the sacred edifice on the Lord's-day, and mark his behaviour in the house of God. He conducted the public services of the Church with becoming solemnity; yet with an ease and freedom sufficient to arrest attention and awaken devotional feeling. In reading the incomparable Liturgy, he "endeavoured to avoid that dead and unpleasing monotony of too many, who speak out of the ground in one heavy tenor, without life or devotion." He also shunned "the other extreme, no less grating on a judicious ear, of unequal cadences and incondite whining; laying weight where there ought to be none," or omitting it where it is requisite. To him, "reading prayers" was a religious privilege and Divine duty to be solemnly enjoyed and performed. He never impressed his congregation that he was going through a piece of religious task-work, "galloping over the office in so much more haste than good speed, as to distance all the congregation, and leave them panting and breathless behind." His constant endeavour was to "read the prayers commendably, to the glory of God and the edification of His people." He regarded psalmody as "the most elevated part of public worship." Notwithstanding his love for "anthems and cathedral music," he was willing to forego his own preferences for the sake of his uneducated flock, and allowed "the novel way of parochial singing." Preferring Brady and Tate to "the sorry Sternhold-Psalms, he nevertheless yielded to the wish of the common people for "Grandsire Sternhold," because, having, as he says, "a strange genius at understanding nonsense," they understood the "Old Version" better than the "New." Discarding the lazy and inharmonious choir of ignorant and self-important rustics, he resolutely set himself to teach the congregation and children the Divine art of sacred song. His efforts were so successful that he declares, "they did sing well after it had cost a pretty deal to teach them." This is the most appropriate place to glance at one or two curious incidents, said to be connected with this part of the public worship. The Epworth parish clerk had a strong touch of vanity in his composition. He regarded his master as the greatest man in the town; and as he stood nearest to him in church ministrations, he seemed to think himself second only in worth and importance, especially when

93

he donned the cast-off clerical coat and wig. The rector's head was broad and massive; John's small and contracted, which the bushy substitute for hair almost buried. Anxious to reprove the old man's vanity, Wesley resolved to mortify him by making him a mirthful spectacle to the congregation. "John," said he, "I shall preach on a particular subject to-day, and shall therefore choose my own psalm. I will give out the first line, and you shall then proceed as usual." When the time arrived for "psalm before sermon," the rector gave out the following line:—

"Like to an owl in an ivy bush:"

and when it had been duly sung, John, peeping out from under the large wig, announced, with audible voice and appropriate connecting twang, the ready response, "That rueful thing am I." The coincidence was too striking not to arrest the attention even of that somewhat stolid congregation, and a general, hearty laugh was the result. John was mortified, and the rector rejoiced in the success of his stratagem. This is the version of the story as given by Doctor Clarke, who says he received it from John Wesley. He also regards it as characteristic of the rector of Epworth, and an "innocent," as well as "appropriate and efficient" means of curing a simple man of his vanity. The rector had certainly a keen sense of the ridiculous, and heartily relished a little broad fun. Had the scene been any other than the sanctuary of God, and the employment of the moment unassociated with solemn public worship, we can readily believe he would not hesitate to arrange a scheme for curing a simpleton of excessive self-conceit. But his reverential regard for everything connected with public worship, and the extreme care which he took to perform it in a solemn and becoming manner, convince us that he would never premeditate and commit such an unseemly act in the house of God. John Wesley no doubt related correctly what had been reported to him; and it may be that Clarke has penned the story, as "nearly as he can remember," in the narrator's "own words." But even then, there are circumstances which incline us to think that there may have been glosses and inaccuracies

94

before it reached John Wesley's ear. The clerk was an oddity, and in his ignorant simplicity was more than once the occasion of a general smile in the congregation. He sometimes took unwarrantable liberties in his precentorship, and gave out doggerel far worse than the "sorry Sternhold-Psalms." One Sunday, determined to celebrate the King's recent return to London, he startled the assembly by exclaiming, in a loud voice,

"Let us sing to the praise and glory
of God, an hymn of mine own composing:—
King William is come home, come home!
King William home is come!
Therefore let us together sing
The hymn that's called *Te D'um!*"

This abounding simplicity would utterly unfit the worthy clerk for any ready appreciation of ludicrous coincidences, and we should not be surprised even if he did give out the curious lines about "an owl in ivy bush," without perceiving their striking application to his own grotesque appearance. We have given ourselves a great deal of trouble to find the psalm in which these lines occur, and a few friends learned in "old versions" have rendered us their ready help. But our united researches have failed to discover it. There is certainly nothing like it in Sternhold and Hopkins, whose version was used in the Epworth church. We never saw more of it than the two lines quoted, and the most confident advocates of the genuineness of the story have not condescended to hint at its authorship, or point to the Version, or Collection, in which it may be found. Was it another of the worthy clerk's "hymns of his own composing?" Judging from the authentic specimen of his poetic powers already quoted, it would be somewhere about his mark; and if any such couplet ever greeted the ears of the congregation, this, as far as we can now see, is the most probable explanation. At the risk, therefore, of being called "a petulant critic, worthy of little notice, unacquainted with the whole business, mislead by report, and should have held his peace," we do believe that the part attributed to Samuel Wesley in Doctor Clarke's version of the anecdote, implicates him in an
95

irreverent act in the house of God of which he was incapable, and which, if true, would deserve the severest possible reprehension, rather than the slightest praise. We have taken considerable pains to form a just estimate of Samuel Wesley's pulpit services,—a somewhat difficult task with the scant materials at our disposal. Our general impression is that, as a preacher, he was "thoroughly furnished;" a "workman that needeth not to be ashamed, rightly dividing the word of truth." The Bible, which, in his own words, "contains an unfathomable mine of heavenly treasure, capable so richly to recompense and overbalance all our pains and labour," was the subject of his deepest study. His knowledge of the originals of the Sacred Text was extensive. The study of Hebrew and its cognate languages was with him, a strong passion. Without a competent skill in these, he says, "we must take God's meaning upon trust from others. And if we borrow our bucket, or make use of canals, the water may be, and generally is, tinged in the drawing or passage; which we may have much clearer and sweeter if we ourselves will but be at the pains to fetch it at the fountain-head; without which I should look upon the most famed and popular preacher to be little better than a retailer in divinity." In addition to a creditable knowledge of the works of the Fathers and the earlier writers, he had read and studied the best theological treatises issued from the English press. His notices of the leading writers of all denominations, clearly shew that he was not merely well up in title-pages and tables of contents; but that he had mastered the works themselves. He was no smatterer in theology, but a sound, able, well-read divine. His discourses, generally carefully prepared, were delivered with considerable freedom, and often without notes. Most sincerely hating, as he tells us, "what some people call a fine sermon with just nothing in it," he strove, in good and vigorous English, to make the common people understand "the Gospel of God our Saviour." Here a sprightly turn of thought; there a homely illustration, drawn from the scenes and occupations around him; and, anon, a weighty appeal to the conscience, all tended to interest and impress his hearers. In a "warm and practical sermon," some prevailing sin or superstition of the neighbourhood was frequently exposed and denounced.

Perhaps he dwelt at disproportionate length upon denying ungodliness and worldly lust, instead of giving greater prominence to the privilege of a present and conscious salvation. Yet, thoroughly believing the blessed truth that, by the grace of God, Jesus Christ tasted death for every man, he shunned not to declare the whole counsel of God. The fact that he was frequently sent to London as "convocation man," indicates that he was of good standing and a minister of some note in his own diocese: while the request to preach the annual sermon before the Society for the Reformation of Manners, clearly shews that he stood forth as one of the best and most prominent preachers of his day. The public festivals of the Church were most carefully observed by the rector of Epworth. "Every Holiday, Wednesday, and Friday," prayers were read, "and the Second Service at the altar." Instead of an annual Sacramental gathering, there was a regular monthly administration of the Lord's Supper. Although Sunday-schools are of much later growth, the religious training of the rising generation was not overlooked. They were instructed in Bishop Beveridge's Catechism, and publicly catechised at intervals according to the requirements of the Rubric. They were also directed and encouraged to commit large portions of Scripture to memory, and in many cases with the most encouraging results. "I have known children," he says, "and some of them not of the best memories,"—the lack of which "they made up with an indefatigable industry,–who in twelve months' time, or less, have perfectly got the whole New Testament memoriter, and yet not intermitted their spinning, or ordinary work." Occasionally he singled out a poor boy, who gave early promise of more than ordinary mental power, taught him the elements of classical learning, opened his way to the University, and secured him a position in the ministry of the Church of England. These were the services that Samuel Wesley rendered, through a long life, to the people of his charge. As we calmly examine them in detail or in combination, the conviction forces itself irresistibly upon us, that he was one of the most exemplary and laborious parish priests of his times. And what were the results of this untiring, faithful, and long-continued ministry? For many years, it was indeed like ploughing the

97

rock, where there is no depth of earth; or casting the precious seed of the kingdom upon the hard-trodden way-side, where the birds of the air soon caught it away. "Yet, herein God hath humbled many painful pastors, in making them to be clouds to rain, not over Arabia the Happy, but over the Stony, or Desert." This non-success in the highest human calling often caused grave thoughts in the Epworth parsonage; and not least so in the mind of Mrs Wesley. She was sometimes strongly tempted to doubt whether her husband were in his right place. "Did I not know that Almighty Wisdom hath views and ends, in fixing the bounds of our habitation, which are out of our ken, I should think it a thousand pities that a man of his brightness and rare endowments of learning and useful knowledge in the Church of God, should be confined to an obscure corner of the country, where his talents are buried, and he determined to a way of life for which he is not so well qualified as I could wish." The preaching of the word is, in some places, "like the planting of woods, where, though no profit is received for twenty years together, it comes afterwards." This was never more applicable to the labours of any man, than to those of Samuel Wesley at Epworth. He sowed with unfaltering hand, and for many years saw no fruit. But ere he departed the Autumn came. He saw "the full corn in the ear," and a few patches of the golden harvest ready for the reaper's sickle. The congregations had largely increased. The dozen communicants had multiplied to more than a hundred, and many happy deaths had antedated his own triumphant end. His son comforts him with the cheering words,—"As for the flock committed to your care, many of them the Great Shepherd has, by your hand, delivered from the hand of the Destroyer; some of whom are already entered into peace, and some of whom remain unto this day. For yourself, I doubt not, when your warfare is accomplished, when you are made perfect through sufferings, you shall come to your grave, not with sorrow, but as a ripe shock of corn, full of years and victories. And He that took care of the sheep before you were born, will not forget them when you are dead." He had outlived all hostility; conciliated and won the good-will of his formerly troublesome charge. A new generation, widely different from their fathers, mainly as the result of his own godly

98

ministry, had grown up around him; and amidst their tenderest sympathy he passed the quiet evening of life. Many years after his decease, Doctor Clarke sought out some of the aged parishioners who had known him and his communications in the days of his pastorate. His memory was still precious and fragrant in their recollection, and they spake of him with the strongest affection and regard. While he thus steadily pursued his pulpit and pastoral toils, he continued a most diligent student. He is confessedly allowed a good place, though not in the foremost rank, among the most learned men of his times in the sacred tongues and the literature of the Divine Word. He modestly speaks, indeed, of his "own sorry Latin;" and, while thanking God that his three sons had the knowledge of the languages in a very laudable degree, he says he "had never more than a smattering of any of them," and was "but indifferently learned in Hebrew." But the recondite studies in which he so much delighted, and the works which he published, are such as no mere "smatterer" could accomplish. When old and gray headed, he went over the Pentateuch four times in one year, "collating the Hebrew and the two Greek, the Alexandrine and the Vatican, with what he could get of Symmachus and Theodotion." He had made large preparations for a new and critical edition of the original Scriptures, for which he is believed to have possessed the requisite learning, industry, and carefulness. His "Dissertations on the Book of Job," written in good and vigorous Latin, have been declared by competent critics, to "evince profound learning." If in reading his more elaborate writings, he does not always gain our assent to his views, he never fails to command our admiration of the learning and ability with which they are expounded and enforced. Pope, who knew him well, says, in a letter to Swift, "I call him what he is,—a learned man." He had the rare if not unparalleled honour of dedicating works to three successive Queens of England; namely, to Mary, Anne, and Caroline, Queen of George the Second.

He was an early "dabbler in rhyme," and the poetic passion, sometimes wild and ungovernable, glowed to the last. His essays in this beautiful art have, we think, been somewhat underrated. Had he written less and used the pruning-knife

99

with a more relentless hand, his verse would have gained much in strength, compactness, and polish. But we could cull many a beautiful and fragrant flower from among the weeds of his poetic wilderness. There are passages whose vivid conceptions, even rhythm, well-finished rhyme, and vigorous diction, indicate the presence and working of the true poetic power. His boyish pieces sparkle with wit and are occasionally somewhat coarse; but his maturer verse is devout and earnestly religious. It fully deserves his son's eulogium:—

"Whate'er his strains, still glorious was his end,—
Faith to assert, and virtue to defend."

And it must not be forgotten that from him, rather than from their Mother, his gifted sons and daughters inherited their genius in "the noble art of poesy." While industriously fulfilling the duties of the parish and the study, the thoughts of this country clergyman stretched themselves into the regions beyond, where there is no open vision, and where many people perish for lack of knowledge. Deeply affected with the wretched condition of the Eastern nations, he drew up an important missionary scheme, and offered his personal service to initiate and establish it. He proposed to "make a particular inquiry into the state of Christianity in all our factories and settlements, from Saint Helena to the further Eastern countries." Where he could not personally visit the settlements, he would fix a correspondence "from Surat, it being a mart of so many nations." He would make it his "faithful endeavour to revive the spirit of Christianity among them, by spreading good books, bringing them to catechising, or any other means, as God should enable him." He would then open up a correspondence with Abyssinian Churches, or "even try to pierce into that country himself;" and "enquire into the state of the poor Christians of Saint Thomas, and settle a correspondence between them and the Church of England." He thought it probable that he might "light on some opportunity" to convey books to the Romanists, "translated into the language of the countries where they are, and even as far as China, whereby the Jesuits' half-converts might be better instructed in the

100

principles of our religion, or made more than almost Christians." As for the pure heathen, he proposed to "learn the Hindostan language; and when he had got master of their notions and way of reasoning, endeavour to bring over some of their Brahmins and common people to the Christian religion." He felt he was not sufficient for the least of these noble designs, "much less for all together. But as it would be worth dying for to make some progress in any of them," he would cheerfully surrender himself for the exalted enterprise, looking for "the same assistance as to kind, though not to degree, which was granted of old to the first planters of the Gospel." "If," he says in conclusion, "one hundred pounds per annum might be allowed me, and forty I must pay my curate in my absence, either from the East India Company or elsewhere, I should be ready to venture my life on this occasion, provided any way might be found to secure a subsistence for my family, in case of my decease in those countries." He was not permitted to carry out this great project. But surely the Lord said unto him, as He said unto David of old time: "Whereas it was in thine heart to build an house unto My name, thou didst well that it was in thine heart. Nevertheless thou shalt not build the house; but thy son, that shall come forth out of thy loins, he shall build the house unto My name." Within a century after this elaborate scheme had been pondered by the humble rector, a company of noble men, the spiritual children of this good man's own son, landed on those far off shores to "learn the Hindostan language," and "preach among the Gentiles the unsearchable riches of Christ." In those very lands to which his own thoughts so eagerly turned in vain, a goodly band of missionaries, bearing his own name as their denominational badge, are striving to accomplish the work which it was in his heart to do. Their labours are not in vain. They have mastered the Hindoo "notions and way of reasoning," and "brought over some of their Brahmins and common people to the Christian religion." The personal character of this eminent clergyman of Epworth would well repay, did our limits allow, a critical and extended examination. He has been too commonly regarded as harsh and unfeeling; imperious in his household; ruling his wife with sternness and his family with unmitigated rigour; careless of his children in their early years,

101

leaving their entire education to their Mother; and largely inattentive to the temporal well-being of those dependent upon him. This probably arises from a superficial acquaintance with the facts of his history. The notion possibly finds some defence in a few strong expressions in the letters of some of his sprightly daughters, who, like many other young ladies, were occasionally impatient of control. It may also derive further countenance from one or two anecdotes, circulated with great industry, and remembered only for their extravagance or oddity. A careful study of all the available sources of information will prove that the popular estimate of his character does Samuel Wesley a serious injustice. And we hope that the narrative of his life and labours contained in these pages will lead to a more righteous decision. The anecdotes so often quoted against him we believe are either destitute of foundation, or enormously exaggerated to his disparagement. Loved by his wife and revered by his children, his somewhat strict domestic rule must have been tempered with manifestations of the best affections of a fatherly nature. His lively disposition, sparkling wit, and wise sayings were the delight of his domestic circle. There was a sharpness of temper not always under control, and a slight dash of eccentricity, which a stranger might wrongly interpret; but we cannot endorse the statement of the American historian of Methodism, that "the energy of his character and the tenacity of his opinions were, doubtless, faulty virtues. They led him into not a few unnecessary sufferings, and bordered sometimes on insanity." Were we disposed to be critical, we might ask this writer what he means by "faulty virtues." Are they not something very nearly allied to vices? And why should "energy of character," which we have been accustomed to regard as a precious gift of God, be classed among these "faulty virtues?" And why should a firm holding of opinions, confessedly not heretical or sinful, formed on what appears to the man himself, after the most careful study, good and sufficient evidence, be placed in the same category?

We are not disposed to hold up this good man as a paragon of perfection, free from all blemish. He had his faults and failings; but we see no reason to question the following comprehensive and candid judgment of Doctor Clarke, who had deeply studied his character:— "He was earnest, conscientious, and indefatigable in his search after truth. He thought deeply on every subject, which was either to form an article of his creed, or a principle for his conduct. And having formed these, he boldly maintained them, conscious of his own integrity, and zealous of what he conceived to be the orthodox faith. His orthodoxy was pure and solid; his religious conduct strictly correct in all respects; his piety towards God ardent; his loyalty to his King unsullied; and his love to his fellow creatures strong and unconfined. Though of High-Church principles and High-Church"* politics, he could separate the man from the opinions which he held and the party he had espoused; and when he found him in distress, knew him only as a friend and brother."

* This term must not be interpreted as identifying Samuel Wesley in doctrinal sentiments with our modern Puseyites.

Editor's note: A 'Puseyite' is a follower of the theological doctrine of the English theologian Edward Pusey (1800-1882) and his associates. In reviving the doctrine of the Real Presence in the Lord's Supper, Pusey contributed to the rise of ritualism in the Church of England.

In addition to orthodox opinions and upright conduct, there was in Wesley of Epworth a vigorous spiritual life. There is no record of any distinct conversion, of his passing through that great change which the Bible represents as our being washed, and sanctified, and justified "in the name of the Lord Jesus and by the Spirit of our God." Yet, the son of parents who did their best in the days of his childhood to "teach him the good and the right way," he "feared the Lord from his youth." It is possible that for many years he was, according to John Wesley's well-known distinction, a "servant," rather than a "son," of God; serving the Lord from a strong conviction of duty, more than from a principle of Divine, filial love. His state was probably very much like that of his sons at Oxford, before they experienced what is properly regarded as their conversion. But as life advanced, his views of conscious pardon and the renewing of the Holy Ghost became clear and strong. Either suddenly or by slow degrees, almost imperceptible perhaps to himself, he was made the happy possessor of these inestimable blessings. He knew God as a pardoning God, and felt the great transformation which made him "a new creature in Christ Jesus." We cannot trace the light from its earliest dawn, through all its advancing brightness; but we are anxious to fix attention upon its grand culmination in his peaceful and blessed departure, recorded in a subsequent chapter. The clearness of his setting sun flings a cheerful light upon all the path which he traversed in gaining such an illustrious close.

# VII. MODES OF EDUCATION.

The great part of family care and government consists in the right education of children. —BAXTER.

IT is generally known that Providence blessed Mrs Wesley and her husband with what the rector himself calls "a numerous offspring, eighteen or nineteen children." The scattered allusions in various family letters and other documents, leave no doubt as to the lower number, and the higher, in all probability, is correct. One was born in London, six at South Ormsby, and the rest at Epworth. Every one of them found an entrance into life within the limits of twenty-one years. It is difficult to ascertain how many of this large number were living at one time. Only seven daughters and three sons grew up to maturity. But John Wesley speaks with profound admiration of the serenity with which his Mother wrote letters, attended to business, and held conversations while surrounded by THIRTEEN children. More than ten, therefore, must have survived the period of infancy, though the nine departed ones evidently died young. The first breach in the domestic circle—an event never to be forgotten wherever it occurs—was made in the spring of 1693, when Susanna, the second child and first daughter, only two years old, was summoned away. The following year the grave again closed; this time over the twin brothers, Annesley and Jedidiah, children of a few weeks. Then at intervals, probably too short to allow the wounded heart to heal, others fell by the hand of the destroyer, until the trial culminated in the loss of an infant accidentally suffocated by the nurse. These repeated bereavements were borne with becoming resignation to the Divine will; but they, nevertheless, deeply wrung the Mother's heart. One sentence, penned many years after they had taken place, discloses the feeling with which she remembered her losses:—"I have buried many —but here I must pause!" Poor sorrowing Mother, weeping over the graves of thy early dead,—

"Think what a present thou to God hast sent,
And render Him with patience what He lent:
This if thou do, He will an offspring give,
That till the world's last end shall make thy name to
live!"— Milton

Mrs Wesley's care for those who died in childhood was soon over: but the ten survivors claimed her untiring attention and industry for many years. Her marvellous ability and success in their education and training, have won for her a proud, if not pre-eminent position among the many illustrious mothers of the wise and good. On all hands, her sons and daughters are acknowledged to form one of the most remarkable family groups in the history of English households; and their eminence is largely attributed to their early domestic training. It therefore becomes a deeply interesting inquiry,–what were the means by which their various powers were so admirably developed, and their character so well and firmly built up? The present chapter aims to give some reply to this question. It must not be regarded as a defence of every part of Mrs Wesley's plans, nor as a statement of the writer's own views on the important subject to which it relates. It is to be taken simply as an exposition of the principles and plans adopted by the Mother of the Wesleys, in the management and education of the Epworth family. Using the word education in its widest sense, it is obvious that the bodily appetites and wants of the child first demand the parent's careful attention. If these be not properly regulated and met, seeds of sickness are sown during the period, which should be devoted to the cultivation of health. "If the shaft of the column is to be firm, and the sculptured capital to point to the skies, the base resting on the earth must not be neglected." Mrs Wesley was so well persuaded of this important truth that, no sooner were her children born into the world, than their infant life was regulated by method. Even their sleep was meted out in strict accordance with rule. The appointed time for their slumbers,—three hours in the morning and three in the afternoon,—was gradually shortened, until they required none at all during the day-time. Punctual to the moment were they laid in the cradle, awake if possible, and rocked to sleep. The gentle motion was continued until the allotted time had transpired, and then, asleep or awake, they were taken up. This method secured their daily rest, and regulated the time of its duration. The common apology for the peevishness of a child as the evening approaches, was never heard in the Wesley family. At seven o'clock, immediately after supper, they were all prepared for bed; and at eight they were left in their several rooms awake; "for there was no such thing allowed in the house as sitting by a child until it went to sleep." They were also placed under the same rigid regulations concerning food. As soon "as they were grown pretty strong," they were confined to three meals a-day. Eating between the appointed hours was never allowed, "except in case of sickness, which seldom happened." If a child entered the kitchen and obtained food from the servants while they were at meals, "the child was certainly beat, and the servants severely reprimanded." At breakfast, they always had "spoon meat;" supper, as soon as family prayers were over. At these meals, they were never allowed to "eat of more than one thing, and of that sparingly enough." Dinner was a more ample repast. "Their little table and chairs," says Mrs Wesley, "were set by ours, where they could be overlooked." They were allowed to eat and drink,—"small beer,"—as much as they desired. Asking aloud for anything they wished was strictly forbidden. They whispered their wants to the servant who attended them, and she conveyed the request to their Mother. "As soon as they could handle a knife and fork," they were promoted to a seat at the regular family table. In all cases it was an imperative law, that they should eat and drink what was set before them. To this they became so accustomed, that whenever they were ill, there was no difficulty in making them take the most unpleasant medicine, because "they dare not refuse it." But children will give expression to their emotions; and it is as natural for them to cry as to laugh. The merry ring of their voices in a good peal of laughter is always a welcome sound; and we never heard of any rules for its suppression or control, unless it were unseasonable. The opposite expression, when constantly indulged in on the occurrence of some trifling disappointment, is universally regarded as "odious." But Mrs Wesley seems to

107

have regulated the crying of her children, with as much ease and success as either their sleep or their food. We have often heard her censured for "not allowing a child to cry after it was a year old." The censure, however, becomes pointless, when it is known that she had no such regulation in force. Her rule was that when a child reached the first anniversary of its natal day, it should be "taught to fear the rod, and to cry softly." Yet even this has been objected to by some over-gentle parents, as calculated to break a child's spirit, and overshadow what ought to be its most gleeful hours with a perpetual gloom. But these sad consequences never followed in the Wesley family. Every one of the children who grew up had spirit enough; yet "not one of them was heard to cry aloud after it was a year old." They thus escaped much correction, which they might otherwise have received; and "that most odious noise," the crying of children, was never heard in the house. Opinions will continue to differ as to the universal applicability of the principle upon which this rule is founded. John Wesley thinks it may be enforced by "any woman of sense," with "such patience and resolution as only the grace of God can give." It may safely be left an open question. But if, like Mrs Wesley, a mother can gain this difficult point, "no crying children will ever drown her singing of psalms, or put her devotion out of tune." It is generally admitted, that one of the most difficult problems of education is, to form a child to obedience without impairing his freedom; to restrain him alike from the extreme of obstinacy on the one hand, and too great pliancy on the other. It may probably be accepted as a general maxim, that the will determines the amount of individual power; and once it is brought under proper control, obedience to the rightly constituted authority becomes the law of our being. Hence Mrs Wesley attached great importance to the early subjugation and right government of the will. "In order to form the minds of children," she writes, "the first thing to be done is to conquer their will, and bring them to an obedient temper. To inform the understanding is a work of time, and must with children proceed by slow degrees as they are able to bear it. But the subjecting the will is a thing which must be done at once; and the sooner the better. I insist upon conquering the will of children betimes, because this is the only strong and rational foundation of a religious education; without which both precept and example will be ineffectual. But when this is thoroughly done, then a child is capable of being governed by the reason and piety of its parents, till its own understanding comes to maturity, and the principles of religion have taken root in the mind. I cannot yet dismiss this subject. As self-will is the root of all sin and misery, so whatever cherishes this in children, insures their after-wretchedness and irreligion: whatever checks and mortifies it, promotes their future happiness and piety. This is still more evident, if we farther consider, that religion is nothing else than the doing the will of God, and not our own: that the one grand impediment to our temporal and eternal happiness being this self-will, no indulgences of it can be trivial, no denial unprofitable. Heaven or hell depends on this alone. So that the parent who studies to subdue it in his child, works together with God in the renewing and saving a soul. The parent who indulges it does the Devil's work, makes religion impracticable, salvation unattainable; and does all that in him lies to damn his child, soul and body, forever." This thorough mastery of the will at the outset was Mrs Wesley's first important step towards the government of her children. Still, the good old proverb remains true, "He that spareth his rod spoileth his son; but he that loveth him chasteneth him betimes." However painful and difficult the duty, the chastisement of children is sometimes required, even in the best regulated families. "By neglecting timely correction," says Mrs Wesley, "children will contract a stubbornness and obstinacy which are hardly ever after conquered, and never without using such severity as would be as painful to me as to the child. In the esteem of the world they pass for kind and indulgent, whom I call cruel, parents, who permit their children to get habits which they know must be afterwards broken. Nay, some are so stupidly fond, as in sport to teach their children to do things, which, in a while after, they have severely beaten them for doing. Whenever a child is corrected, it must be conquered; and this will be no hard matter to do, if it be not grown headstrong by too much indulgence." Observing that "cowardice and fear of punishment often lead children into

109

lying," till they become so accustomed to it that it settles into a confirmed habit, she enacted that "whoever was charged with a fault, of which they were guilty, if they would ingenuously confess it and promise to amend, should not be beaten." The will being thoroughly subdued, childish follies and inadvertences were passed by, or mildly reproved; but no wilful transgression, however trivial, was ever forgiven without chastisement, less or more, as the nature and circumstances of the offence required. No sinful action, as falsehood, pilfering, playing at church or on the Lord's Day, disobedience, or quarrelling, was allowed to go unpunished. Every signal act of obedience, especially if it crossed the child's own inclinations, was always commended, and frequently rewarded according to its merits. None of the children were ever reprimanded or beaten twice, for the same fault; and "if they amended," they were never upbraided with it afterward. And, finally, if any of them "performed an act of obedience, or did anything with an intention to please, though the performance was not well, yet the obedience and intention were kindly accepted, and the child with sweetness directed how to do better for the future." Based on these important principles, Mrs Wesley's rule over her children became one of absolute authority, blended with the strongest maternal love. She moved among them, not as a mere school-mistress, punctilious only about the observance of routine and rule; but as a mother, allowed of God to be put in trust for their education, and yearning for the welfare of their souls. Duty was never made hateful by being assigned as a punishment. All her commands were pleasant as "apples of gold in baskets of silver." Her rebukes were always well-timed; proportioned as nearly as possible to the offence; never administered in anger, but as the remonstrances of a tender mother. Instead of governing by fear and ruling with a rod of iron, she strove to make obedience only another name for love. The mother who steadily governs on these principles, will seldom have to enforce obedience to her commands. She will find herself in the possession of a love out of which all obedience grows, and which gains its richest reward in the sunshine of her own approving smile. The parental reign is not to be one of terror and stern authority, but of love. The rod may be employed, but in reason and moderation, and never from momentary impulse and anger. Children are not to be provoked to wrath by harsh and unreasonable treatment. If they be uniformly confronted with parental power and menace, their spirit is broken, and the most powerful motive to obedience,— the desire to please, -is completely taken away. The references to the recreations in which Mrs Wesley's principles suffered her children to indulge, are exceedingly few. Her scrupulous care for the preservation of their health, would probably induce her to discountenance all amusements of a sedentary character: and her high Christian principles would restrain her from allowing games which she considered, in the least degree, prejudicial to their moral or spiritual welfare. The little ones had their childish toys, concerning the proprietorship and barter of which the strictest rules were adopted and enforced; and those of riper years had their more vigorous amusements. The almost mechanical rigour, which prevailed in the household method of government, was relaxed at suitable intervals. The nursery, the yard, and "the adjoining croft" occasionally became scenes of "high glee and frolic." But from the stern rule by which Mrs Wesley regulated her own childish amusements,— "never to spend more time in any matter of mere recreation in one day, than she spent in private religious duties,"—we may fairly conclude that the period allotted for play was comparatively short. It has been asserted that games of skill and of chance, such as John Wesley afterward prohibited among the Methodist Community, formed part of the family pastimes at Epworth. The fact is undeniable that, even when the parsonage was ringing with the sound of Jeffery's unwelcome noises, some of the daughters amused themselves and endeavoured to quiet their fears by a game at cards, and their Mother joined in the frivolous play. As far as this ancient game can be brought within the range of an innocent domestic amusement, it would undoubtedly be so far controlled in the Epworth family. It was at that time very common in the most respectable and orderly households: and even John Wesley himself speaks of it with surprising leniency:—"I could not do it with a clear conscience. But I am not obliged to pass any sentence on those that are otherwise minded. I leave them to their own Master. To Him

111

they stand or fall." Regarding card-playing as fraught with a multitude of dangers, especially to the youthful mind, we deeply regret to find it among the occasional pastimes of this godly and well-regulated household. As to Mrs Wesley's general sentiments on the subject of recreations, the following passages ought to be considered in this connexion. "Your arguments against horse-races do certainly conclude against masquerades, balls, plays, operas, and all such light and vain diversions, which, whether the gay people of the world will own it or no, do strongly confirm the lust of the flesh, the lust of the eye, and the pride of life; all which we must renounce, or renounce our God and hope of eternal salvation. I will not say it is impossible for a person to have any sense of religion who frequents these vile assemblies: but I never, throughout the course of my long life, knew as much as one serious Christian that did; nor can I see how a lover of God can have any relish for such vain amusements." Again, she writes, "I take Kempis to have been an honest weak man, who had more zeal than knowledge, by his condemning all mirth or pleasure as sinful or useless, in opposition to so many direct and plain texts of Scripture. Would you judge of the lawfulness or unlawfulness of pleasure; of the innocence or malignity of actions? Take this rule: Whatever weakens your reason impairs the tenderness of your conscience, obscures your sense of God, or takes off the relish of spiritual things; in short, whatever increases the strength and authority of your body over your mind,—that thing is sin to you, however innocent it may be in itself." With such admirable general principles to guide her conduct, Mrs Wesley would not allow games of chance to form any important part of the recreations permitted to her children.

The communication of intellectual instruction must necessarily enter largely into every system of education. And here again there are several remarkable and interesting peculiarities in Mrs Wesley's plans. She never attempted to teach her children even the letters of the alphabet, until they had completed their fifth year. But no sooner was the appointed birth-day with its simple festivities fairly over, than learning began in earnest. The day before the new pupil took his formal place in the school-room "the house was set in order, every

112

one's work appointed, and a charge given that no one should come into the room from nine till twelve, or from two till five." The allotted task of those six hours was for the new scholar to acquire a perfect mastery of the alphabet; and in every case, save two, the evening of the day saw Mrs Wesley's children in full possession of the elements of all future learning.

The next step was quite contrary to modern ideas about the graduated system. Instead of going over a page of uninteresting and unmeaning syllables, which communicate no thoughts to the mind, the pupil was taken at once to the sublime announcement;—"In the beginning God created the heaven and the earth." This he was taught to spell, syllable by syllable, and word by word; "then to read it over and over, until he could read it off-hand without hesitation." He then proceeded with the next verse in the chapter in the same way; and was never allowed to leave off until perfect in the appointed lesson. In these initiatory stages, there was the most resolute perseverance until the child gained a thorough mastery of his task. "I wonder at your patience," said her husband on one occasion: "you have told that child twenty times that same thing." "Had I satisfied myself by mentioning the matter only nineteen times," replied Mrs Wesley, "I should have lost all my labour. You see it was the twentieth time that crowned the whole." Under such teaching, all preliminary difficulties vanished away in a few days, and reading became easy, instructive, and pleasant.

In some of these details, Mrs Wesley was probably influenced by a singular fact in connexion with her eldest child. His hearing was acute and perfect; his intellect apparently keen and active: but there was no power of speech. He never uttered an intelligible word until he was nearly five years old; and his parents began to fear that he was hopelessly dumb. Having been missed longer than usual on one occasion, his Mother sought him in different parts of the house, but without success. Becoming alarmed, she called him loudly by name, and to her joyful surprise he answered from under a table, in a clear distinct voice, "Here I am, Mother!" Suddenly, and without any assignable reason or effort, he had gained the use of speech. This early infirmity in the case of her first-born prevented Mrs

Wesley beginning to teach him, had she been so disposed, before he was five years old. He learned with great rapidity, "and had such a prodigious memory," writes his Mother, "that I cannot remember to have told him the same word twice. What was yet stranger, any word he had learned in his lesson, he knew wherever he saw it, either in his Bible or any other book: by which means he learned very soon to read an English author well." This was her first attempt at teaching; and its great and cheering success probably fixed her future plans of action, from which she never deviated, except in the case of her youngest child. With her she was persuaded to commence teaching before the five years had expired, "and she was more years learning than any of the rest had been months." The school always opened and closed with singing a solemn psalm, and was a scene of perfect order, nothing being permitted to interrupt the regular course of study. "If visitors, business, or accident be allowed to interfere with reading, working, or singing psalms at the appointed times, you will find such impediments multiplied upon you, till at last all order and devotion will be lost." Everything moved according to rule. "Everyone was kept close to their business for the six hours." There was no loud talking or playing, "Rising out of their places, or going out of the room was not permitted, unless for good cause; and running into the yard, garden, or street, without leave, was always esteemed a capital offence." With such teaching and discipline, no wonder that the progress of the learners was uniformly rapid and satisfactory. "And it is almost incredible," adds Mrs Wesley, "what a child may be taught in a quarter of a year, by a vigorous application, if it have but a tolerable capacity and good health." Every one of her children, Kezzy alone excepted, "could read better in that time than the most of women can do so as long as they live." If, therefore, it be open to doubt whether there be any definite rule for the time of commencing, or the best mode of communicating intellectual instruction in all cases: there can be no question that Mrs Wesley's system, as carried out in her own family, was amply justified by its satisfactory results. Education, however, has to do with social relations, as well as intellectual culture. The human being cannot be isolated. "Of all the multitudinous objects the earth contains, his fellow-men are to him the most important. So completely are their interests bound up with his, that his social welfare and theirs are one. The justice, veracity, and compassion which they owe to him, is the standard of his duties towards them. Whatsoever he would that they should do to him, he is to do also to them." The children of to-day cannot live forever in the domestic enclosure. They must go forth and face the world, where they will find correlative claims and duties. Hence another most important part of education is to fit them for their social positions in life. This also was embraced within the range of home education in the Epworth rectory. The children were taught to observe the greatest propriety toward everyone in the house. They were not suffered to ask, even the lowest servant, for anything without saying, "Pray, give me such a thing:" and the servant was reprimanded if she allowed them to omit this customary form of request. . Rudeness to a domestic was never passed over without punishment. The same propriety was observed toward each other. Though homely pseudonyms sparkle in the familiar family letters, the proper Christian names, always with the association of brother or sister, as the case might be, were alone allowed in the family. Promises were to be strictly kept. A gift once bestowed, and the right thus relinquished by the owner, could not be returned on any pretence whatever. None was allowed to invade the property of another in the smallest matter, though it were only the value of a farthing or the worth of a pin. This rule Mrs Wesley regarded as of vital importance. She thought that from the lack of its enforcement upon the minds of children by parents and governors, much of the flagrant disregard of justice which we observe in the world undoubtedly flows. The Epworth family circle thus formed a miniature world, where the child's duty to his superiors, his equals, and those in a lower social condition than himself, was learnt and practised. In this way, the sons and daughters were fitted to enter upon the relations and duties of life, whenever they were required to pass from under the parental roof. Their future conduct was in perfect harmony with the admirable manner in which they had been brought up. Were the same pure principles observed in every family in the land; could all households be instructed and governed after the

115

same fashion, society would no longer be so fearfully corrupted at the fountain head. The young life issuing from the domestic hearth to meet the ever-existing demand, would, as a whole, be vigorous and healthy in social virtues; and how much of the great mass of evil which now afflicts the community would then expire with the present generation | But suppose all this accomplished; is there nothing more in education than to develop the physical powers, store the intellect, and enforce the practice of all moral virtues? "To open the mind to human science; to awaken the pleasures of taste; and to decorate the external man with all the adorning of civil and refined life, might be sufficient to occupy the office of education, were there no God, no Saviour, and no future being. Were this life not a state of probation; had man no peace to make with his God, no law of His to obey, no pardon to solicit from His mercy, then this would be education. But most affectingly deficient will the knowledge of that youth be found, and negligent in the highest degree must they be considered who have charge of his early years, if his mind be left unoccupied by other subjects, and un-familiarised to higher considerations." There is nothing deserving the name of education, which is wholly apart from religion. Every child has a soul, which makes him consciously akin to the unseen and the eternal. And this soul, fallen in Adam but redeemed in Christ, must be educated in the truth as it is in Jesus; instructed in all that relates to its responsibility to God, and its necessary preparations for the life to come. These truths had a firm hold upon Mrs Wesley's mind, and she resolutely set herself to meet the solemn responsibilities, which they involved. Before her children could kneel or speak, they were taught to ask a blessing upon their food by appropriate signs; thus learning, at the very beginning, to recognise their dependence upon Him in whom "we live, and move, and have our being." They soon learnt to be still and to behave devoutly during family worship. In short and simple prayers they were instructed, as soon as they could speak, to give utterance to those sentiments of devotion which slumbered in their breast, and which no other language could embody. The Lord's Prayer "they were made to say at rising and bedtime constantly; to which, as they grew bigger, were added a short prayer for their

116

parents and some collects, a short Catechism, and some portion of Scripture, as their memories could bear." As soon as they were capable, they were taught to distinguish the Sabbath from every other day of the week; and to reverence the sanctuary by a constant attendance upon its services, and a quiet and devout behaviour during public worship.

As they increased in years and intelligence, Mrs Wesley felt that their religious teaching made still greater demands upon her time and exertions. She was not willing that while they advanced towards a perfect acquaintance with all other branches of learning, they should know nothing more than the elements of religious truth. "The main thing which is now to be done," she writes to one of her daughters, "is to lay a good foundation, that you may act upon principles, and be always able to satisfy yourself, and give a reason to others of the faith that is in you. For anyone who makes a profession of religion only because it is the custom of the country in which they live, or because their parents do so, or their worldly interest is thereby secured or advanced, will never be able to stand in the day of temptation; nor shall they ever enter into the kingdom of heaven." Her own early mental conflicts had forced her to search to their very foundations the principal doctrines of Divine Revelation. She could not rest until she was able to give a reason for her belief in the truths she received. Convinced that, as far as possible, she ought to place her children in the same position, she set herself to the important work of giving them a thorough theological training. Instead of taking some manual of doctrine ready to her hand, she resolved to prepare one for herself. That which properly forms the first part of it, is an important treatise on natural theology, written at the beginning of 1712; a similar one having perished in the destruction of the parsonage. The argument for the Divine existence, arising from the creation of matter, the arrangement of the world, the stability of the order of nature, and the constitution of the human being, is elaborated with great minuteness and skill: and the theories of the eternity of matter, chance, and a "fortuitous concourse of atoms," are rebutted by good and sufficient reasons. The absolute perfection of the Divine nature and attributes is illustrated with much beauty of

117

expression, and demonstrated by appropriate arguments. The document closes with discussions on the origin of evil; the fact of the fall; the province of reason in matters of religion; the moral virtues; the necessity of Divine Revelation; natural religion; and the theory of innate ideas. This important production of her pen once mastered, the youthful mind would find itself in possession of the main arguments in the entire controversy relating to Christian Theism. This well-meant and well-executed task, however, as Mrs Wesley clearly understood, was only introducing her children into the porch of the great temple of truth. There, indeed, they might stand in awe of Him whose eternal power and Godhead may be understood by the things that are made. But they could learn nothing of His abounding mercy in the redemption of the world by our Lord Jesus Christ. She resolved, therefore, to conduct them into the temple itself, and lead them directly to the propitiatory, where, beneath the wings of adoring cherubim and the clear shining from the heavenly Shekinah, they might learn the doctrines of redemption and salvation. Taking as her text-book that ancient form of sound words, the Apostles' Creed, she prepared a comprehensive exposition of the leading truths of the Gospel. The introduction embraces observations on the defectiveness of the light of nature; the evil of sin; the necessity of an atonement; the value of the Scriptures; the creation and fall of angels; the formation of man, probably to fill up the place of the angels who sinned; the probation, temptation, and fall of the first human pair, and its effects upon their posterity; the provision of redemption; and the nature of faith in Christ. The articles of the Creed are then expounded in regular order; and many of them are illustrated with much beauty and force. On one or two important topics connected with experimental religion the teaching is defective; and there are opinions on other points which do not always commend themselves to our judgment. But, as a whole, it is a good and Scriptural exposition of the principal truths of religion. The child who carefully digested its instructions, would have a far more minute and comprehensive acquaintance with the doctrines of the Gospel, than thousands of well-educated people who profess and call themselves Christians. But religion is not a matter of

118

mere creeds, however orthodox; or of beliefs, however intelligent and correct. It is a thing of practice, and has to do with the right government of the life. It is a walking before God in the observance of all holy duties toward Him, and toward our fellow-men. This view entered largely into all Mrs Wesley's ideas of personal religion; and hence she was not likely to leave her children without some definite teaching concerning the practice of the life. At the close of her work on the Creed, she says to her daughter, "I shall only add a few words to prepare your mind for the second part of my discourse,—Obedience to the laws of God,—which I shall quickly send you." The document to which this reference is made, was soon afterwards completed. Regarding the Moral Law as a permanent and universal enactment, as well as the Divine rule of life, Mrs Wesley prepared a beautiful and searching exposition of the Ten Commandments. Their meaning is set forth with much clearness; and their observance, as the standard of morals and the sovereign rule of conduct, is pressed upon the conscience with great tenderness and power. These three treatises, which do so much honour to Mrs Wesley's extensive reading, comprehensive acquaintance with the entire circle of religious truths, and ready expression of her thoughts, formed the theological manual for her children. They were first written for some of the elder ones who had, for a time at least, passed from under her immediate care and instruction. But she soon adopted them as text-books in her regular system of teaching. "It is necessary to observe some method," she writes, "in instructing and writing for your children. Go through your brief exposition of the Creed, and the Ten Commandments, which are a summary of the moral law: then your brief exposition of the principles of revealed religion; then the being and perfections of God." With such able and systematic theological teaching, the children of the Epworth parsonage could not fail to be well brought up "in the nurture and admonition of the Lord." There is, however, something more in religion than a correct knowledge of Christian doctrine and duty. The heart must be brought to the penitent reception of the blessings which those doctrines set forth, that we may have grace to discharge the duties which the law of God commands. Mrs Wesley did not

119

suppose that she had filled up the measure of religious instruction, when she had expounded the truths and duties of Christianity. She knew that if the Gospel was to become the power of God unto the salvation of her children, she must press the reception of its blessings upon their heart and conscience. For this purpose she arranged a special private conference with each child, once in every week. "I take such a proportion of time," she writes, "as I can best spare every night to discourse with each child by itself, on something that relates to its principal concerns. On Monday, I talk with Molly; on Tuesday, with Hetty; Wednesday, with Nancy; Of Anne (Nancy) we know less than any [of the girls,] but she alone seems to have had a happy marriage. About 1725 she married John Lambert, a land surveyor, highly intelligent and respected. (Maldwyn Edwards, *The Astonishing Youth: A Study of John Wesley as Men Saw Him,* Epworth Press, 1959). Thursday, with Jacky; Friday, with Patty; Saturday, with Charles; and with Emilia and Sukey together, on Sunday." These private conferences disclosed to the Mother the real thoughts and feelings of her children in reference to personal religion. They enabled her to meet any real doubts; to dispel many difficulties by which the mind was perplexed; and to lead the child more thoroughly into the good and the right way. They exerted a most salutary influence, and were gratefully remembered by her children. Nearly twenty years after her son John passed from under her immediate care he wrote,—"In many things you have interceded for me and prevailed. Who knows but in this too,"—a complete renunciation of the world,—"you may be successful? If you can spare me only that little part of Thursday evening, which you formerly bestowed upon me in another manner, I doubt not it would be as useful now for correcting my heart, as it was then for forming my judgment." There was also one more important and salutary arrangement adopted by Mrs Wesley, for promoting the religious welfare of her children. When, after the sad dispersion occasioned by the calamitous fire, the family assembled in the new rectory, she ordered a general retirement as soon as the school duties for the day were closed. The eldest child took the youngest that could speak, and the second the next; and so with the rest, until they passed, two and two, into private rooms, where they read a chapter in the New Testament and the Psalms for the evening of the day. In the morning they

120

were also directed to read a chapter in the Old Testament and the Psalms for the forenoon. They then "went to their private prayers, before they got their breakfast, or came into the family." This remarkable practice, whatever visitors they might have, was uninterruptedly observed for nearly thirty years. Who can estimate the influence for good that it exerted over the entire household ? These were the plans adopted by the Mother of the Wesleys in the education and training of her children, while they were under the parental roof. But when they left home she never ceased to follow them with her prayers and godly instructions. Her letters are such as probably no other mother ever wrote to her children. The ability with which she lays open the temptations, which would inevitably assail them; the lucid expositions of religious doctrine and practice; and the yearning tenderness of her appeals to the heart, excite the highest admiration, and stir the deepest emotions of the soul. One or two passages from letters to her eldest son must suffice as a sample. "I am concerned for you, who were, even before your birth, dedicated to the service of the sanctuary, that you may be an ornament of that Church of which you are a member, and be instrumental, if God shall spare your life, in bringing many souls to heaven. Take heed, therefore, in the first place, of your own soul, lest you yourself should be a castaway. . . . . . I hope that you retain the impressions of your education, nor have forgot that the vows of God are upon you. . You know that the first-fruits are Heaven's by an unalienable right; and that as your parents devoted you to the service of the altar, so you yourself made it your choice when your father was offered another way of life for you. But have you duly considered what such a choice and such a dedication imports? Consider well, what separation from the world, what purity, what devotion, what exemplary virtue are required in those who are to guide others to glory ! I say exemplary, for low, common degrees of piety are not sufficient for those of the sacred function. You must not think to live like the rest of the world. Your light must so shine before men, that they may see your good works, and thereby be led to glorify your Father which is in heaven. For my part, I cannot see with what face clergymen can reprove sinners, or exhort men to lead a good life, when they themselves

121

indulge their own corrupt inclinations, and by their practice contradict their doctrine. If the Holy Jesus be indeed their Master, and they are really His ambassadors, surely it becomes them to live like His disciples; and if they do not, what a sad account must they give of their stewardship! . . . . . I exhort you, as I am your faithful friend; and I command you, as I am your parent, to use your utmost diligence to make your calling and election sure; to be faithful to your God; and after I have said that, I need not bid you be industrious in your calling. I have a great and just desire that all your sisters and your brothers should be saved as well as you; but I must own, I think my concern for you is much the greatest. What you my son; you ! who was once the son of my extremest sorrow, in your birth and in your infancy, who is now the son of my tenderest love; my friend, in whom is my inexpressible delight, my future hopes of happiness in this world; for whom I weep and pray in my retirements from the world, when no mortal knows the agonies of my soul upon your account, no eye sees my tears, which are only beheld by that Father of spirits, of whom I so importunately beg grace for you, that I hope I may at last be heard. Is it possible that you should be damned? O that it were impossible! Indeed, I think I could almost wish myself accursed, so I were sure of your salvation. Still I hope; still I would fain persuade myself that a child, for whom so many prayers have been offered to Heaven, will not, at last, miscarry. To the protection of the ever-blessed God I commit you, humbly beseeching Him to conduct you by His grace to His eternal glory." These passages disclose the true parental yearning for the salvation of children; the real travailing in birth again until Christ be formed in them. Had they been written to a wild, dissipated youth, piercing the soul of his parents with many sorrows, and wasting his substance in riotous living, who would not have commended their earnestness? But why all this solicitude about an amiable, moral, industrious, and intelligent boy, who gave her not a moment's concern, except about his conversion to God? Ah, she well knew that, in comparison with heart-felt, personal religion, all other things are as the small dust of the balance;—and she bent her best endeavours to the great work of bringing the soul of her child to the knowledge of the truth. Were this example followed by all godly parents, the conversion of children would not be so long delayed. Years of terrible anxiety would be averted, and religious households, like that at Epworth, would be multiplied a thousand-fold. The foregoing narrative of Mrs Wesley's educational plans suggests some of the main principles upon which she acted in the discharge of this important duty. First of all, she began early. She delayed the commencement of their literary education until her children were five years old. But from their birth they were made to feel the power of her training hand; and before they could utter a word they were made to understand that there was a Supreme Being to whom their gratitude and homage must be reverently rendered. "Some parents," says Christopher Anderson, "talk of beginning the education of their children. The moment they were capable of forming an idea, their education was already begun,— the education of circumstances; insensible education, which, like insensible perspiration, is of more constant and powerful effect, and of far more consequence to the habit than that which is direct and apparent. This education goes on at every instant of time; it goes on like time itself—you can neither stop it, nor turn its course. . . . . . Here, then, is one school from which there are no truants, and in which there are no holidays." Childhood is the most impressible period of life. Every object soon becomes a book; every place a school-house; and every event ploughs in some winged seeds which will be bearing their appropriate fruit for thousands of ages yet to come. The young plant is bent with a gentle hand; and the characters graven in the tender bark grow deeper and larger with the advancing tree. Parents, in their religious teaching especially, should seize upon these golden hours of prime, so hopeful and important. If they wait for intellectual development, and delay to cast the good seed of the Kingdom into the virgin soil, the enemy will sow his tares and preoccupy the ground. Another manifest principle observed by Mrs Wesley in the education and training of her family, was that of thorough impartiality. There was no pet lamb in her deeply interesting flock: no Joseph among her children, to be decked out in a coat of many colours to the envy of his less-loved brethren. It was supposed by some of her sisters that

123

Martha was a greater favourite with Mrs Wesley than the rest of her children; and Charles expressed his "wonder that so wise a woman as his Mother, could give way to such a partiality, or did not better conceal it." This, however, was an evident mistake. Many years afterwards, when the saying of her brother was mentioned to Martha, she replied, "What my sisters call partiality was what they might all have enjoyed if they had wished it; which was permission to sit in my Mother's chamber when disengaged, to listen to her conversation with others, and to hear her remarks on things and books out of school-hours." There is certainly no evidence of partiality here. All her children stood before her on a common level, with equal claims, and all were treated in the same way. There was no such evil habit in the parsonage as that which prevailed in the ancient patriarchal tent —"Isaac loved Esau, but Rebekah loved Jacob." The principles of equity combine with the dictates of nature to forbid an unequal distribution of parental favours and affections. It may not be always easy to suppress the feeling of preference; but parents must studiously avoid giving any expression of it, either by word or deed. Favouritism kindles the flames of jealousy and resentment, and renders the heart, which should be the seat of every gentle and holy emotion, the habitation of anger, malice, and revenge. The education in the Epworth parsonage was preeminently home-education. God had blessed Mrs Wesley with signal ability for teaching; and the pecuniary circumstances of the family compelled her to undertake the literary instruction of her children. But had it even been otherwise, she would have felt that their souls were committed to her special charge, and that the solemn responsibilities could not be transferred to another. This conviction led her to give herself to this one work as the supreme duty of her life; and by its successful performance she served her own generation,—and even all the future generations of the world,—far more effectually than if she had left the care of her children to others, and consecrated her remarkable abilities to the most untiring activity in some department of service in connexion with the Church. He who made the parents the instruments of the child's existence, has placed in their hands the key to the recesses of its heart. Education in the various branches of secular learning may be delegated to the governess, or the public teacher; but on no account, without a grave dereliction of duty and viola. tion of the most solemn responsibilities, can parents altogether transfer to a stranger the task of religious instruction. Mrs Wesley found her work sufficiently arduous and trying; but she encouraged herself with thoughts of the future. "Though the education of so many children must create abundance of trouble, and will perpetually keep the mind employed as well as the body; yet consider 'tis no small honour to be entrusted with the care of so many souls. And if that trust be but managed with prudence and integrity, the harvest will abundantly recompense the toil of the seed-time: and it will be certainly no little accession to the future glory to stand forth at the last day and say, 'Lord, here are the children which Thou hast given me, of whom I have lost none by my ill example, nor by neglecting to instill into their minds, in their early years, the principles of Thy true religion and virtue !'" Thus far attention has been entirely directed to Mrs Wesley's own efforts in the education of her children. Most previous writers have claimed for her the exclusive honour of all the instruction given in the parsonage, and represented her husband as taking no part whatever in this important duty. There is no evidence, however, that he was so indifferent to his children's welfare as this representation implies. Would he who took the poor boy Whitelamb into his study and prepared him, both in general and classical knowledge, for the University, put forth no personal effort in the education of his own children? Two or three of the daughters evidently possessed some classical learning, and the sons had undoubtedly obtained the elements of Latin and Greek before they went to Westminster and the Charterhouse. Who, then, instructed them in these ancient tongues? Mrs Wesley, as we have already seen, was unacquainted with these branches of learning. There was no governess for the daughters, or tutor for the sons, except in the case of Samuel for a short time. To whom, then, could they be indebted for their classical knowledge but their father? Mrs Wesley had the care of the school, and the greater part of the instruction, especially in the earlier stages, was communicated by her, assisted by her elder daughters as they grew up. But the

125

study, as well as the schoolroom, was a place where many a lesson was given, and the classical learning, at least, was entirely under the rector's charge. His concern for the religious instruction and spiritual welfare of his children was only second to that of Mrs Wesley herself. His long and elaborate letters of advice, encouragement, and warning display the genuine yearning of a father's heart. "Now, my boy," he writes to Samuel, "it is likely begins that conflict whereof I have so often warned you, and which will find you warm work for some years to come. Now vice or virtue; God or Satan; heaven or hell! which will you choose? What, if you should fall on your knees this moment, or as soon as you can retire, and choose the better part? If you have begun to do amiss, resolve to do better. Give up yourself solemnly to God and to His service. Implore the mercy and gracious aid of your Redeemer, and the blessed assistance, perhaps the return, of the Holy Comforter. You will not be cast off. You will not want strength from above, which will be infinitely beyond your own, or even the power of the enemy.

Why should you not make your parents' hearts rejoice? You know how tenderly they are concerned for you, and how fain they would see you virtuous and happy; one of which you cannot be without the other. In short, use the means which God has appointed, and He will never forsake you." As his children grew up around him, the good man rejoiced in their superior education, their stern principles, and consistent conduct. His own humorous defence, in reply to his brother's accusations, is too characteristic to be omitted. "If God has blessed him with a numerous offspring, he has no reason to be ashamed of them, nor they of him, unless perhaps one of them: and if he had but that single one, it might have proved no honour or support to his name and family. Neither does his conscience accuse him, that he has made no provision for those of his own house; which general accusation includes them all. But has he none,— nay, not above one, two, or three,—to whom he has, and some of them at very considerable expense, given the best education which England could afford; by God's blessing on which they

126

live honourably and comfortably in the world? some of whom have already been of considerable help to the others, as well as to himself: and he has no reason to doubt the same of the rest, as soon as God shall enable them to do it; and there are many gentlemen's families in England who, by the same method, provide for their younger children. And he hardly thinks that there are many of greater estates, but would be glad to change the best of theirs, or even all their stock, for the worst of his. Neither is he ashamed of claiming some merit in his having been so happy in breeding them up in his own principles and practices; not only the priests of his family, but all the rest, to a steady opposition and confederacy against all such as are avowed and declared enemies to God and His clergy; and who deny or disbelieve any articles of natural or revealed religion; as well as to such as are open or secret friends to the Great Rebellion; or to any such principles as do but squint towards the same practices: so that he hopes they are all staunch High Church, and for inviolable passive obedience; from which if any of them should be so wicked as to degenerate, he can't tell whether he could prevail with himself to give them his blessing; though, at the same time, he almost equally abhors all servile submission to the greatest and most overgrown tool of state, whose avowed design it is to aggrandise his Prince at the expense of the liberties and properties of his free-born subjects." The reader's attention cannot fail to be arrested by a very significant sentence at the commencement of this quotation. When the rector boasts that he has no reason to be ashamed of any of his children, he adds, "Unless perhaps one of them; and if he had but that single one, it might have proved no honour or support to his name or family." And the following touching passage from Mrs Wesley's pen, seems to glance in the same direction: —"O sir! O brother! Happy, thrice happy are you; happy is my sister, that buried your children in infancy; secure from temptation; secure from guilt; secure from want, or shame, or loss of friends! They are safe beyond the reach of pain or sense of misery. Being gone hence, nothing can touch them further. Believe me, sir, it is better to mourn ten children dead than one living; and I have buried many." It is in the power of our hand to lift the veil; but this allusion, which historic fidelity demanded, must suffice. The erring one was recovered, and the future career of Mrs Wesley's children amply rewarded the pains bestowed upon their general and religious education. Some of the daughters, it is true, were most unhappily married. But the conduct they displayed under their wrongs and provocations proved them to be women of noble principle,—true daughters of Susanna Wesley. The surrounding darkness of their circumstances only served to make the light of their character shine with increasing brightness. As, one by one, these many children reached the goal of life, their last hours testified that they had not neglected the grand purpose of their earthly existence,—a preparation for the life to come. Their father, feeling that the promise was unto him, and to his children, was often heard to say, "God has shown me that I should have all my nineteen children about me in heaven. They will all be saved; for God has given them all to my prayers!" And as far as we can judge, his hopes have been realised. In all human probability, the family of the Epworth parsonage are now collected in the many-mansioned house above. Oh, who can estimate the fulness of their joy! With a gladness intenser far than when he saw them rescued from the burning parsonage, will the good rector exclaim, "Let us give thanks to God! He has given me all my children." The present life was to them a scene of temptation, of tremulous anxiety, and hard struggle; but now all are rescued from every danger and snare, —their souls from death, their eyes from tears, their feet from falling. With what thankfulness do they "revert to the altar around which they knelt; to the abode where they were sheltered from the arrow of temptation and the pestilence of vice; to the prayer in which they joined; to the example by which they were incited; to the love which sweetened and sanctified all! Yet never were they so truly one as now,-their sentiment so agreed, and their song so harmonious. Never were their feelings so true, and their concord so intimate. They are at HOME with the Lord. Every breach is repaired; every broken tie is reunited. Christianity can achieve nothing more than this. It is according to its purest, kindest spirit. It notes habitations; it saves by families, in its sacrificial Passover of mercy. It is moved by the spirit of Him who hateth putting away; who blessed each

128

bond and followed each yearning of the heart; who Himself mourned that death should reign; who gave back from the grave an only brother to the sisters of Bethany, an only son to the widowed mother of Nain." Happy the families whose earthly life is cheered by the prospect of such a final and eternal reunion!

# VIII. EMBARRASSMENTS.

*If you listen to David's harp, you shall hear as many hearse-like airs, as carols: and the pencil of the Holy Ghost hath laboured more in describing the afflictions of Job than the felicities of Solomon. Prosperity is not without many fears and distastes; and adversity is not without comforts and hopes. —BACON.*

EVEN in our own days, the position of many clergymen in the Church of England, and many ministers in other Churches, is nothing more than a position of respectable poverty. With incomes—we cannot call them salaries— notoriously low, and a status in society, which compels them to shew outward respectability, and brings upon them pecuniary demands unknown to persons in private life, there is a perpetual struggle between keeping up appearances and providing for the usual domestic wants. But in the times of which we write, the worldly circumstances of the inferior clergy were far worse than they are now. The living of South Ormsby, which, when held by Samuel Wesley, was worth fifty pounds per annum, now brings in more than five times that amount; and the rectorship of Epworth, then of the nominal annual value of two hundred pounds, is now worth nine hundred and fifty-two. The Wesley family must, therefore, have felt all the evils incident to an expensive position combined with a scant and insufficient income. The full story of their thrift, sufferings, and manifold contrivances to make ends meet, can never be told; but there are facts enough to shew that they had far more than an ordinary share of the common struggles for life. When, in the spring of 1701, Mrs Wesley and her husband "clubbed and joined stocks to send for coals," all they could muster was six shillings. A quarter of a century later, five pounds was all they had to "keep the family from May-day till after harvest." Thirteen years from the date of the disastrous fire, the house was not half furnished, nor the family half clothed. No wonder that when he paid his friendly visit in 1731, the rector's wealthy brother was "strangely scandalised at

131

the poverty of the furniture, and much more so at the meanness of the children's habit."

"Tell me, Mrs Wesley," said the good Archbishop Sharp, "whether you ever really wanted bread."

"My Lord," replied the noble woman, "I will freely own to your Grace that, strictly speaking, I never did want bread. But then, I had so much care to get it before it was eat, and to pay for it after, as has often made it very unpleasant to me. And I think to have bread on such terms is the next degree of wretchedness to having none at all."

"You are certainly in the right," replied his Lordship, and made her a handsome present, which she had "reason to believe afforded him comfortable reflections before his exit."

This testimony of Mrs Wesley is fully corroborated by the letters of some of her children. When Emilia, the eldest daughter, approached womanhood, she realised the terrible fact that the family were involved in heavy pecuniary embarrassment. She tells us, that her father's journeys to London to obtain money from his friends, or to attend "convocations, of blessed memory!" took him from home, more or less, for seven successive winters. The family was "in intolerable want and affliction." Through one entire "dismal winter," she had to take the sole management of the household. Her Mother was sick, confined even to her room, and daily expected to die. Her father was in constant danger of arrest and imprisonment for debt, and Emilia had to provide for a large family with the smallest possible means. "Then," she adds,— and O, what an amount of grief is condensed into this one sentence —"Then I learnt what it was to seek money for bread, seldom having any without such hardships in getting it, that much abated the pleasure of it."

With these illustrations before his eye, the reader will readily receive Mrs Wesley's own statement,—"It is certainly true that I have had a large experience of what the world calls adverse fortune."

The real cause of these painful circumstances, the heritage of Mrs Wesley's entire married life, may easily be discovered. Her husband had no personal property, and she received no goodly marriage portion. The greater part of her father's private

132

resources was exhausted or lost before her marriage. In his will, he speaks of his "earthly pittance," and says, "My just debts being paid, I give to each of my children one shilling, and all the rest to be divided between my son Benjamin, my daughter Judith, and my daughter Anne." Mrs Wesley probably received this magnificent fortune of one shilling; but it is evident that she and her husband had no provision made for their temporal comfort at the time of their marriage. The income of the London curacy had to be supplemented by the vigorous but uncertain efforts of the pen. The tale of South Ormsby is best told in the rector's own words. "Twill be no great wonder that when I had but fifty pounds per annum for six or seven years together; nothing to begin the world with ; one child at least per annum, and my wife sick for half that time, that I should run one hundred and fifty pounds behind hand; especially when about a hundred of it had been expended in goods, without doors and within." When he received the living of Epworth, it cost him fifty pounds for his journey to London, the affixing of the broad seal to his title, and removing his family. He had to borrow money for additional furniture, and for "setting up a little husbandry" when he took the tithes into his own hands. His barn fell, and cost him eighty pounds to rebuild it. His aged mother, who for many years during his earlier struggles, was largely dependent upon him, must have gone to prison had he not assisted her with more than forty pounds. He also made her a yearly allowance of ten pounds. The two disastrous fires at the parsonage cost him five hundred pounds, at least, exclusive of replacing the furniture. His living had a nominal value of two hundred a-year; but it never reached that sum; and the taxes to "Saint John of Jerusalem" and other parties, amounted to thirty pounds. The parishioners took advantage of his "dislike to go to law," and robbed him of portions of those tithes and offerings on which his income so much depended. The authorities kindly "bestowed an apprentice" upon him, whom he supposed he must "teach to beat rime," whatever that particular phrase may mean. His family was large, and his medical expenses heavy. His old friends the Dissenters had influence enough to secure his removal from the chaplaincy of a regiment conferred upon him by the Duke of Marlborough. The living of Wroote, which he held for a short time in connexion with Epworth,-and now worth four hundred a-year with residence,—hardly did more than pay the expenses of the additional curate; and he soon relinquished it in favour of Whitelamb, the husband of his daughter Mary. These notices are amply sufficient to account for the straitened financial circumstances, which so long oppressed the Epworth family. The greatest carefulness was exercised, and the utmost efforts made to "provide things honest in the sight of all." For a considerable time, only one maid-servant was kept; and never more than two. The daughters were all educated at home and without the aid of a governess, except one or two who were educated by their uncle Matthew. As they grew up, they had their regular departments of house-work, which they readily performed. The three sons, with the exception of Samuel for a short time, were all educated at home, until they were ready for the public schools, and were a considerable demand upon the father's resources for years while they were at school and college. No company was kept; and the strictest economy was practised in food and raiment. The only extravagant tendencies we discover in the rector are a moderate love of his pipe, and rather an "immoderate fondness for snuff;" for the latter of which very questionable habit he received a smart poetical castigation from his eldest son. These luxuries might, and ought to have been dispensed with under the circumstances. But in all other respects, the minister of Epworth stands before us as a most temperate and frugal man. Replying to his brother's unkind letter, "he challenges an instance to be given of any extravagance, in any single branch of his expenses, through the whole course of his life, either in dress, diet, horses, recreation, or diversion, either in himself or family. . . . He can struggle with the world, but not with Providence: nor can he resist sickness, fires, and inundations." The true secret of these embarrassments was stated by Lord Oxford, in 1730, when he requested Dean Swift to subscribe for the rector's work on the Book of Job:— "The person concerned is a worthy, honest man; and by this work of his, he is in hopes to get free of a load of debt which has hung upon him some years. This debt of his is not owing to any folly or extravagance of his, but to the calamity of his house having been twice burnt, which he was obliged to rebuild; and having but small preferment in the Church, and a large family of children, he has not been able to extricate himself out of the difficulties these accidents have brought upon him. Three sons he has bred up well at Westminster," and they are excellent scholars. The eldest has been one of the ushers in Westminster school since the year 1714. He is a man in years, yet hearty and able to study many hours in a day. This, in short, is the case of an honest, poor, worthy clergyman, and I hope you will take him under your protection." But did not Mrs Wesley's husband largely augment these pecuniary embarrassments, by his own imprudence and "sorry management?" Did he not spend much money in publishing books and attending convocations, which he ought to have husbanded for the use and comfort of his family? These questions are generally answered greatly to the good man's disparagement. But if they be fairly examined, some of the charges will fall to the ground, and the severity of the rest will probably be mitigated. When he was presented to Epworth, the living was let for a hundred and sixty pounds a-year. Thinking he could make it more productive, he took the management of it into his own hands. For this he had neither the proper qualifications, nor the requisite capital. "He is not fit for worldly business," wrote his brother Annesley, who had employed him in one or two matters during his own absence in India. "This I likewise assent to," replies Mrs Wesley, "and must own I was mistaken when I did think him fit for it. My own experience hath since convinced me that he is one of those who, our Saviour saith, are not so wise in their generation as the children of this world." His long-established habits, and the ardent love of more congenial pursuits, disqualified him for the careful and energetic management of glebe and cattle; and the borrowed money necessary to set him up in this little husbandry, brought upon him an annual expenditure for interest, which his income could not well bear. By this attempt to better his fortune he probably lost many pounds a year. The step was both unwise and unprofitable. During his Lincolnshire incumbencies, he was three times elected a member of convocation. This required him to spend a considerable time in London at his own expense. He sets down the cost of the three journeys at a hundred and fifty

135

pounds. He could probably have declined the appointment; and censures have been rather liberally awarded him for incurring such heavy expenditure when his present liabilities were so great. But may not something be said in mitigation of these censures? He was an able, prominent, and active clergyman, taking a deep interest in everything connected with his Church. He earnestly advocated carrying out to the full the usages and discipline of the Establishment; and embraced every opportunity to shew his sincere and strong love for ecclesiastical observance and order. His brother clergymen of the Diocese selected him as their fit representative in the deliberations of the most august and important assembly of his own Church. How difficult for a man of his disposition and habits to decline an appointment so congenial to his own feelings, and probably, after all, not very easy to refuse!

Were our censure to fall anywhere, it would be upon the system which required a poor parish priest to pay his own expenses while attending to the business of a public appointment, rather than upon the man who made heavy personal sacrifices to discharge, what he believed to be, an important duty to his Church at the request of his brethren. As to the money spent in publishing books, we believe it was the only profitable investment the Epworth rector ever made. During his London curacy he doubled his income by the efforts of his pen; and these vigorous literary exertions continued to his last hours. When bending beneath the infirmities of seventy years, he still bravely toiled to "mend in some sort his fortune," and make a little provision for his family. His right hand stricken with paralysis, and compelled to drop the pen, he says, "I have already lost one hand in the service; yet, I thank God, *non deficit altera,"* (the other does not fail me) and I begin to put it to school this day to learn to write, in order to help its lame brother." His larger works, published mainly by subscription and dedicated to royal and noble personages, were important sources of income. Let all be taken into account, and his noble boast is amply justified:— "No man has worked truer for bread than I have done; and few have lived harder, or their families either. I am grown weary of vindicating myself: not, I thank God, that my spirits sink, or that I have not right on my side;

136

but because I have almost a whole world against me; and therefore shall, in the main, leave my cause to the Righteous Judge." But were there not large subscriptions made at different periods to rescue him from financial pressure? Good Archbishop Sharp and others did render him considerable help in the time of need; and his letters in acknowledgment of their kindly liberality disclose to us one of the most grateful hearts God ever made. "When I received your Grace's first letter, I thanked God upon my knees for it; and have done the same I believe twenty times since, as often as I have read it; and more than once for the other, which I received yesterday." Again; "I am pretty confident your Grace neither reflects on, nor imagines how much you have done for me; nor what sums I have received by your Lordship's bounty and favour; without which I had been, ere this, mouldy in a jail and sunk a thousand fathoms below nothing." After giving a list of various sums, –amounting to a hundred and eighty-four pounds, in which Queen Anne is represented by forty-three pounds,—received through the Archbishop at different times, he adds: "A frightful sum, if one saw it all together. But it is beyond thanks, and I must never expect to perform that as I ought till another world; where, if I get first into the harbour, I hope none shall go before me in welcoming your Lordship into everlasting habitations; where you will be no more tried with my follies, nor concerned with my misfortunes. However, I may pray for your Grace while I have breath, and that for something nobler than this world can give. It is for the increase of God's favour, of the light of His countenance, and of the foretastes of those joys, the firm belief whereof can only support us in this weary wilderness." The entire of these contributions, from all sources, did not amount, we believe, to more than the cost of rebuilding the parsonage, leaving all the other losses to fall upon a man with a large family and a frightfully low income. We are no advocate for contracting debts; but when a man, with an income, which, with the utmost economy, hardly meets his daily necessities, has his house burnt down and is compelled to rebuild it, what can he do but borrow money on the best security he has, and struggle to repay it? This Wesley of Epworth did. None of his debts were repudiated, and none were forgiven. With his noble wife's thrift in the house and his own persevering toil in the study, all were honestly and honourably paid. The struggle was long and painful; but when, at the close of forty-five years' married life, the rector died, his liabilities were little more than a hundred pounds; and the furniture in the house and the stock on the glebe (also known as church furlong, rectory manor or parson's close(s)) is an area of land within an ecclesiastical parish used to support a parish priest. were nearly, if not quite sufficient to meet the demand. With these explanations before us, we leave others to censure good Samuel Wesley's "imprudence and sorry management." Convinced that, without attempting to vindicate him in all things, we have represented his true circumstances in relation to these painful pecuniary matters, "our sympathies gather around the busy bee whose active industry and zeal could not shield his hive from spoliation and misfortune, while many a contemporary drone surfeited in abundance, and wore out a useless life in luxury, self-indulgence, and criminal ease."

Mrs Wesley's deportment under these manifold and long-continued trials was everything that could be required of a wife and a Christian. What can exceed the beautiful spirit indicated in the following passage from one of her meditations? "Our blessed Lord reproves Martha's care because it cumbered and perplexed her mind. She erred not in caring for a decent reception for her Saviour, but in being too anxious and solicitous about it, insomuch that she was not at liberty to attend on His instructions as her sister did. It requires great freedom of mind to follow and attend on Jesus with a pure heart, ever prepared and disposed to observe His example, and obey His precepts. To manage the common affairs of life so as not to misemploy or neglect the improvement of our talents; to be industrious without covetousness; diligent, without anxiety; to be as exact in each punctilio of action as if success depended upon it, and yet so resigned as to leave all events to God, still attributing the praise of every good work to Him; in a word, to be accurate in the common offices of life, yet, at the same time, to use the world as though we used it not, requires a consummate prudence, great purity, great separation from the world, much liberty, and a firm and steadfast faith in Christ." In the darkest hour of their fortunes, her husband exclaims, "All

138

this, thank God, does not in the least sink my wife's spirits." She "bears it with that courage which becomes her, and which I expected from her."

Sometimes, however, the pressure seemed almost too heavy for her, and she writes, "I have enough to turn a stronger head than mine. And were it not that God supports me, and by His omnipotent goodness often totally suspends all sense of worldly things, I could not sustain the weight many days, perhaps hours. But even in this low ebb of fortune, I am not without some kind interval."

Then the momentary gloom passes away, and beautiful sentences drop from her pen. "Upon the best observation I could ever make, I am induced to believe, that it is much easier to be contented without riches than with them. It is so natural for a rich man to make his gold his god,—for whatever a person loves most, that thing, be it what it will, he will certainly make his god;— it is so difficult not to trust in it, not to depend on it for support and happiness, that I do not know one rich man in the world with whom I would exchange conditions."

When disappointed of expected resources and the balance is again on the wrong side, she writes, "I think myself highly obliged to adore and praise the unsearchable wisdom and boundless goodness of Almighty God for this dispensation of His Providence towards me. For I clearly discern there is more of mercy in this disappointment of my hopes, than there would have been in permitting me to enjoy all that I had desired; because it hath given me a sight and sense of some sins which I had not before. I would not have imagined I was in the least inclined to idolatry, and covetousness, and want of practical subjection to the will of God." The dark cloud again gathers; but she is prepared for its steepening gloom. "Now all things are sufficiently uneasy, and the incommodities of a little house and great family are great impediments, when the body is weak and the mind not strong. But all things must be endured with patience, seeing the end of all trouble is at hand: for life wears apace, and in a few years,—perhaps a few days, -we shall pass into another state, very different from this, wherein we shall alway enjoy that tranquillity which is in vain sought for in any temporal enjoyment. Nor shall we find sin or sorrow more.

139

Courage, then! Think on Eternity!" All this bespeaks a home needy, but not sordid; poverty-stricken, yet garnished by high principle and unflinching resolution; full of anxieties for temporal provision, yet free from the discontent that dishonours God. And from beneath these clouds, which unceasingly hovered over her, she calmly looked for the blessed even-time with its promised light. "Those dark and mysterious methods of Providence which here puzzle and confound the wisest heads to reconcile them with His justice and goodness, shall be there un-riddled in a moment; and we shall clearly perceive that all the evils which befall good men in this life were the corrections of a merciful Father: that the furnace of affliction, which now seems so hot and terrible to nature, had nothing more than a lambent flame, which was not designed to consume us, but only to purge away our dross, to purify and prepare the mind for its abode among those blessed ones that passed through the same trials before us into the celestial Paradise. And we shall forever adore and praise that infinite power and goodness which safely conducted the soul through the rough waves of this tempestuous ocean, to the calm haven of peace and everlasting tranquillity. Nor shall we have the same sentiments there which we had here; but shall clearly discern that our afflictions here were our choicest mercies. Our wills shall no longer be averse from God's; but shall be forever lost in that of our blessed Creator's. No conflicts with unruly passions, no pain or misery shall ever find admittance into that heavenly kingdom. God shall wipe away all tears from our eyes; and there shall be no more death, neither sorrow, nor crying; neither shall there be any more pain; for the former things are passed away. Then shall we hunger no more, neither shall we thirst anymore; neither shall the sun light upon us, nor any heat; for the Lamb who is in the midst of the throne shall feed us, and shall lead us unto living fountains of water. Far be it from us to think that the grace of God can be purchased with anything less precious than the BLOOD OF JESUS: but if it could, who that has the lowest degree of faith, would not part with all things in this world to obtain that love for our dear Redeemer which we so long for, and sigh after? HERE we cannot watch one hour with Jesus without weariness, failure of spirits, dejection of mind, worldly regards which damp our devotions and pollute the purity of our sacrifices. What Christian here does not often feel and bewail the weight of corrupt nature, the many infirmities which molest us in our way to glory? And how difficult is it to practise as we ought that great duty of self-denial; to take up our cross and follow the Captain of our salvation without ever repining or murmuring! If shame or confusion could enter those blessed mansions, how would our souls be ashamed and confounded at the review of our imperfect services, when we see them crowned with such an un-proportionable reward. How shall we blush to behold that exceeding and eternal weight of glory, that is conferred upon us for that little, or rather nothing, which we have done or suffered for our Lord! That God who gave us being, that preserved us, that fed and clothed us in our passage through the world; and, what is infinitely more, that gave His only Son to die for us, has, by His grace, purified and conducted us safe to His glory! Oh, blessed grace, mysterious love! How shall we then adore and praise what we cannot here apprehend aright! How will love and joy work in the soul! But I cannot express it; I cannot conceive it!" With these earnest longings for the coming redemption from every affliction, Mrs Wesley joyfully bore the inconveniences and sorrows of the present time, knowing in herself that she had in heaven a better and an enduring substance. Notwithstanding its many and heavy trials, we believe that the married life in the Epworth parsonage was one of hearty affection and mutual helpfulness. Between persons of so much decision and firmness as Mrs Wesley and her husband, no doubt differences of opinion and probably conflicts of temper occasionally arose. But they were neither many nor serious. There is, however, a very current story about a singular and protracted breach of their conjugal harmony, which must not be passed over in silence. The anecdote, as given by John Wesley and Doctor Clarke, states that, the year before the death of William the Third, the rector observed that his wife did not respond to the prayer for the King, in their daily domestic worship. When he remonstrated with her, and required her reason for the omission, she justified herself by declaring that she did not believe the Prince of Orange to be King. "Sukey," replied her husband, somewhat

141

tartly, "if that be the case, you and I must part; for if we have two Kings, we must have two beds;" and declared he would not continue to live with her unless she renounced these objectionable opinions. He retired to his study immediately after this hasty speech, and remained alone for a considerable time. He then, without another word, mounted his horse and rode for London, where, being "convocation man" for the Diocese of Lincoln, he resided a whole year without any communication with his family. When Anne came to the throne, about whose title to the kingdom there was no difference of opinion, he returned; and John Wesley was the first child born after the restoration of conjugal harmony. "This very singular incident," writes the American Methodist historian, "seems not to have been attended with any severe recrimination. It was as cool as it was determined and foolish. It was made a matter of conscience by both parties, and both were immovably, but calmly resolute in all conscientious prejudices. As an illustration of character, it indicates worse for the good sense than the good heart of the rector. It would be incredible if related on less authority than that of John Wesley himself."

The truth of this damaging anecdote has never been questioned; but we are satisfied that, even if it have any foundation in fact, it is grossly exaggerated in its details. Far be it from us to impeach the veracity of one so  transparent and truthful as the Founder of Methodism. But as the circumstances were not within the range of his personal knowledge, he could only report to others what had first been reported to him. When even real incidents are transmitted from one generation to another in an oral manner, how soon does fiction become blended with fact! John Wesley heard the anecdote on what he considered reliable authority, and recorded it as it was told to him. But a careful examination of the various alleged circumstances will clearly prove that the fictitious element, to say the least, largely prevails.

There undoubtedly was a strong difference of opinion between Mrs. Wesley and her husband on the abstract lawfulness of the Revolution in 1688. Writing in reference to the continental wars in 1709, she says, "As for the security of our religion, I take that to be a still more unjustifiable pretence for war than the other"—namely, checking the power of France. "For, notwithstanding some men of a singular complexion may persuade themselves, I am of opinion that, as our Saviour's kingdom is not of this world, so it is never lawful to take up arms merely in defence of religion. It is like the presumption of Uzzah, who audaciously stretched out his hand to support the tottering ark, which brings to mind those verses of no ill poet:— "In such a cause 'tis fatal to embark, Like the bold Jew, that propped the falling ark; With an unlicensed hand he durst approach, And though to save, yet it was death to touch."

And truly the success of our arms hitherto has no way justified our attempt; but though God has not much seemed to favour our enemies, yet, neither has He altogether blest our forces. But though there is often many reasons given for an action; yet there is commonly but one true reason that determines our practice,—and that, in this case, I take to be the securing those that were the instruments of the Revolution from the resentments of their angry master, and the preventing his return and settling the succession in an heir. Whether they did well in driving a Prince from his hereditary throne, I leave to their own consciences to determine; though I cannot tell how to think that a King of England can ever be accountable to his subjects for any mal-administrations or abuse of power: but as he derives his power from God, so to Him only he must answer for his using it. But still I make a great difference between those who entered into a confederacy against their Prince, and those who, knowing nothing of the contrivance, and so consequently not consenting to it, only submitted to the present government,- which seems to me to be the law of the English nation, and the duty of private Christians, and the case with the generality of this people. But whether the praying for a usurper, and vindicating his usurpations after he has the throne, be not participating his sins, is easily determined." With a political creed like this, admitting to its fullest extent and consequences "the right Divine of Kings," Mrs Wesley could not regard William of Orange as the lawful Sovereign of England. And from the same manuscript we learn another principle which she held most tenaciously, and which will throw some light upon the other important point in the incident now under discussion,—

namely, a positive refusal to join in praying for a blessing on that which she did not recognise as strictly lawful. "Since I am not satisfied of the lawfulness of the war, I cannot beg a blessing on our arms till I can have the opinion of one wiser, and a more competent judge than myself, in this point,— namely, whether a private person that had no hand in the beginning of the war, but did always disapprove of it, may, notwithstanding, implore God's blessing on it, and pray for the good success of those arms which were taken up, I think, unlawfully. In the meantime, I think it my duty, since I cannot join in public worship, to spend the time others take in that, in humbling my soul before God for my own and the nation's sins; and in beseeching Him to spare that guilty land, wherein are many thousands that are, notwithstanding, comparatively innocent, and not to slay the righteous with the wicked; but to put a stop to the effusion of Christian blood, and, in His own good time, to restore us to the blessing of public peace. Since, then, I do not absent myself from church out of any contempt for authority, or out of any vain presumption of my own goodness, as though I needed no solemn humiliation; and since I endeavour, according to my poor ability, to humble myself before God, and do earnestly desire that He may give this war such an issue as may most effectually conduce to His own glory, I hope it will not be charged upon me as a sin; but that it will please Almighty God, by some way or other, to satisfy my scruples, and to accept of my honest intentions, and to pardon my manifold infirmities." If, then, according to this statement from her own pen, Mrs Wesley refused to join in public worship on a national fast-day because she did not believe in the lawfulness of the object for which prayer was to be made ; we may readily believe that she would refuse to respond to the prayers for William the Third, when she did not recognise him as the lawful King of England. But while we admit all this, there are two or three facts which prove that several of the statements in the anecdote, as given by Wesley and Clarke, cannot be sustained. William Prince of Orange died on 8 March 1702; and the separation, which occurred the year before his demise, must have taken place sometime in 1701. On 18 May in the latter year, the rector writes from Epworth, announcing to Archbishop

Sharp the addition of two infants to his family. We may fairly presume, therefore, that the difference and desertion could not arise before July 1701. If Mrs Wesley did not hear anything of him for a twelvemonth, her husband could not return earlier than the middle of the following year. In that case, the statement that he came back on the accession of Queen Anne, in the previous March, must fall to the ground. The first fire at the parsonage occurred in July 1702. The rector was then at home, quietly pursuing his usual parochial duties. Writing to his friend the Archbishop, he gives a full account of this fiery trial, and describes a journey to London in search of pecuniary help among his friends. This journey, which in that day required a considerable time to accomplish, was completed by the beginning of July. He must, therefore, have been in Epworth early in 1702. In the light of this fact, the statement that Mrs Wesley "did not hear anything of him for a twelvemonth" cannot be true, because he was not absent from home half that time. And, finally, the difference of opinion is said to have been discovered by her husband observing that Mrs Wesley did not say amen to the prayer for the King. But this prayer for His Majesty and the Royal Family was no new thing in the devotions of the Epworth parsonage. It had formed part of the regular domestic worship twice every day for eleven years before the death of William. Is it possible that Mrs Wesley should have refused the usual response to this supplication and her husband never discover it till after the lapse of so long a period? The supposition is utterly incredible. She was on friendly terms with Samuel Wesley when he wrote "several pieces, both in prose and verse," vindicating the valid sovereignty of William and Mary, and was probably his affianced bride at the very time. She must have been acquainted very well with his views; and as she was accustomed from childhood to express her own sentiments with great frankness, and act upon them with prompt decision, we cannot believe that her husband remained ignorant of her real opinions on the subject in question for eleven years after their marriage. These considerations bring us to the conclusion that facts are against the literality of several leading circumstances in this oft-told tale; and when these are taken away, the residuum of truth, if indeed any remain, is

145

exceedingly small. The difference of opinion is candidly admitted; and, for aught we know, altercations occasionally arose. But that "the contention was" ever "so sharp between them, that they departed asunder the one from the other" after the fashion described in the anecdote under discussion, we more than doubt. If a separation ever took place, which is by no means proved, and which in our opinion is exceedingly improbable, it was neither so aggravated nor protracted as is commonly believed. Mrs Wesley was a true-hearted and noble wife, loving her husband with an enlightened and strong affection, ever ready to stand by him and vindicate his consistency and honour. When unjust reflections were cast upon him because he had made no provision for his family, she defended him with an energy and faithfulness that entitle her to the highest praise. "Old as I am," she writes, "since I have taken my husband 'for better for worse, I'll take my residence with him. Where he lives, will I live; and where he dies, will I die; and there will I be buried. God do so unto me, and more also, if aught but death part him and me. Confinement is nothing to one that, by sickness, is compelled to spend great part of her time in a chamber. I sometimes think that, if it were not on account of Mr Wesley and the children, it would be perfectly indifferent to my soul, whether she ascended to the Supreme Origin of being from a jail or a palace, for God is everywhere:

"Nor walls, nor locks, nor bars, nor deepest shade,
Nor closest solitude excludes His Presence;
And in what place soever
He vouchsafes
To manifest His Presence, there is Heaven."

And that man whose heart is penetrated with Divine love, and enjoys the manifestations of God's blissful Presence, is happy, let his outward condition be what it will. He is rich as having nothing, yet possessing all things. This world, this present state of things, is but for a time. What is now future will be present, as what is already past once was. Then, as Pascal observes, a little earth thrown on our cold head will forever determine our hopes and our condition. Nor will it signify much who personated the prince or the beggar, since, with respect to the exterior, all must stand on the same level after death." These strong attachments were reciprocated by her husband. He speaks of her in tender and earnest words as you can," he writes to Samuel. "For, though I should be jealous of any other rival in your breast, yet I will not be of her. The more duty you pay her, and the more frequently and kindly you write to her, the more you will please your affectionate father." The following poetic picture of a good wife, in his *Life of Christ*, is an ideal description of the blessed Virgin; but there is reason to believe that the original from which it was drawn was near the rector's side, in the humble parsonage at South Ormsby:—

"She graced my humble roof, and blest my life,

Blest me by a far greater name than wife:

Yet still I bore an undisputed sway,
Nor was't her task, but pleasure to obey:
 Scarce thought, much less could act, what I denied;
In our low house there was no room for pride:
Nor need I e'er direct what still was right,
Still studied my convenience and delight.
Nor did I for her care ungrateful prove,
But only used my power to shew my love:
Whate'er she asked I gave, without reproach or grudge,
For still she reason asked,—and I was judge:
 All my commands requests at her fair hands,
And her requests to me, were all commands:
To others' thresholds rarely she'd incline;
Her house her pleasure was, and she was mine;
Rarely abroad, or never, but with me,
Or when by pity called, or charity."

147

# IX. LAST DAYS OF THE RECTOR.

The weary sun hath made a golden set.
—SHAKESPEARE.

THE long course of married life in the Epworth parsonage, so eventful in domestic vicissitudes and so full of blessing to the world in all future time, was now hurrying to its close. The many children had been well educated. The sons were young men of extraordinary promise. The daughters were sprightly and clever. All were serious, and some of them religious in an eminent degree. The heaviest debts were paid; and several of the family were provided for. "Thank God!" writes the rector, "I creep up hill more than I did formerly, being eased of the weight of four daughters out of seven, as I hope I shall be of the fifth in a little longer." Almost for the first time in financial matters, "A bow was in the cloud of grief."

The burden of embarrassment under which he had so long been bowed down, was rapidly lightening, and the goodly land of rest seemed to lie full before his gaze. He saw it with his eyes, but was not allowed to go over and possess it.

During the last decade of his life, the old man's health, "with time's injurious hand crushed and o'erworn," had been seriously failing. The grasshopper became a burden, and the strong man began to totter. Memorable sentences, indicating that he, at least, was looking for the coming crisis, were ever and anon dropping from his ready pen. For the greater part of the last ten years he had been "closely employed in composing a large book," whereby he hoped he might have done some benefit to the world and in some measure amended his own fortunes. By sticking so close to this, he had broken a strong constitution and fallen into the palsy and gout." "Time has shaken me by the hand, and death is but a little behind him. My eyes and my heart are now almost all I have left; and bless God for them!"

"What will be my own fate before the summer is over, God knows."

The right hand was fast forgetting her cunning. The pen of the ready writer was, for the most part, committed to an amanuensis. The fertile brain which, in the days of its vigour, had sometimes "beaten rhyme" at the rate of two hundred couplets a day, had now to dictate its slow-coming thoughts to another. His whole appearance was so wasted and changed that his most familiar friends, who had not seen him for a time, would hardly recognise him. Sometimes he was quite confined to the house by pain and weakness; unable to "venture to church on a Sunday," and far "too weak to be at the visitation."

While compassed about with these infirmities, a new sorrow pierced his heart. His only grandson, whom he had fondly hoped to see serving God in the Gospel of His Son, was removed by death. He seems from the following lines to have felt the bereavement most keenly: —"Yes, this is a thunderbolt indeed to your whole family; but especially to me, who now am not likely to see any of my name in the third generation, though Job did in the seventh, to stand before God. However, this is a new demonstration to me that there must be a hereafter; because when the truest piety and filial duty have been shewed, it has been followed by the loss of children, which therefore must be restored and met with again, as Job's first ten were, in another world. As I resolve from hence, as he directs, to stir up myself against the hypocrite, I trust I shall walk on my way and grow stronger and stronger, as well as that God will support you both under this heavy and unspeakable affliction. But when and how did he die? And where is his epitaph?" The rector's somewhat novel argument for a future life may not carry much weight; but who can fail to appreciate the characteristic references to Job, and the manly tenderness that the extract discloses? About the same time, the venerable man met with an alarming accident, which jeoparded his life, and from the effects of which it is a wonder that he ever recovered.

Riding with Mrs Wesley, his daughter Matty, and the servant-maid, to look at a field, which he rented at Low Melwood, the horses suddenly started into a gallop. The rector was thrown out of the wagon, and fell heavily on his head. Two neighbours, who providentially met near the spot at the time, raised his head and held him backward, "by which means he began to respire." The "blackness in the face" indicated that he had "never drawn breath" from the moment of the fall till they lifted him up. He was so stunned by the blow that, when Mrs Wesley came up and asked him how he was, he looked "prodigiously wild," denied all knowledge of the fall, and declared he was "as well as ever he was in his life." They bound up his head, "which was very much bruised, and helped him into the wagon again, and set him at the bottom of it." Mrs Wesley supported his head between her hands, and the man led the horses softly home. After being bled, he began to "feel pain in several parts, particularly in his side and shoulders." Further remedies were applied and he rallied. On Whitsunday, only a very few days after the accident, "he preached twice, and gave the Sacrament, which was too much for him to do; but nobody could dissuade him from it." The following day, he was very ill, and slept for many hours. On Tuesday, his old enemy the gout came; but with proper attention for two or three nights, "it went off again. We thought at first," continues Mrs Wesley, "the wagon had gone over him. But it only went over his gown sleeve; and the nails took a little skin off his knuckles, but did him no further hurt." The shock to his constitution from this terrible fall was very severe; and the four remaining years of his life were full of feebleness. Yet, with the two terrible enemies of palsy and gout laying vigorous siege to his shaken frame, he was still cheerful in spirit, and even gay in his pleasantries. The dearest interests of his parishioners were as fully on his heart as ever. He moved among them from house to house, as he had done aforetime. There was the same kindly greeting and earnest endeavour to do them good. His pulpit, from which he had so long preached the Gospel to a stiff-necked and gainsaying people, still exerted its wonted influence over him. No weakness could induce him to forego the privilege of declaring to his flock the way of salvation. "Your father," writes his devoted wife, "is in a very bad state of health. He sleeps little, and eats less. He seems not to have any apprehension of his approaching exit; but I fear he has but a short time to live. It is with much pain and difficulty that he performs Divine service on the Lord's Day, which sometimes he is obliged to contract very much. Everybody observes his decay but himself; and people really seem very much concerned for him and his family." These manifold weaknesses and sufferings were graciously sanctified to his spiritual good. By a marvellous process, in union with the true grace of God, they were working for him "a far more exceeding and eternal weight of glory." They were not joyous, but grievous, yet afterwards yielding the peaceable fruit of righteousness. Certain metals require strong fires to fuse them down; and, by these somewhat protracted sorrows, a temper naturally harsh and irritable was chastened into patient, and even joyful submission. Replying to a very reproachful and unnecessarily severe letter of his brother Matthew, he describes the grateful change in his own humorous way:—"I was a little surprised that he did not fall into flouncing and bouncing, as I have often seen him do on far less provocation; which I ascribe to a fit of sickness which he hath lately had, and which I hope may have brought him to something of a better mind." This "fit of sickness," whatever the nature of the disease might be, was of great violence and duration. It "held him half a year," during the greater part of which he was attended by three physicians, and his life despaired of. It brought him to the verge of the grave, "And left the strong man, when it passed, Frail as the sere leaf in the blast." The chastening, however, was eminently sanctified to his spiritual good. The first time he again entered the pulpit, he made grateful acknowledgments of the Divine goodness. He preached an impressive sermon, with special reference to his recovery, on that most appropriate text, "Jesus findeth him in the temple, and said unto him, Behold, thou art made whole: sin no more, lest a worse thing come unto thee." Happy is the man who so endures the afflictions of this present mortal life, as to render them subservient to his spiritual interests and his everlasting welfare. Meditating upon the patience of Job, and working harder than his failing strength would warrant, in order to complete the dearest project of his heart, and satisfy the clamour of some of his subscribers, he was now compelled to ponder very seriously what ought to be done for the well-being of his parishioners and his own family, in the appointment of his successor. He was naturally anxious that one of his sons should obtain the living, and thus provide a home for his widow and unmarried daughters. The following passage from a letter to Samuel suggests the grounds of his desire —"The deplorable state in which I should leave your Mother and the family, without an almost miraculous interposition of Providence, which we are not to presume upon, when we neglect the means, if my offer should be rejected till it were too late. The loss of near forty years', I hope honest, labour in this place, where I could expect no other but that the field which I have been so long sowing with, I trust, good seed, and the vineyard which I have planted with no ignoble vine, must be soon rooted up, and the fences of it broken down. For I think I know my successor, who, I am morally satisfied, would be no other than Mr P., if your brothers both slight it; and I shall have work enough, if my life should last so long, to accomplish it: and, behold, there seems to be a price now put into their hands, or, at least, some probability of it. If they go on to reject it, I hope I am clear before God and man, as to the whole affair." After all his earnest entreaty they did "go on to reject it;" and having done his best to ensure the continuance of the same Gospel to his parishioners which he himself had so long preached, he felt that he must now leave everything in the hands of Him who is "Head over all things to His body, the Church." He writes, "I hinted at one thing which I mentioned in my letter to your brother, whereon I depend more than upon all my own simple reasoning; and that is, earnest prayer to HIM who smiles at the strongest resolutions of mortals, and can, in a moment, change or demolish them; who alone can bend the inflexible sinew, and order the irregular wills of us sinful men to His own glory, and to our happiness. And while the anchor holds, I despair of nothing, but firmly believe that He who is best will do what is best, whether we earnestly will it, or appear never so averse from it. And there I rest the whole matter, and leave it with Him to whom I have committed all my concerns, without exception and without reserve, for soul and body, estate and family, time and eternity." The strong tabernacle, however, is not to be overthrown with the suddenness of a whirlwind's rush. The cords thereof are gradually loosened during eight weary months, until, in the springtime of 1735, the hour of dissolution, so momentous in its issues, draws near. On March 25, we have the following passage in a manuscript letter of Charles to his brother Samuel: —"This spring we hoped to follow our inclinations to Tiverton, but are now loudly called another way. My father declines so fast, that before next year he will, in all probability, be at his journey's end; so that I must see him now, or never more with my bodily eyes. My Mother seems more cast down at the apprehension of his death than I thought she could have been; and, what is still worse, HE seems so too. I wish I durst send him Hilarion's words of encouragement to his departing soul; —"Go forth, my soul; what art thou now afraid of? Thou hast served thy God these threescore and ten years, and dost thou tremble now to appear before Him?' Methinks that such a man as he should 'rejoice with joy unspeakable and full of glory,' while he enters his haven after such a succession of storms: or rather, to use M. de Renty's words, while his spirit is applied to that joy which a creature ought to have, to see itself upon Whatever the apprehensions referred to in this letter as clouding the rector's mind when he saw death approaching, it is certain that when the eventful moment arrived, his lamp was trimmed, his light burning, his loins girded, and he himself like unto them that wait for their Lord. Sons and daughters gather around his bed, and the dying man rejoices in the "clear sense of his acceptance with God." More than once he exclaims, "The inward witness, son! The inward witness; that is the proof, the strongest proof of Christianity!" As his afflictions abound, his consolations abound also by Christ Jesus. "Are you in much pain?" asks his son John. "God does chasten me with pain," he answers aloud with a smile; "yea, all my bones with strong pain. But I thank Him for all! I bless Him for all! I love Him for all!" "Are the consolations of God small with you?" "No! No! No! The weaker I am in body, the stronger and more sensible support I feel from God." All anxiety for the future welfare of those he so much loved vanishes away before his strong faith in God's Providence and covenant. "Do not be concerned at my death. God will then begin to manifest Himself to my family." Like Christian and Hopeful, the nearer he comes to the Celestial City the brighter view he has of it. Heavenly prospects, in all their ravishing

154

splendour, burst upon his soul, and he summons his children and attendants to celestial discourse. "Now let me hear you talk of heaven. Think of heaven; talk of heaven! All the time is lost when we are not thinking of heaven. Nothing is too much to suffer for heaven." Like some ancient patriarch, the Divine afflatus seems to visit him for a moment, and prophetic visions of that glorious Revival, in which the mourning sons now bending over his pillow, are to be God's chosen instruments, cheer him with their glowing brightness. More than once, he lays his hand upon the head of his youngest son, and utters the weighty words, "Be steady! The Christian faith will surely revive in this kingdom. You shall see it, though I shall not." The mind now adverts to another Death than his own; and he is anxious to commemorate the Lord's cross and passion once more. "There is but a step between me and death. To-morrow I would see you all with me round this table that we may once more drink of the cup of blessing, before I drink of it new in the Kingdom of God. With desire have I desired to eat this Passover with you before I die." The morrow comes; but the sufferer is "so weak and full of pain, that he receives the elements with much difficulty," often repeating, "Thou shakest me! Thou shakest me!" With the communicating act, there is an apparent revival of physical strength. He is "full of faith and peace;" and the family almost dare to hope for his recovery. The reviving is illusory as far as the outer man is concerned; but the sting of death is taken away, and all fear of eternity is banished forever. His latest human desires, of finishing Job, paying his debts, and seeing his eldest son once more, are cheerfully relinquished. The tide ebbs apace. The flame flickers fitfully in the socket. The last sands are quickly dropping from the glass. His son John whisperingly asks, "Are you not near heaven?" He answers distinctly, and with the most hope and triumph that could be expressed in words, "Yes, I am !" The group kneel around his bed for the last solemn duty. With deep emotion and faltering accents, the same son offers the solemn Commendatory Prayer "for a sick person at the point of departure":— "O Almighty God, with whom do live the spirits of just men made perfect, after they are delivered from their earthly prisons; we humbly commend the soul of this Thy

155

servant, our dear FATHER, into Thy hands, as into the hands of a faithful Creator, and most merciful Saviour; most humbly beseeching Thee, that it may be precious in Thy sight. Wash it, we pray Thee, in the blood of that immaculate Lamb, that was slain to take away the sins of the world; that whatsoever defilements it may have contracted in the midst of this miserable and naughty world, through the lusts of the flesh, or the wiles of Satan, being purged and done away, it may be presented pure and without spot before Thee. And teach us who survive, in this and other like daily spectacles of mortality, to see how frail and uncertain our own condition is; and so to number our days, that we may seriously apply our hearts to that holy and heavenly wisdom, whilst we live here, which may in the end bring us to life everlasting, through the merits of Jesus Christ Thine only Son our Lord! Amen."

There is a momentary pause, and the sinking saint, referring to this final office of his Church toward her departing children, says, "Now you have done all !" It is "about half an hour after six; from which time till sunset he makes signs of offering up himself." The Commendatory Prayer again fills the death-chamber with its solemn sound; and as its last sentences rise to the throne of the Eternal, the ransomed spirit of Samuel Wesley passes from its shattered home of clay. "With a cheerful countenance he falls asleep without one struggle, or sigh, or groan." His passage is so smooth and imperceptible, that, "notwithstanding the stopping of his pulse, and ceasing of all sign of life and motion," his children continue bending "over him a good while, in doubt whether the soul were departed or no." Alas, it is a solemn, stern reality. The Father of the Wesleys is dead. Just as the golden beams of that bright April day shot their last glances upon the dear old parsonage, the sun of the venerable rector completed its circuit, and, all-radiant with celestial hues, gently declined behind the western hills of old age to shine in a higher, holier, more empyrean sky for evermore.

"Not in the fiery hurricane of strife,
"Midst slaughtered legions, he resigned his life;

156

But peaceful as the twilight's parting ray,
His spirit vanished from its house of clay,
And left on kindred souls such power impress't,
They seemed with him to enter into rest."

Near the east end of the sacred edifice in which he so long ministered the word of life, a plain grit tombstone, supported by brickwork, marks the spot where his mortal remains are committed to the dust "in sure and certain hope of the resurrection unto eternal life." It bears the following inscription, composed by Mrs Wesley herself, but the lines of which, as graven on the stone, are divided with a curious disregard of all propriety and meaning:

HERE LIETH ALL THAT WAS
MORTAL OF SAMUEL WESLEY, A.M.
HE WAS RECTOR OF EPWORTH
39 YEARS, AND DEPARTED
THIS LIFE 25TH OF APRIL, 1735,
AGED 72:
AND AS HE LIVED SO HE DIED
IN THE TRUE CATHOLIC FAITH
OF THE HOLY TRINITY IN UNITY,
AND THAT JESUS CHRIST IS GOD INCARNATE;
AND THE ONLY SAVIOUR OF MANKIND,
ACTS IV. J 2.
BLESSED ARE THE DEAD
WHICH DIE IN THE LORD,
YEA SAITH THE SPIRIT
THAT THEY MAY REST
FROM THEIR LABOURS AND
THEIR WORKS DO FOLLOW THEM.
REV. XIV. 13.

Seven years pass away, and one bright summer evening a grave man, little of stature and in full canonicals, stands on that plain grit tombstone, preaching to dense crowds who cover all the place of the dead. It is the son of the venerable man over whose ashes he now stands. He has been denied the use of the church by one who owes his very position as curate of Epworth and all that he has, to the sire of that son whom he now excludes from the pulpit, and rudely repels from the table of the Lord. Eight successive nights does John Wesley cry aloud from the same hallowed spot. Surrounding villages pour forth their inhabitants to swell the ever-increasing congregations. Hundreds are pricked in their heart by the preacher's word, and ask what they must do to be saved. As the zealous evangelist, to whom this out-door preaching is now no novelty, surveys the results of his week's hallowed toil, thinks of the past, and looks upon the whitening harvest-field inviting the sickle of the reaper, he exclaims:—"O let none think his labour of love is lost because the fruit does not immediately appear. Near forty years did my father labour here; but he saw little fruit of his labour. I took some pains among this people too; and my strength also seemed spent in vain. But now the fruit appeared. There were scarce any in the town on whom either my father or I had taken any pains formerly, but the seed sown so long since, now sprang up, bringing forth repentance and remission of sins." How true is the prophetic word, "For as the rain cometh down, and the snow, from heaven, and returneth not thither, but watereth the earth, and maketh it bring forth and bud, that it may give seed to the sower, and bread to the eater; so shall My word be that goeth forth out of My mouth: it shall not return unto Me void; but it shall accomplish that which I please, and it shall prosper in the thing whereto I sent it. . . . . Instead of the thorn shall come up the fir-tree, and instead of the brier shall come up the myrtle-tree; and it shall be to the Lord for a name, for an everlasting sign that shall not be cut off." These moral renovations took place at Epworth just seven weeks before Mrs Wesley departed to rejoin her husband in the Paradise of God. How would the blessed tidings gladden her few remaining days I Among those converted under the preaching of her son from his father's tomb, were persons whose names were familiar to her memory. And may we not suppose that this blessed revival of religion in a town where she and her husband had toiled so hard and long, would hold a foremost place among those themes of meditation and thankfulness upon which her very latest days were employed.

# X. WIDOWHOOD.

But it shall come to pass, that at evening time it shall be light. —
BOOK OF ZECHARIAH.

> The death of Samuel Wesley, Sr. in 1835 signaled the
> beginning of a new life-phase for Susanna. In addition
> to the loss of her husband of some 46 years, it also
> meant her removal from the Epworth rectory (a place
> that for all the disruptions had been home for nearly
> as long). Now she would no longer be mistress of a
> household, but would sojourn for a seven-year period
> as a guest, albeit a welcome one, with various of her
> children. She first stayed with Emily, now a
> schoolmistress in nearby Gainsborough. Then she
> moved southwest to live with Samuel, Jr., a
> headmaster in Tiverton, Devon, leaving him two years
> before his unexpected death in 1739 to be with her
> daughter Martha (called Patty) and her clergyman
> husband, Westley Hall, in three locations (Wooton,
> Wiltshire, Malborough; Fisherton near Salisbury' and
> London). From that last brief arrangement, it was an
> easy step to finally take up residence with her son,
> John, at his London headquarters, the Foundery,
> within hailing distance of her birthplace. (*Susanna
> Wesley: The Complete Writings,* Charles Wallace, Jr.,
> Editor., London: Oxford University Press, 1997).

DEEPLY affected was Mrs Wesley during those sad and
protracted watchings which saw her husband slowly sinking
into the arms of death. Anxious, above all things, to fulfil her
duty and serve him to the last with her tenderest ministries,
she frequently visited the chamber where the dying man lay.
But for several days before his death, the sight was too much
for her to bear; and she was carried away faint and breathless.
Her grief, however, was a still rain, which gently distils itself for
many hours, rather than a tropic shower, rushing down in
floods and past in a few moments. When all was over, she was

"far less shocked" than her children expected. "Now I am heard," said she calmly, "in his having so easy a death, and my being strengthened so to bear it." The rector no doubt died intestate, "not for lack of time to make a will, but for lack of means to bestow." One of his last "human desires was to pay his debts." These, as we have already seen, only amounted to a little over a hundred pounds, besides some slight obligations to one of his own relatives; and the stock and other property would probably meet the entire liabilities. But rapacious creditors are proverbially impatient; and on the very day the rector was "buried, very frugally, yet very decently, in the churchyard, according to his own desire," a merciless creditor— a woman and a widow— seized "all the quick stock, valued at above forty pounds, for fifteen pounds," the rent due on a field at Low Melwood. The matter was adjusted by the intervention of John Wesley, who gave a note for the money. The very beginning of Mrs Wesley's widowhood was thus overcast with clouds. Destitute of income, and most of her other children unable to help her, she was compelled to turn to her eldest son, whose noble liberality had so richly abounded, out of the depths of his own poverty, in past days. "If you take London in your way," writes Charles to Samuel, "my Mother desires you will remember that she is a clergyman's widow. Let the Society give her what they please, she must be still, in some degree, burdensome to you, as she calls it. How do I envy you that glorious burden, and wish I could share it with you! You must put me in some way of getting a little money, that I may do something in this shipwreck of the family, though it be no more than furnishing a plank." Happy indeed is the widow who has such sons to whom she can look in the hour of her deepest need! The parsonage, built mainly out of their own means, had now become desolate. The well-known form and genial conversation of the rector are seen and heard no more. The old armchair is vacant. The study is no longer visited by him who found it a peaceful refuge from so many cares. The books on the shelves are untouched by the wonted student-hand. The nursery, the schoolroom, and the parlour are all fertile in vivid reminiscences. There her children had grown up around her; and thence sons and daughters had gone forth, many of them

160

to heaven in their infancy, where the paternal head of the family had now rejoined them forever, and the rest to brave the bleak winter of a rude and hostile world. The wall-fruit growing up by the sides of the house; the mulberry, cherry, and pear trees in the garden, and the stately walnuts "in the adjoining croft," were now full of sap, and blithe in their gay dresses of vernal foliage and blossom. On her own head, the snows of winter were falling fast, and an icy chill lay at her heart. With what sad emotion would the new-made widow take her farewell look at these mementoes of her husband's foresight and care! The time has come when she must quit forever a place where many of the greatest events in her life had occurred. With what feelings would she leave the many associations, painful and pleasing, which clustered around that memorable spot! Epworth had been no paradise of unmixed delights to her. The serpent had often lurked within its enclosures. Poverty, like an armed man, had stood at the gate and sometimes crossed the threshold; and death, with his merciless scythe, had mown down many a fair and beautiful flower. As, in widow's weeds and sable dress, she passes out of the dear old parsonage never more to return, "Some natural tears she dropp'd, but dried them soon." Her first resting-place, after she left the long-loved rectory, was the neighbouring town of Gainsborough. But it was not in some pretty little rose-mantled cottage, nestling among shrubs and flowers, that she found a home. Her daughter Emilia had opened a school, and amidst the din and bustle of a public establishment, the widow had to take up her abode. Nor was it on means adequate to her frugal wants, and insuring freedom from care, that she retired to wait the remaining days of her appointed time. Her circumstances were those of absolute dependence upon her children, or upon the charity of benevolent friends. It is stated by Kezzy, in a letter to John, that the widow of Mrs Wesley's eldest brother left her a thousand pounds, the interest of which she was to receive, and the principal to be divided among the children at her death. But, even if the money were so left, there is no evidence that it ever came into the family's possession. With such an investment, supposed to have been left about a year before the rector's death, would Charles Wesley have entreated Samuel to pass

161

through London and press her claims upon the charity of a Society for the relief of clergymen's widows? And would he have declared that whatever the Society might grant, "she must be still, in some degree, burdensome" to her eldest son? The thing is exceedingly improbable. For all that the Church, which her husband so long and faithfully served, has done for her, her few remaining years must be years of dependence and penury. After the lapse of more than a century there are still poor livings in the Establishment and miserable parsimony among thousands of Churches belonging to other Denominations. Wealthy congregations freely accept the full ministerial services of able and godly men, who have given up all worldly enterprise for the cure of souls, on such a poor paltry pittance, that it is utterly impossible for them to make any provision for the time of old age, or the necessities of widows and children who may survive them. Should exhausting work break up the minister's constitution and bring him to a premature grave, are not his children paupers and his widow destitute? Or if he toil on until his work becomes a burden which he can no longer bear, has he not to retire in age and feebleness, not having wherewith to make ends meet, even with the most self-denying economy? And all this, too, where there are among the Churches men of wealth who spend more on the mere luxuries of their table and the decorations of their mansions in one year than they contribute to the ministry in half a century ! Ought these things so to be? Are the churches to hold the principle that ministerial support simply means a scant provision for the supply of daily wants; and then, when the man of God, who has contributed so largely to their spiritual enrichment, can no longer work, think that they fulfil the measure of their duty by casting him upon the care of Providence, or coolly reminding him that his reward is in heaven? "If we have sown unto you spiritual things, is it a great thing if we shall reap your carnal things?" Happily, Mrs Wesley had her three noble-hearted sons to lean upon, and they were no brittle or thorny staff. Charles, it is true, had no means of furnishing "even a plank in this shipwreck of the family." John's salary, as a college tutor, was small: and Samuel's income, when the needs of his own family are considered, was by no means ample. But they were men who would work their

162

way; willing to bear any burden to relieve their Mother of care, and smooth the path of her declining days. To them the widow could look with confidence and hope. No sooner, however, was she safe in her temporary home at Gainsborough, than circumstances arose which compelled her to bid her two younger sons farewell, with but slight hopes of seeing them again in the flesh. Toward the close of 1726, or early in the following year, James Edward Oglethorpe,—a soldier, statesman, patriot, and philanthropist,-visited a friend imprisoned for debt. This turned his thoughts towards the hardships of this class of prisoners. He obtained a Parliamentary Committee to inquire into their condition and the best means of providing for them some effectual relief. It was ascertained that not less than four thousand persons were every year immured in jails from this cause alone. As the poor debtor entered the dungeon, rapacious keepers extorted money under the name of fees; robbed him of any clothing or supplies of food which he might happen to possess; loaded him at their pleasure with irons; tormented him with stripes above measure; and, in many cases, compelled him to sleep upon the damp earth-floor of his cell. These disclosures led to the formation of the colony of Georgia, to which these unfortunate beings might emigrate and live by honest industry. An ample extent of land was granted to trustees by Royal Charter. Ten thousand pounds were voted from the public funds; a like sum was raised by the trustees; and public collections and private subscriptions were obtained from various quarters. The first company of emigrants consisted of thirty-five families, or one hundred and sixteen persons. They embarked in November 1732, under the command of General Oglethorpe; and in the middle of the following January, they arrived at their destination, where they had "the best motives for industry, a possession of their own, and no possibility of subsisting without it." Meanwhile, Protestant exiles from various continental countries, driven from their homes by Popish persecution, were invited to share the benefits of this promising settlement, and liberal contributions were given for their outfit and passage. This benevolent enterprise was warmly supported by young Samuel Wesley. Ever ready at the call of charity, he gave a subscription of one guinea, and a donation of five. He could not lay vessels of silver or vessels of gold upon the altar, but he gave a "pewter chalice and patine for present use in Georgia, until silver ones are had." The next year, "an unknown benefactor, by the hands of the Reverend Samuel Wesley," presented "two silver chalices and two patines for the use of the first church in the town of Savannah." The father of the Wesleys was also among the first to congratulate Oglethorpe on "raising a new country, or rather a little world of his own, in the midst of almost wild woods and uncultivated deserts, where men may live free and happy, if they are not hindered by their own stupidity and folly, in spite of the unkindness of their brother mortals." And only six short months before his death, he wrote the following noble sentences: "I am at length, I thank God, slowly recovering from a long illness, during which there have been few days or nights but my heart has been working hard for Georgia. I had always so dear a love for your colony, that if it had but been ten years ago, I would gladly have devoted the remainder of my life and labours to that place, and think I might, before this time, have conquered the language, without which little can be done among the natives,—if the Bishop of London would have done me the honour to have sent me thither, as perhaps he then might. But that is now over. However, I can still reach them with my prayers, which I am sure will never be wanting." Little did he imagine that, in less than twelve months from the date of this letter, he would be called to his final reward; his wife left a dependent widow; and his two younger sons embarked as missionary ministers to this very sphere of labour. But so it was. The trustees and managers were most anxious to secure the regular observance of all religious ordinances among the settlers, and to make the colony a base of evangelical operations among the surrounding aborigines. They were, therefore, anxious to secure some earnest and self-denying ministers for this distant and difficult field. John Wesley and his companions at Oxford had already acquired a good reputation for the very qualities supposed to be most needed for such an appointment. While visiting London to present his father's work on Job to Queen Caroline, Wesley heard that the trustees had fixed their attention upon him and his Methodist associates, as men who possessed the requisite habits and character for preaching the Gospel to the Georgian settlers and the neighbouring Indians. Doctor Burton, who knew Wesley well, introduced him to General Oglethorpe, just returned from the colony. But when the mission was proposed, he decidedly refused to accept it. Some of his objections were obviated, and the firmness of his resolution seemed shaken. Still he urged the case of his widowed and dependent Mother. What a grief it would be to her, if he, the staff of her age, and probably her chief support and comfort, should go to a land so very far off! Would he go if her consent could be obtained? asked the persevering negotiators. This he thought extremely improbable; but consented that the trial should be made, and secretly determined that he would accept her decision as the decision of Providence. He went to Gainsborough, where he spent three days, and laid the whole case before his Mother and eldest sister. The consent of both was obtained; and the noble widow declared, "Had I twenty sons, I should rejoice that they were all so employed, though I should never see them more." Surely if there ever were circumstances to justify a mother in using her utmost efforts to keep her sons at home, these circumstances now met in the case of Mrs Wesley! A widow dependent and penniless, the sacrifice on her part cannot be measured. But she had trained up those very sons for God and not for herself. He calls them to a life of glorious hardship and honour among distant and heathen peoples, and she gladly surrenders them for missionary service in a colony for which their father's last efforts were made, and his last prayers offered. This is a wide contrast to the way in which the same demand is sometimes met by professedly religious parents in our own day. Worldly families make no demur when their sons go forth in quest of military honour or monetary gains. They submit willingly to years of separation and sacrifice for these mere earthly trifles. But when the Master calls for the sons and daughters of the Church for missionary service in foreign lands, how often do Christian parents interpose their authority and pronounce their veto ! Has God put it into the heart of your son to go far hence unto the Gentiles as an ambassador for Christ? Has He disposed your daughter to link her fortune and her life with the youth who gives up all to preach the Gospel in the regions beyond? Will you, dare you interpose your authority between them and their noble mission? Would you not freely yield them up for other services? And will you withhold them from this? Why should the "offer of a cadet's commission, a merchant's partnership, or a civilian's appointment be hailed as "a good thing,' and the commission to preach Christ to the Gentiles be yielded to reluctantly with speeches about hardships and sacrifices?" What honour greater than that which will crown their holy toil? When the wreath of fame woven by military prowess, or political sagacity, or literary effort, shall wither in the dust; the coronet won by self-denying missionary service shall be "a crown of glory that fadeth not away." "He that winneth souls is wise;" and "they that be wise shall shine as the brightness of the firmament; and they that turn many to righteousness, as the stars for ever and ever." If, then, your children are called of God to this noble service, come not between them and their high destiny. Entwine not around them the silken threads of affection to bind them to yourselves. Loose them and let them go; for the Lord hath need of them to extend the peaceful triumphs of His spiritual dominion. Think of the widow's words, "Had I twenty sons, I should rejoice that they were all so employed, though I should never see them more." O, bind the noble "sacrifice with cords, even unto the horns of the altar." After spending some months with her daughter at Gainsborough, Mrs Wesley went, in September 1736, to reside with her eldest son at Tiverton, where she remained until July 1737. Thence she removed to the pleasant little village of Wootton, Wiltshire, where her son-in-law, the afterward notorious Hall, who had married her daughter Martha,—was curate.

Hall is called "notorious because of his sexual promiscuity. He had several children out of wedlock, whom Martha raised. Hall had once been highly esteemed by the family as an Oxonian and convert. He would later become a polygamist and preach that it was not wrong. [See Wesley, Works, 16:269-73.]

Here she received the greatest possible kindness. "I tell you because I know you will be pleased with it," she writes to a friend at Tiverton, "that Mr Hall and his wife are very good to me. He behaves like a gentleman and a Christian, and my daughter with as much duty and tenderness as can be expected; so that on this account I am very easy." Her residence in this sequestered spot was evidently happy and profitable. The unhappy Hall had not yet entered upon those paths of licentious profligacy in which he afterwards wandered so far and so long. His ministry seems to have been gentle and tender; his conversation godly and pleasant; his conduct as becometh the Gospel of Christ. Here, too, she occasionally enjoyed the fellowship and ministry of one of her sons. Charles speaks of spending two days there, one of them the Sabbath, on which he no doubt preached, and he calls them "days never to be forgotten." In the course of a few months, Mr and Mrs Hall removed to Salisbury, and Mrs Wesley accompanied them. While resident in this ancient cathedral city, there occurred several important circumstances, which it would be unpardonable to pass over. Both her sons had returned from their bootless mission to Georgia. Broken down in health and constitution, as well as sorely distressed in spirit, they nevertheless thought of returning to the scene of their severest trials. But their Mother, however ready to give them up in the first instance, violently opposed their return. She probably saw that their mission had so far been a failure; and when she learnt, as she undoubtedly did from their own lips, the hardships they had undergone, the snares which had been unblushingly laid for their ruin, and the scandalous treatment they had received from their father's friend, who ought to have been their defence, she did perfectly right when, in the words of her son Charles, "she vehemently protested against our returning to Georgia." After a long night of deep penitential sorrow, her two sons, John and Charles, conveyed to her the glad tidings that they had obtained the blessing of conscious forgiveness, by faith in Jesus Christ. John's account, drawn up with his usual clearness and care, and accompanied by personal explanations, she fully endorsed, and expressed her thankfulness for the great spiritual change which he had

167

experienced. Charles seems to have used terms in describing his former and present condition which somewhat startled her. She thought he had done himself injustice, and "fallen into an odd way of thinking" in stating that, till within a few months, he had "no spiritual life, nor any justifying faith." But she heartily rejoiced that he "had now attained to a strong and lively hope in God's mercy through Christ. Blessed be God," she continues, "who shewed you the necessity you were in of a Saviour to deliver you from the power of sin and Satan,—for Christ will be no Saviour but to such as see their need of one,—and directed you by faith to lay hold of that stupendous mercy offered us by redeeming love. Jesus is the only physician of souls; His blood, the only salve that can heal a wounded conscience. . . . . There is none but Christ—none but Christ who is sufficient for these things. But, blessed be God, He is an all-sufficient Saviour! and blessed be His Holy name, that thou hast found Him a Saviour to thee, my son! O, let us love Him much, for we have much forgiven."

The time of her residence at Salisbury now ended, and about April 1739, she returned to the place of her birth, and spent the rest of her days in London. Fifty years before, in the very bloom and freshness of early-married life, she had left the great and busy city to encounter the hardships, and share the honours of a parochial minister's wife. She now returns to it a lone widow, aged and infirm, eyesight dim, and frame tottering on the verge of the grave. At her departure, her father, mother, sisters, and brothers were still in the land of the living; now all are numbered with the dead. She alone survives out of that "two dozen, or a quarter of a hundred children" which once bore her maiden name. These former days were probably called to remembrance as she entered her native city to spend, as she no doubt hoped, her remaining months in peace, undisturbed by further trouble. Alas, heavy trials still awaited her. She soon had to mourn the death of her first-born, who had been her comfort in manifold sorrows; to whose noble-hearted generosity the whole family had been so long and largely indebted; and in whose life her own seemed almost bound up. His health, never very robust, seriously failed in the autumn of 1739. "It has pleased God," he says, "to visit me with sickness; else I should not have been so backward in writing. Pray to Him for us, 'That He would give us patience under our sufferings, and a happy issue out of all our afflictions; granting us in this world knowledge of His truth, and in the world to come life everlasting!'" Still, he declares himself "on the mending hand in spite of foul weather." But his constitution, worn by slowly-rolling years, was evidently exhausted. On the evening of 5 November, he retired to rest "about as well as he had been for some time." But at three in the morning, he became alarmingly ill, and at seven, "he resigned his soul to God." This was a heavy stroke to Mrs Wesley. She had given Samuel the pre-eminence over his brothers, as her counsellor and friend. She had looked up to him as her natural protector, since his father's death; and she had always fondly spoken of him as "Son Wesley." How keenly she felt, and nobly she sustained this bereavement, the following beautiful passages from her letter to Charles clearly shew:—"Upon the first hearing of your brother's death, I did immediately acquiesce in the will of God, without the least reluctance. Only I somewhat marvelled that Jacky did not inform me of it before he left, since he knew thereof. But he was unacquainted with the manner of God's dealings with me in extraordinary cases, which indeed is no wonder: for though I have so often experienced His infinite power and mercy in my support and inward calmness of spirit, when the trial would otherwise have been too strong for me: yet His ways of working are to myself incomprehensible and ineffable. Your brother was exceeding dear to me in his life; and perhaps I have erred in loving him too well. I once thought it impossible for me to bear his loss; but none know what they can bear till they are tried. As your good old grandfather often used to say, 'That is an affliction, that God makes an affliction!' For surely the manifestation of His presence and favour is more than an adequate support under any suffering whatever. But if He withhold His consolations, and hide His face from us, the least suffering is intolerable. But blessed and adored be His holy name, it hath not been so with me, though I am infinitely unworthy of the least of all His mercies ! I rejoice in having a

169

comfortable hope of my dear son's salvation. He is now at rest, and would not return to earth, to gain the world. Why then should I mourn? He hath reached the haven before me; but I shall soon follow him. He must not return to me; but I shall go to him, never to part more. I thank you for your care of my temporal affairs. It was natural to think that I should be troubled for my dear son's death on that account, because so considerable a part of my support was cut off. But, to say the truth, I have never had one anxious thought of such matters: for it came immediately into my mind, that God, by my child's loss, had called me to a firmer dependence on Himself; that though my son was good, he was not my God; and that now our heavenly Father seemed to have taken my cause more immediately into His own hand; and therefore, even against hope, I believed in hope that I should never suffer more." It has often been observed that, just before the Lord Jesus was called to endure His protracted temptation, He received the brightest manifestation of His heavenly Father's approval and love. The heavens were opened unto Him; the Spirit of God descended like a dove and abode upon Him; and, lo, a voice from heaven, saying, "Thou art my beloved Son; in Thee I am well pleased." Thus animated and strengthened, He was blessedly prepared to encounter the forty-days' conflict in the wilderness. And does not God often so deal with His adopted children, as well as with His only-begotten Son? To fit us for trials, which He foresees, must come, He vouchsafes times of special refreshing and grace that we may not be overwhelmed, and swallowed up of overmuch sorrow. He so dealt with Mrs Wesley. A very short time before the heavy tidings of her son's death reached her ear, she had a most remarkable visitation to her soul. "Two or three weeks ago," she said, "while my son Hall was pronouncing those words, in delivering the cup to me, 'The blood of our Lord Jesus Christ, which was given for thee!' the words struck through my heart, and I knew that God, for Christ's sake, had forgiven me all my sins." Who can tell how much of that blessed calmness and resignation, so transparently reflected in the preceding letter, was due to the refreshing communications of grace through that Sacrament of the Supper? Truly "the Lord is good,

170

a stronghold in the day of trouble; and He knoweth them that trust in Him."

Late in the autumn of 1739, John Wesley took the old Foundery in Moorfields, which had been shattered almost to pieces by a terrific explosion. He had it repaired and fitted up as a place of worship. In connexion with it, there was a dwelling house, where Wesley, his friends, and his "helpers" found a home. To this townhouse of the Founder of Methodism, at the very top of the building, Mrs Wesley ultimately removed, and spent the few additional months of her life. Here she enjoyed the society of her sons and several of her daughters. She was a diligent attendant upon all the means of grace in connexion with the infant Methodist Community; and had the privilege of communion with "many good Christians, who refreshed, in some measure, her fainting spirits." In the death of her son Samuel this much-tried, but calm and trusting widow, had dismissed the eleventh of her children to the heavenly Paradise,— a series of heavy bereavements which few mothers have been called to sustain. Eight sons and daughters remain. Will they all survive her? Has her heart been riven oft enough? or must it pass through the pangs of bereavement once more, before it throbs for the last time? The first-born has gone, and now, in the course of a few months, the latest-born must follow. Sickly from her infancy, her youngest daughter passed thirty years of life in much feebleness; and on 9 March 1741, "full of thankfulness, resignation, and love, without pain or trouble, she commended her spirit into the hands of Jesus, and fell asleep." Kezzy had the unfortunate experience of having been courted by Mr. Westley Hall, who later married her sister, Martha. She never married.

The death of Kezzy was the widow's last great trial.

The violence of the last enemy was no more heard in her tabernacle; nor his wasting and destruction within her family borders. The days of her mourning were ended. Feeding in green pastures and led forth by the waters of comfort; with the shadows of death gathering around her; supported by the rod and staff of her good Shepherd; and ever ready to cheer with

171

her counsel and blessing the apostles of Methodism, this Mother in Israel waited, as in the Land Beulah, until the messenger came from the King of the Celestial City, and delivered unto her the welcome summons;—"Hail, good woman I bring thee tidings that the Master calleth for thee, and expecteth that thou shouldest stand in His presence in garments of immortality."

# XI. THE RELEASE.

Shortly, for I can scarce take off my pen from so exemplary a subject, her life and her death were saint-like. —BISHOP HALL.

Susannah Wesley as an older woman. W. H. Gibbs engraving.

THE most prominent facts in Mrs Wesley's personal history which arrest the attention at a cursory glance, are, her extraordinary care in the education of her many children; her untiring attention to the management of the affairs of her household; her extensive and accurate reading; the large amount of time spent in private devotion; and the persevering use of her pen. It is felt that to discharge these manifold duties as she discharged them, and bear for fifty years the burden of care, which daily came upon her, would be a heavy exaction upon the strongest constitution, and enough to fill up every moment of a long life without the slightest interruption from affliction or any other cause. This, probably, is the principal reason of the strong and general impression that Mrs Wesley was a woman of robust constitution, rejoicing in a rich and constant flow of health; knowing nothing of wearisome weeks of confinement to her own room in consequence of feebleness or personal affliction. This impression rests entirely upon an imaginary foundation.

She was a woman of comparatively delicate frame. Not only in the time of old age, but also in her years of prime, throughout her entire married life her health was very precarious, and she was frequently laid aside. Her first-born might have been called Jabez; for "she bare him with sorrow." His birth was preceded and followed by "deep affliction, both of body and mind."

A few years later she was confined to her room for many months, utterly "incapable of any business in the family," or the least attention to household affairs. As she passes over to "the right side of fifty," she represents herself as "infirm and weak; rarely in health; now and then having some very sick fits." Heavy tidings of her feebleness often reached the ears of her affectionate sons, who filled their letters with "compliments of condolence and consolation, on the supposition of her near-approaching end." The patient submission and even joyfulness with which she bore these tribulations is beautifully described in one of her morning meditations: "Though man is born to trouble, yet I believe there is scarce a man to be found upon earth, but, take the whole course of his life, hath more mercies than afflictions, and much more pleasure than pain. I am sure it has been so in my case. I have many years suffered much pain, and great bodily infirmities; but I have likewise enjoyed great intervals of rest and ease. And those very sufferings have, by the blessing of God, been of excellent use, and proved the most proper means of reclaiming me from a vain conversation; insomuch that I cannot say I had better have been without this affliction, this disease, this loss, want, contempt, or reproach.

174

All my sufferings, by the admirable management of Omnipotent Goodness, have concurred to promote my spiritual and eternal good. And if I have not reaped the advantage of them which I might have done, it is merely owing to the perverseness of my own will, and frequent lapses into present things, and unfaithfulness to the good Spirit of God; who, notwithstanding all my prevarications, all the stupid opposition I have made, has never totally abandoned me. Glory be to Thee, O Lord!"

This general debility and repeated sickness, which one of her daughters declares was "often occasioned by want of clothes or convenient meat," formed the subject of frequent meditation, and led her to realise most vividly the solemn fact that this was not her rest. She seemed to stand on the verge of eternity, glancing at the past with its crowded omissions and sorrowful memories, and looking earnestly into the future with its dread solemnities and awful issues. What can exceed the touching beauty of the following passage?—"Ah! my dear son, did you with me stand on the verge of life, and saw before your eyes a vast expanse, an unlimited duration of being, which you might shortly enter upon, you can't conceive how all the inadvertencies, mistakes, and sins of youth would rise to your view ; and how different the sentiments of sensitive pleasures, the desire of sexes, and pernicious friendships of the world, would be then, from what they are now, while health is entire and seems to promise many years of life. "Believe me, youth, for I am read in cares, And bend beneath the weight of more than fifty years.'" As in many other cases, these anticipations of a comparatively early dissolution were not realised. She lived to a good old age; but the earthly house was ready to shake with every passing breeze. The records of her closing hours are not so ample as we could desire; but they are precious and suggestive, affording every evidence of a blissful and triumphant close. When her son John, after a hurried ride from Bristol, where the tidings of her approaching end probably reached him, arrived in London on 20 July 1742, he wrote the touching sentence, "I found my Mother on the borders of eternity!" Nature was rapidly giving way, and the bourne of life was reached. A few days before, her bodily sufferings were severe, and her mental conflicts fierce and torturing: but now

175

all doubts and fears are fled forever. There remains but one desire, "to depart, and be with Christ, as soon as God shall call." Her husband and twelve of her children are already with the Lord, and why should she longer tarry? On the twenty-third, just as the eyelids of the morning open upon her, and about twelve hours before her departure, she wakes from a quiet slumber, rejoicing "with joy unspeakable and full of glory." Her exultant expressions attract the attention of her children. They listen, and hear her saying, "My dear Saviour! art Thou come to help me in my extremity at last?" From that moment "she is sweetly resigned indeed. The enemy has no more power to hurt her. The remainder of her time is spent in praise." Just after the customary mid-day intercession meeting, —where fervent supplications were no doubt offered for her departing spirit,—"her pulse is almost gone, and her fingers are dead." Her "change is near, and her soul on the wing for eternity." That solemn Commendatory Prayer which, more than seven years before, rose over her dying husband at Epworth, and told that the hour of her widowhood was at hand, now rises from the lips of the same beloved son, commending her own soul into the hands of Him with whom "are the issues from death." Her look is "calm and serene, and her eyes fixed upward." From three to four the silver cord is loosing; the wheel is breaking at the cistern; and those who look out of the windows are being darkened. Her son and all her surviving daughters, – Nancy, Emilia, Hetty, Patty, and Sukey, sit down "on her bed-side and sing a requiem to her dying soul." And what is the death-song which, in its beautiful burden of praise, rises from these tremulous, but well-trained voices, as the grand accompaniment of the ascending spirit to the harmonies of heaven? Some of those strains "for one departing," subsequently written by the dying widow's own minstrel son, would have been a most appropriate expression of the grateful sorrow of these devout children before Him who had been "pleased to deliver the soul of this their dear Mother out of the miseries of this sinful world." Well might they have sung in her closing ears,—

"Happy soul, thy days are ended, All thy mourning days below: Go, by angel guards attended, To the sight of Jesus, go!

Waiting to receive thy spirit, Lo! the Saviour stands above; Shews the purchase of His merit, Reaches out the crown of love." When the sound of their song had ceased, "she continued," says John, "in just the same way as my father was, struggling and gasping for life, though,—as I could judge by several signs,—perfectly sensible, till near four o'clock. I was then going to drink a dish of tea, being faint and weary, when one called me again to the bedside. It was just four o'clock. She opened her eyes wide, and fixed them upward for a moment. Then the lids dropped, and the soul was set at liberty, without one struggle, or groan, or sigh. We stood around the bed and fulfilled her last request, uttered a little before she lost her speech;—"Children, as soon as I am released, sing a psalm of praise to God!'" "As soon as I am RELEASED!"—blessed, beautiful, most appropriate word! No wonder that, after such an utterance, it should be enshrined in more than one of Charles Wesley's noble funeral hymns:—

"Lo! the prisoner is released,
 Lighten'd of her fleshly load;
 Where the weary are at rest,
 She is gather'd into God!"

Yes! death is not annihilation; not an eternal sleep; not a temporary suspension of conscious existence and enjoyment. It is the sanctified spirit's final enfranchisement; its release from the bondage of corruption into the glorious liberty of the children of God: its dismissal from the sorrows of time to the "fulness of joy" in the heavenly Paradise. "And oh, the immediateness of that joy! There is not a computable point of time. It is not a sand-fall. It is scarcely the twinkling of an eye. There lies my friend. He hastens to depart. Death is upon him. The change has well-nigh come. How little intervenes between his present humiliations and his awaiting glories! I tremble to think what in an instant he must be How unlike all he was ! How extreme to all he is! I bend over thee, and mark thy wasted, pallid frame,—I look up, and there is ascending above me an angel's form! I stoop to thee, and just can catch thy feeble, gasping whisper,-I listen, and there floats around me a

177

seraph's song! I take thy hand, tremulous and cold,—it is waving to me from yonder skies! I wipe thy brow, damp and furrowed,—it is enwreathed with the garland of victory! I slake thy lip, bloodless and parched, —it is drinking the living fountains, the overflowing springs, of heaven!" "Therefore we are always confident, knowing that, whilst we are at home in the body, we are absent in the Lord;—for we walk by faith, not by sight, —we are confident, I say, and willing rather to be absent from the body, and to be present with the Lord. Wherefore we labour, that, whether present or absent, we may be accepted of Him." How beautiful and impressive, in the light of Mrs Wesley's death-scene, are the following words to her son John fifteen years before! "You did well to correct that fond desire of dying before me, since you do not know what work God may have for you to do ere you leave the world. And besides, I ought surely to have the preeminence in point of time, and go to rest before you. Whether you could see me die without any emotions of grief, I know not. It is what I have often desired of the children, that they would not weep at our parting, and so make death more uncomfortable than it would otherwise be to me. If you, or any other of my children were likely to reap any spiritual advantage by being with me at my exit, I should be glad to have you with me. But, as I have been an unprofitable servant during the course of a long life, I have no reason to hope for so great an honour, so high a favour as to be employed in doing our Lord any service in the article of death. It were well if you spake prophetically, and that joy and hope might have the ascendant over the other passions of my soul in that important hour. Yet, I dare not presume, nor do I despair; but rather leave it to our Almighty Saviour to do with me in life and death just what He pleases; for I have no choice." Better than all her anticipations, when the appointed time arrived she had a death by which she "glorified God," and an exit from which her children might reap much "spiritual advantage." "When faith and love, which parted from thee never, Had ripen'd thy just soul to dwell with God, Meekly thou didst resign this earthly load Of death, call'd life; which us from life doth sever. Thy works, and alms, and all thy good endeavour, Stay'd not behind, nor in the grave were trod;

But, as faith pointed with her golden rod,
Follow'd thee up to joy and bliss forever.

Love led them on, and faith, who knew them best Thy handmaids, clad them o'er with purple beams And azure wings, that up they flew so drest, And spake the truth of thee on glorious themes Before the Judge, who thenceforth bid thee rest, And drink thy fill of pure immortal streams." Eight days after her peaceful departure, "almost an innumerable company of people gathered together" in that great Puritan Necropolis,— the Bunhill-Fields burying-ground. Between four and five o'clock on the Sabbath afternoon, the exanimated clay of Susanna Wesley was borne from the old Foundery to its final resting place, until the morning of the resurrection. The funeral ceremonies, conducted by her son John, were most solemn and affecting. With faltering voice he pronounced;—"Forasmuch as it hath pleased Almighty God of His great mercy to take unto Himself the soul of our dear MOTHER here departed, we therefore commit her body to the ground; earth to earth, ashes to ashes, dust to dust; in sure and certain hope of the Resurrection to eternal life, through our Lord Jesus Christ !" A witness of the solemn ceremony, whose stray note has fallen into our hands, says, "At the grave there was much grief when Mr Wesley said, 'I commit the body of my MOTHER to the earth!'". She came to her grave "in a good old age," and the people made great lamentation for her. As soon as the funeral service was ended, that same son stood up and preached a sermon over her open grave. His selected text had more reference to warning the living to flee from the wrath to come, than to the eulogy of her who had just finished her course. The solemn and appropriate Scripture was, "I saw a great white throne, and Him that sat on it, from whose face the earth and the heaven fled away; and there was found no place for them. And I saw the dead, small, and great, stand before God; and the books were opened: and the dead were judged out of those things that were written in the books, according to their works." O that the sermon had been published! O that the warmhearted and loving references to the life and character of the Mother of the Wesleys had been preserved to us! What they were we are left to conjecture. But, says the preacher, "It was one of the most solemn assemblies I ever saw, or expect to see, on this side Eternity." Standing in the presence of this impressive scene, surrounded by the associations which this place of the dead so vividly awakens, one thought in connexion with the history of the departed Susanna Wesley, forcibly impresses the mind. Forsaking Nonconformity in early life, and maintaining for many years a devout and earnest discipleship in the Established Church, which in theory she never renounces; in the last two years of her life she becomes a practical Nonconformist in attending the ministry and services of her sons, in a separate and unconsecrated "conventicle." The two ends of her earthly life, separated by so wide an interval, in a certain sense embrace and kiss each other. Rocked in a Nonconformist cradle, she now sleeps in a Nonconformist grave. There, —in close contiguity to the dust of Bunyan the immortal dreamer; of Watts one of the Church's sweetest psalmists; of her sister Dunton, and many of her father's associates; and directly opposite the spot where some of her children quietly rest in the sister cemetery around City Road Chapel,—her mortal remains await the "times of the restitution of all things." "We set up a plain stone at the head of her grave," says her son John in closing his brief, but beautiful re. cord,—"inscribed with the following words:—

HERE LIES THE BODY
OF MRS SUSANNA WESLEY
YOUNGEST AND LAST SURVIVING DAUGHTER OF
DR SAMUEL ANNESLEY.

In sure and steadfast hope to rise,
And claim her mansion in the skies,
A Christian here her flesh laid down,
The cross exchanging for a crown.
True daughter of affliction, she,
Inured to pain and misery,
Mourn'd a long night of griefs and fears,
A legal night of seventy years.
The Father then reveal'd His Son,

Him in the broken bread made known;
She knew and felt her sins forgiven,
And found the earnest of her heaven.
Meet for the fellowship above,
She heard the call, "Arise, My love!'
'I come!" her dying looks replied,
And lamb-like as her Lord, she died."

# XII. RELIGIOUS LIFE.

Her assiduity in her religious course, the seasons, order, and constancy whereof seemed to be governed by the ordinances of heaven, that ascertain the succession of day and night; so that one might as soon divert the course of the sun, as turn her from her daily course in religious duties; this argued a steady principle and of the highest excellency, that of Divine love. —John Howe.

THE life of Mrs Wesley, crowned with a death so peaceful and triumphant, was pre-eminently religious. As we contemplate her amidst those diversified scenes and circumstances through which she was called to pass, the mind becomes forcibly impressed with the devoutness of her spirit and the steadfastness of her heart in the fear of God. Religion mingled with all her joys, and shed its serene and heavenly lustre upon all her sorrows. She possessed great natural calmness and fortitude; but the joy of the Lord was her strength. This was the secret power which sustained her in every trial, and finally gave her a happy issue out of all her afflictions. Her religious life, therefore, is a subject of deepest interest, and deserves a careful consideration. Ample materials for such a purpose may be found in her meditations and letters; and the best use we can make of them will be to throw a careful selection of passages into something like order, accompanied by a few connecting and expository remarks. Mrs Wesley will thus become the biographer of her own inner life, and the reader will have the advantage of receiving the description of her religious state mainly from her own nervous and honest pen.

In the spiritual experience of believers there is, generally speaking, a particular crisis, called conversion, which distinctly marks the commencement of the new life in the soul. Yielding in a moment to long-resisted convictions, they experience an instantaneous spiritual change. Thenceforth they look back upon that hour as the date of their new birth. This, however, is by no means a uniform law in the economy of grace. Some persons who do not doubt the fact of their own conversion, cannot point to any particular moment when they passed from death unto life. This, as the reader has already been told, was the case with Mrs Wesley's father, who often declared that he did not remember the time when he was not converted. And this, in all probability, was the case with Mrs Wesley herself. When her son Charles, in the fervour of his own new-found peace with God, was disposed to insist upon a knowledge of the exact moment of the great change as essential to its possession, she wrote,—"I do not judge it necessary to know the precise time of our conversion."

Surrounded from infancy by religious influences, and favoured with a godly training, the seeds of truth probably took root imperceptibly, and ultimately brought forth fruit. Even the years of her childhood were years in which she resolved not to spend more time in amusements in any one day, than she spent in meditation and prayer. From the first, religion was the one great subject of her thoughts; and the practice of piety was her daily effort. As she advanced in years there was no change, except that of increasing strictness and care in all spiritual things. There is a beautiful oneness in her religious experience and conduct, which is seldom found even among the most devout disciples of the Lord Jesus. The constant prayerfulness of her spirit commends itself to our strongest admiration. She believed that, under all circumstances, it was her privilege to seek and obtain Divine guidance and help. Not only her own personal wants, but the various events affecting the household, or any particular member of the family, had special seasons appointed, in which she might spread them before the Lord. When her eldest son was doubtful about his election from Westminster to an Oxford scholarship, she besought him to "beg God's favour in this great affair;" and observed,—"If you can possibly, set apart the hours of Sunday afternoon, from four to six, for this employment, which time I also have determined to the same work." Prayer was, indeed, her very life. In it her great strength lay, and by it she overcame. In order that this devotional spirit might be more thoroughly cultivated and sustained, she coveted certain set times for retirement, that she might "have leisure to worship and adore the Supreme Fountain of being." Surrounded by so many domestic cares,

184

and with such heavy demands upon her attention, this might appear almost impossible. But before her calmly-resolute will and admirable method of redeeming the time, all obstacles vanished away. Two hours of the day, one in the morning and another in the evening, with an occasional interval at noon, were consecrated to secret communion with God. There may be some danger that, as an old writer observes, "when devotion is thus artificially plaited into hours, it may take up our thoughts in formalities to the neglect of the substance." But this was not the case with Mrs Wesley. These seasons of retirement were seasons of rich baptism and holy blessing. She came from her closet like Moses from the mount, her face radiant with the beauties of holiness. Having conversed with God, she appeared in her family bright, cheerful, and calm; like Mary in the fervour of her devotion, and akin to Martha in the activity of her secular duties. If, in the order of His Providence, God "did sometimes plainly interrupt or prevent such retirement, the same love to Him which inspired her with a desire for it" calmed and guided her soul, and "caused it humbly to acquiesce and submit to whatever He saw best for her to do or suffer." How rigidly she adhered to these set times of devotion, the following passage clearly indicates:—"It is now about nine years since you more solemnly devoted yourself to His will, and since you resolved to spend at least one hour morning and evening in private duty, which resolution you have peremptorily adhered to. And though by sickness, and sometimes unavoidable business, you have occasionally contracted your devotions, yet your conscience cannot accuse you of omitting them."* With Mrs Wesley, prayer was not simply assuming a devotional attitude the moment she entered her closet, and uttering a few warm expressions. She regarded it as a most solemn act of worship, not to be entered upon without serious and considerate preparation. She charged herself to take, at least, a quarter of an hour to collect and compose her thoughts before she attempted to approach the throne of grace. "If but some earthly prince," she argued, " or some person of eminent quality were certainly to visit you, or you were to visit him, would you not be careful to have your apparel and all about you decent, before you came into his presence? How much more should you take care to have your mind in order, when you take upon yourself the honour to speak to the Sovereign Lord of the Universe! Upon the temper of the soul, in your addresses to Him, depends your success in a very great measure. HE is infinitely too great to be trifled with ; too wise to be imposed on by a mock devotion; and He abhors a sacrifice without a heart. An habitual sense of His perfections is an admirable help against cold and formal performances. Though the lamp of devotion is always burning, yet a wise virgin will arise and trim before going forth to meet the Bridegroom." She also charged herself against vain mirth, immoderate anger, the least diversion, or even walking in the open air, –"because it discomposed her head,"— before the morning worship of the household had been offered. "If possible," she writes, "redeem some time for preparation for family prayer." Mrs Wesley also attached great importance to the duty of self-examination, as a means of spiritual improvement. A considerable portion of her hours of retirement was employed in communing with her own heart, as well as in fellowship with God. She endeavoured to keep her "mind in a temper of recollection, often in the day calling it in from outward objects, lest it should wander into forbidden paths. Make an examination of your conscience," she continues, "at least three times a day, and omit no opportunity of retirement from the world." This was her practice for many years, until, in consequence of increasing infirmities, she "could not observe order, or think consistently, as formerly." The following quotation illustrates the searching manner in which she performed this self-inquisition. "You, above all others, have most need of humbling yourself before the great and holy God, for the very great and very many sins you daily are guilty of, in thought, word, and deed, against His Divine Majesty. What an habitual levity is there in your thoughts! How many vain, impure thoughts pass through the mind in one hour! And though they do not take up their abode for any long continuance, yet their passing through often leaves a tincture of impurity. How many worldly regards, even in sacred actions, with habitual inadvertence; seldom any seriousness, or composure of spirit; the passions rude and tumultuous, very susceptible of violent impressions, from light and inconsiderable accidents, unworthy a reasonable being, but

186

more unworthy a Christian. Keep thy heart with all diligence,— thy thoughts, thy affections,—for out of them are the issues of life. Who can tell how oft he offendeth in this kind? Oh, cleanse Thou me from secret faults | Out of the abundance of the heart the mouth speaketh. How many unnecessary words are you guilty of daily? How many opportunities of speaking for the good of the souls committed to your care are neglected? How seldom do you speak of God with that reverence, that humility, that gravity that you ought? Your words, as well as your thoughts, are deficient. You do not conceive or speak of God aright. You do not speak magnificently or worthily of Him who is the high and lofty One that inhabiteth eternity, the Creator of the Universe!"* In these deep searchings of heart, Mrs Wesley probably did herself some injustice by rating her spiritual condition lower than it really was. But who does not admire the thoroughness with which she sought to find out any way of wickedness, wherein her thoughts, affections, or words might, perchance, be still wandering?

As the appointed time for receiving the Lord's Supper drew near, there was a special examination of her soul to ascertain whether she possessed the grace, which fitted her to eat and drink worthily at the table of the Lord. "The Church," she observes, "replies to that question,— What is required of those that come to the Lord's Supper? To examine themselves whether they repent them truly of their former sins; steadfastly purposing to lead a new life; have a lively faith in God's mercy through Christ, with a thankful remembrance of His death; and be in charity with all men." In self-humbling terms she discusses her experience in relation to every one of these points, and concludes, "You have, of late, often experienced that the more accurate you have been in the work of preparation for the Sacrament, the more indisposed you have been for meditation and reflection, for sometimes one, two, or three days after. And this hath been a great discouragement to you; and you have thought that your soul has received no benefit from that sacred Ordinance. Now, the reason of it I apprehend to be this,—long, intense thinking, keeping the mind for a considerable time to hard exercise does necessarily impair the bodily strength, where persons are of a weak constitution, and the mind being under the influence of the body in this imperfect state, it cannot exert itself until that hath again recovered its vigour, which requires some time; and you may observe that as the body is refreshed, the soul is strengthened. Therefore be not discouraged; but endeavour to keep your mind as composed as possible, and pray to God to preserve you from temptation during this bodily indisposition, and that, as your day is, so your strength may be." Religious meditation, which an old writer defines as "a sort of spiritual rumination," and which is so little practised in our own bustling age, was another duty to which Mrs Wesley attached considerable importance. "I see nothing," she writes to her son John, "in the disposition of your time but what I approve, unless it be that you do not assign enough of it to meditation; which is, I conceive, incomparably the best means to spiritualise our affections, confirm our judgment, and add strength to our pious resolutions, of any exercise whatever." Her manuscripts shew that, in connexion with self-examination and prayer, she meditated deeply upon the works of Creation, and the ways of Providence; the human frame, so fearfully and wonderfully made, and the powers and passions of the soul; the nature of vice and virtue; the necessity, fulness, and boundless efficacy of the atoning work of Christ, on which she observes, that "were there as many worlds to save as Omnipotence could create, His own sacrifice of Himself would be sufficient to save them all;" the operations of the Holy Spirit as the only source of all inward religion; and the profound mysteries connected with the Divine existence and perfections. The last of these subjects seems to have possessed an irresistible charm for her mind. As she meditates upon the glory of God many beautiful sentences fall from her pen. "What is it," she asks, "to have a just sense of Almighty God, as He is distinguished into three subsistences,—namely, Father, Son, and Holy Ghost? Indeed I cannot tell! After so many years' inquiry, so long reading, and so much thinking, His boundless essence seems more inexplicable, the perfection of His glory more bright and inaccessible. The farther I search, the less I discover; and I seem now more ignorant than when I first began to know something of Him." "But to behold Him in Jesus Christ reconciling the world unto Himself; to see by faith that infinite,

188

all-glorious Being assuming the character of a Saviour, a Repairer of the lapse, a Healer of the diseases and miseries of mankind, is— what? It is something that penetrates and melts the soul. It is something the heart feels and labours under, but the tongue cannot express. I adore, O God! I adore!" "Praise God for illuminating your mind, and for enabling you to prove demonstratively that His wisdom is as infinite as His power! The use you are to make of these discoveries is to praise, and love, and obey. Therefore, be exceedingly careful that your affections keep pace with your knowledge; for if you study the Divine perfections as matters of mere speculation, your acquests of knowledge will but enhance your guilt and increase your future torments. You must know, that you may adore and love! And if you are now more rationally persuaded that God is infinitely wise, then learn by this knowledge to practise a more hearty and universal subjection to Him; more cheerfully submit to the order of His Providence; submit your reason so far to your faith, as not to doubt or scruple those points of faith which are mysterious to us through the weakness of our understanding, and adore the mystery you cannot comprehend."

Mrs Wesley's delight was also in the law of the Lord, and diligently did she meditate upon all its precepts. She hailed with thankfulness the least degree of additional light upon any of its precious sentences, and used it as the means of attaining still more comprehensive views of truth. "What shall I call it," she asks, "Providence or chance, that first directed my eye to the first verse of the thirteenth of Zechariah,-'In that day there shall be a fountain opened to the house of David, and to the inhabitants of Jerusalem, for sin and for uncleanness,'—when, for several nights, the Bible always opened on that place when I took it to read in the evening? Whatever it was, I have found a good effect of it; for by that means I have for so long a time had an opportunity of praising the eternal, infinite God for sending His Son into the world,—nor can I see that verse without. Glory be to Thee, O Lord!" And from this apparently trivial circumstance of her Bible opening at the same place on several successive evenings, she draws the following instructive conclusion: "That if the temper and disposition of the mind be good, there are very few things that occur in the ordinary

189

course of life, however trivial or inconsiderable they may seem in their own nature, but what may prove a means of conveying grace into the soul. And it is only want of advertence, and a due care to implore the Divine blessing and direction in all our ways, that makes us so little the better for those little accidents we meet with in our daily converse in the world."

The holy vigilance and resolute control, which Mrs Wesley exercised over herself, meet us at every turn of her history. Knowing that the "still small voice of the Divine Spirit is not heard amidst the thunder and noise, the storms and tempests of tumultuous passions, be they raised either by intemperate joys or griefs," she strove to keep her mind perpetually composed and stayed on God. "If you desire to live under the continual government and direction of the Holy Spirit, preserve an equal temper," was one of her most cherished rules of self-government. She also held her mouth as with a bridle, lest she should offend with her tongue. "It is, perhaps, one of the most difficult things in the world to govern the tongue; and he that would excel herein must speak but seldom; rarely, if ever, in passion of any kind. For it is not only in anger we are apt to transgress; but all excess of other passions,—whether love, hate, hope, fear, desire,—does often unwittingly cause us to offend in words. Our blessed Lord hath told us that "out of the abundance of the heart, the affections, 'the mouth speaketh.' The best way, therefore, to prevent evil-speaking of any sort is to purify the heart; for till that be done, all resolves and cautions will be ineffectual." "It always argues a base and cowardly temper to whisper secretly what you dare not speak to a man's face. Therefore be careful to avoid all evil-speaking, and be ever sure to obey that command of our Saviour in this case as well as others,—'Whatsoever ye would that men should do unto you, do ye even so unto them." Therefore be very cautious in speaking of these three sorts of persons, namely, the innocent, the dead, and the absent."

"In telling a story, or relating past actions, be careful to speak deliberately and calmly; avoiding immoderate mirth or laughter on the one hand, and un-charitableness and excessive anger on the other, lest your invention supply the defect of your memory. Ever remember you are in the presence of the great and holy God. Every sin is a contradiction and offence to some Divine attribute. Lying is opposite and offensive to the truth of God." These are golden rules; and they were sacredly observed by her who formed them for the government of her own conversation. She opened her mouth with wisdom, and in her tongue was the law of kindness. The same vigilant government was exercised over all her appetites and passions. "It is necessary for you," she writes, "if you would preserve your liberty and live free from sin, to mortify your appetites; for if they remain in power, restrain them as you will or can, still some circumstances or seasons will occur wherein they will betray you, and compel you to act contrary to your better judgment." She believed that "any passion in excess does as certainly inebriate as the strongest liquor immoderately taken." "The great difficulty we find in restraining our appetites and passions from excess, often arises from the liberties we take in indulging them in all those instances wherein there does not, at first sight, appear some moral evil. Occasions of sin frequently take their rise from lawful enjoyments; and he that will always venture to go to the utmost bounds of what he may, will not fail to step beyond them sometimes; and then he uses his liberty for a cloak of his licentiousness.

He that habitually knows and abhors the sin of intemperance, will not stay too long in the company of such as are intemperate; and because God is pleased to indulge us a glass for refreshment, will therefore take it when he really needs none. It is odds but this man will transgress; and though he should keep on his feet, and in his senses, yet he will perhaps raise more spirits than his reason can command; will injure his health, his reputation or estate; discompose his temper, violate his own peace, or that of his own family; all which are evils which ought carefully to be avoided. It holds the same in all other irregular appetites or passions; and there may be the same temptations in other instances, from whence occasions of sin may arise. Therefore, be sure to keep a strict guard, and observe well lest you use lawful pleasures unlawfully. Fly from occasions of evil." According to the rector's testimony, temperance was not the reigning virtue of the Isle of Axholme. This probably, among other considerations, led Mrs Wesley to

191

regard with horror any practices, which might lead to the sin of intoxication. "Proper drunkenness," she observes, "does, I think, consist in drinking such a quantity of strong liquor as will intoxicate, and render the person incapable of using his reason with that strength and freedom as he can at other times. Now, there are those that, by habitual drinking a great deal of such liquors, can hardly ever be guilty of proper drunkenness, because never intoxicated. But this I look upon as the highest kind of the sins of intemperance." Mrs Wesley was probably in no danger of falling into this lamentable habit; but she determined to guard every avenue to its approach. The common practice of the times was for the members of any social party to "keep the rounds in drinking healths." Regarding this as a strong temptation to many, she resolved never to countenance the custom by joining in it; and she publicly made known her reasons for refusing. She also made a solemn vow that she would never drink more than two glasses at one time." As a student and admirer of Herbert, she probably based her resolution on his homely exhortation:— "Drink not the third glass:—which thou canst not tame When once it is within thee; but, before, May'st rule it as thou list:—and pour the shame Which it would pour on thee, upon the floor. It is most just to throw that on the ground, Which would throw me there, if I keep the round." If ever she made the least approach to any infringement of this rule, she severely chided herself for the indiscretion. "I do not approve," she writes, "of your drinking twice of ale in so short a time. Not that I think it unlawful for another to do so, or that it is a direct breach of your vow; but it is injurious to your health, and so does not fall under your own rule,— namely, never to drink anything strong but merely for refreshment. You have great reason to adore the great and good God that hath given you so mice a constitution as will not bear the least degree of intemperance. He might have made you strong to endure the excess that others run into, and so you might often have been exposed to temptations to offend; whereas you are now doubly guarded, both by His wise and holy laws, and an infirm body. Glory be to Thee, O Lord!'" Temptation is the common lot of the Lord's people; and Mrs Wesley was sometimes violently assailed by the enemy of her soul. But when the dark hours came, she endeavoured to encourage herself by a review of God's merciful loving-kindness towards her. "If He had been willing you should perish," she argues with herself, "He might have let you perish without the expense of so many miracles to save you. Why did He give you birth in a Christian country, of religious parents, by whom you were early instructed in the principles of religion? Why hath He waited so long to be gracious? Why hath His Providence so often prevented you? And why hath the same good Providence so often reclaimed you by punishments and mercies? Why hath His Spirit so long striven with you, co-operating with the means of grace, illuminating your mind, purifying your affections, in some measure awakening your conscience, not suffering you to enjoy any rest or quiet in the course of sin? And though sometimes you have been impatient under checks of conscience under less miscarriages, yet He hath not given you over till He hath brought you to repentance. You may remember the time when you were strongly inclined to — ; t and you cannot forget that state of temptation that you were in for two whole years, and what a doubtful conflict you then sustained. But yet the good Spirit of God never totally left you; but the better principle at last prevailed, to the eternal glory of free grace. And may you not argue as Manoah's wife;—If the Lord were pleased to destroy me, were willing that I should perish, would He have at all regarded my prayers? Would He have enabled me, through the assistance of His Holy Spirit, to conquer this temptation, and to break such an inveterate habit of evil thinking?" But did Mrs Wesley merely live a sort of cloister-life, whose quiet contemplations were unbroken by any care or activity for the spiritual welfare of others? Was she entirely absorbed in the concerns of her own soul? She believed that "religion is not to be confined to the church or closet, nor exercised only in prayer and meditation." It must be remembered, however, that our present facilities for Christian effort, where the humblest talents may find some appropriate sphere of usefulness, were mostly unknown in her day. The family was almost the only vineyard in which she could work; and here she toiled well and successfully, employing every talent and gathering an ample vintage. There is, however, one interesting season of holy

193

activity to which special reference must be made. Toward the close of 1711, her husband went to London, where he remained several months. His place was supplied by a very inefficient curate, and public worship was held only on the Sabbath morning. Mrs Wesley felt that, as the mistress of a large family of children and servants, it was her duty to hold some religious service in the parsonage, lest the greater part of the Lord's-day should be spent in idleness or frivolity. "And though the superior charge of the souls contained in the household lies upon you, as the head of the family and as their minister," she writes to her husband; "yet, in your absence, I cannot but look upon every soul you leave under my care as a talent committed to me, under a trust, by the great Lord of all the families of heaven and earth. And if I am unfaithful to Him, or to you, in neglecting to improve these talents, how shall I answer unto Him, when He shall command me to render an account of my stewardship? As these and other such like thoughts, made me at first take a more than ordinary care of the souls of my children and servants; so, knowing that our most holy religion requires a strict observation of the Lord's Day, and not thinking that we fully answered the end of the institution by only going to church, but that likewise we are obliged to fill up the intermediate spaces of that sacred time by other acts of piety and devotion; I thought it my duty to spend some part of the day in reading to, and instructing my family, especially in your absence, when, having no afternoon's service, we have so much leisure for such exercises. And such time I esteemed spent in a way more acceptable to God, than if I had retired to my own private devotions." The tidings of these services soon spread abroad. The servant boy told his parents, who earnestly desired to be present; and others solicited the like privilege, until the number amounted to thirty or forty. With this little company she sang psalms, read prayers, and also a short sermon. She did this with the utmost self-diffidence. "I never durst positively presume to hope," she observes, "that God would make use of me as an instrument in doing good. The farthest I ever durst go was, It may be; who can tell? With God, all things are possible. I will resign myself to Him.

Mrs Wesley herself also became the subject of a gracious spiritual quickening, produced in a most remarkable way. At the beginning of the eighteenth century, Frederick, King of Denmark, resolved to establish a mission for the conversion of the heathen at Tranquebar. He sent out Ziegenbalg and Plutscho, two noble Christian ministers whose gifts and grace eminently fitted them for this sacred enterprise. The little volume containing an account of their self-denying labours in the commencement of the mission, found its way into the Epworth parsonage, and very probably suggested to the rector the missionary scheme, which he propounded and offered to initiate by his personal labours. It also fell into the hand of Mrs Wesley, and none but her own words can describe the blessed effects which it produced upon her mind. "Soon after you went to London," she writes to her husband, "Emilia found in your study the account of the Danish missionaries, which, having never seen, I ordered her to read to me. I was never, I think, more affected with anything than with the relation of their travels; and was exceeding pleased with the noble design they were engaged in. Their labours refreshed my soul beyond measure; and I could not forbear spending good part of that evening in praising and adoring the Divine goodness for inspiring those good men with such an ardent zeal for His glory, that they were willing to hazard their lives and all that is esteemed dear to men in this world, to advance the honour of their Master, Jesus. For several days I could think or speak of little else. At last it came into my mind, though I am not a man nor a minister of the Gospel, and so cannot be employed in such a worthy employment as they were; yet, if my heart were sincerely devoted to God, and if I were inspired with a true zeal for His glory, and did really desire the salvation of souls, I might do somewhat more than I do. I thought I might live in a more exemplary manner in some things; I might pray more for the people, and speak with more warmth to those with whom I have the opportunity of conversing. However, I resolved to begin with my own children." She immediately commenced those private conferences with each child, described in a previous chapter; and discoursed more freely and affectionately with the few neighbours who attended her Sabbath-services in the parsonage. She read to them the best and most awakening sermons the rector's library could supply, and spent a greater amount of time in these holy exercises. Many of the hearers became deeply impressed; the spirit of religious inquiry was excited in the town, until two hundred persons crowded into the parsonage, "while many went away for want of room." There was, in fact, a great and blessed revival; and the results were extensive striking. Some families who seldom attended Divine service, began to go constantly; and one man who had not entered the church for seven years, became a regular hearer of the word. "Besides the constant attendance on the public worship of God," continues Mrs Wesley, "our meeting has wonderfully conciliated the minds of this people towards us, so that we now live in the greatest amity imaginable. And, what is still better, they are very much reformed in their behaviour on the Lord's-day. Those who used to be playing in the streets, now come to hear a good sermon read, which is surely more acceptable to Almighty God. Another reason for what I do is, that I have no other way of conversing with this people, and, therefore, have no other way of doing them good. But by this I have an opportunity of exercising the greatest and noblest charity, that is, charity to their souls. There are many other good consequences of this meeting, which I have not time to mention." These remarkable services were approved and appreciated by the generality of the parishioners; but a few, headed by the curate, sent heavy complaints to the rector and entreated him to stop such questionable proceedings in his own house. Mrs Wesley received a letter from her husband, stating the complaints and making some further inquiries. He reminded her that the whole affair was regarded as very singular; and she replied;—"As to its looking particular, I grant it does. And so does almost everything that is serious, or that may any way advance the glory of God or the salvation of souls, if it be performed out of a pulpit, or in the way of common conversation; because, in our corrupt age, the utmost &re and diligence have been used to banish all discourse of God or spiritual concerns out of society; as if religion were never to appear out of the closet, and we were to be ashamed of nothing so much as of professing ourselves to be Christians." But was

there not some objection taken to these services, on the ground that they were conducted by a female? Apparently there was; and Mrs Wesley herself felt the objection to some extent. "There is one thing," she observes, "about which I am much dissatisfied; that is, their being present at family prayers. I do not speak of any concern I am under barely because so many are present; for those who have the honour of speaking to the great and holy God, need not be ashamed to speak before the whole world: but because of my sex. I doubt if it be proper for me to present the prayers of the people to God. Last Sunday, I fain would have dismissed them before prayers; but they begged so earnestly to stay, that I durst not deny them." Why, then, if her doubts troubled her, did she not get someone else to perform the service? Her own reply is sufficiently cogent: "Alas! you do not consider what a people these are. I do not think one man among them could read a sermon, without spelling a good part of it; and how would that edify the rest? Nor has any of our family a voice strong enough to be heard by such a number of people." Had Mrs Wesley ascended the pulpit and assumed the sacred office, like some of the modern sisterhood, the objection, in our judgment, would have been a valid and Scriptural one. But she held the services in her own house, without ever attempting to take a text or preach a sermon. She simply read an awakening discourse and allowed the neighbours to remain at her customary family worship. In this way she strove after usefulness, and, to some extent, resembled those honourable women of whom Saint Paul declared that they helped him much in the Lord. Did not this proceeding, however, turn the parsonage into a conventicle and damage the regular services at the church? This was alleged at the time; and what was Mrs Wesley's reply? "I shall not inquire how it was possible that you should be prevailed on, by the senseless clamours of two or three of the worst of your parish, to condemn what you so lately approved. But I shall tell you my thoughts in as few words as possible. I do not hear of more than three or four persons who are against our meeting, of whom Inman" is the chief. He and Whitely, I believe, may call it a conventicle; but we hear no outcry here, nor has any one said a word against it to me. And what does their calling it a conventicle signify? Does it alter the
197

nature of the thing? or do you think that what they say is a sufficient reason to forbear a thing that has already done much good, and by the blessing of God may do much more? If its being called a conventicle, by those who know in their conscience they misrepresent it, did really make it one, what you say would be somewhat to the purpose. But it is plain in fact, that this one thing has brought more people to church, than ever anything did, in so short a time. We used not to have above twenty or twenty-five at evening service; whereas we have now between two and three hundred; which are more than ever came before to hear Inman in the morning." But as Mrs Wesley's husband was a minister and a man of note in the Church to which he belonged, would not these irregularities in his own house be likely to bring scandal upon his name? To this objection his wife replied, that the meetings were purely religious, without any worldly design. "And where," she asks, "is the harm of this? If I and my children went a visiting on Sunday nights; or if we admitted of impertinent visits, as too many do who think themselves good Christians, perhaps it would be thought no scandalous practice, though in truth it would be so. Therefore, why any should reflect upon you, let your station be what it will, because your wife endeavours to draw people to the church, and to restrain them by reading and other persuasions, from their profanation of God's most holy day, I cannot conceive. But if any should be so mad as to do it, I wish you would not regard it. For my part, I value no censure on this account. I have long since shook hands with the world, and I heartily wish I had never given them more reason to speak against me." She closes her vindication with the following noble appeal to her husband.

* This was the Epworth curate, concerning whose preaching the following story is recorded. On one occasion when the rector returned from London, the parishioners complained that Inman preached nothing to his congregation except the duty of paying their debts, and behaving well among their neighbours. They added that they thought religion comprehended something more than this.

The rector fully agreed with their views, and resolved to judge for himself. He said to the curate, "You could, I suppose, prepare a sermon upon any text that I should give you?" "By all means, sir," was the ready reply. "Then," said the rector, "prepare a sermon on that text, "WITHOUT FAITH it is impossible to please God." When the Sabbath morning came, the curate ascended the pulpit, and read his text with great solemnity. But, alas, the first sentence of his exordium touched upon the old theme: "It must be confessed, friends, that faith is an excellent virtue; and it produces other virtues also. In particular, it MAKES A MAN PAY HIS DEBTS As soon As POSSIBLE." He vigorously enforced the observance of the social virtues for the usual fifteen minutes, and then concluded. "So," said John Wesley, "my father saw it was a lost case."

"Now, I beseech you, weigh all these things in an impartial balance. On the one side, the honour of Almighty God, the doing much good to many souls, and the friendship of the best among whom we live; on the other—if folly, impiety, and vanity may abide in the scale against so ponderous a weight— the senseless objections of a few scandalous persons, laughing at us, and censuring us as precise and hypocritical. And when you have duly considered all things, let me have your positive determination. I need not tell you the consequences, if you determine to put an end to our meeting. You may easily perceive what prejudice it may raise in the minds of these people against Inman especially, who has had so little wit as to speak publicly against it. I can now keep them to the church; but if it be laid aside, I doubt they will never go to hear him more, at least those who come from the lower end of the town. But if this be continued till you return, which now will not be long, it may please God that their hearts may be so changed by that time, that they may love and delight in His public worship, so as never to neglect it more. If you do, after all, think fit to dissolve this assembly, do not tell me that you desire me to do it, for that will not satisfy my conscience; but send me your positive command, in such full and express terms, as may absolve me from all guilt and punishment for neglecting this opportunity of doing good, when you and I shall appear before the great and awful tribunal of our Lord Jesus Christ." This

199

forcible letter seems to have silenced her husband's scruples, and Mrs Wesley went on her way, rejoicing that she was counted worthy to be an instrument of good to the souls of others. God had made her a blessing to many. Her labours had disarmed the hostility of the parishioners, and laid the foundation of mutual good will between the pastor and the people of his charge. When the rector returned, and the full Sabbath-services at the church were resumed, the gatherings at the parsonage were discontinued; but their hallowing and gracious influences upon the family and the neighbourhood were long felt, and can never be fully estimated. Thus far attention has been chiefly confined to the  external aspects of Mrs Wesley's religious course. But was her religion simply a form of godliness; a mere observance, strict and constant it may be, of the outer duties, without the real inner life? It is clear that her own idea of religion comprehended far more than this. She believed in the personal possession of the Divine favour and image, and felt that all mere speculative knowledge of God and spiritual things came far short of the privileges, which the Gospel offers to them that believe. An occasional sense of the Divine presence was refreshing to her mind; "but how much more delightful is it," she observes, "to find a constant sense of God upon the soul, as Herbert excellently expresseth it, "Not, — thankful, when it pleaseth me;

As if Thy blessings had spare days:
But such a heart whose pulse may be

Thy praise." This, this is the temper of a Christian | This is what you should chiefly endeavour to get and keep. Do not despair; with God all things are possible !" On another occasion she writes in the following beautiful strain: "To know God only as a philosopher; to have the most sublime and curious speculations concerning His essence, His attributes, His Providence; to be able to demonstrate His being from all or any of the works of nature; and to discourse with the greatest elegancy and propriety of words, of His existence or operations, will avail us nothing, unless at the same time we know Him experimentally; unless the heart perceive and know Him to be its supreme good, its only happiness . unless the soul feel and acknowledge that she can find no repose, no peace, no joy, but in loving and being beloved by Him; and does accordingly rest in Him as the centre of her being, the fountain of her pleasure, the origin of all virtue and goodness, her light, her life, her strength, her all; everything she wants or wishes in this world, and forever ! In a word, HER LORD, HER GOD! Thus, let me ever know Thee, O God! I do not despise nor neglect the light of reason, nor that knowledge of Thee which by her conduct may be collected from this goodly system of created beings; but this speculative knowledge is not the knowledge I want and wish for." There are beautiful and satisfactory indications that these intense aspirations of soul were attained. How rich the experience which flows through the following sentences ! "If to esteem and have the highest reverence for Thee; if constantly and sincerely to acknowledge Thee the supreme, the only desirable good, be to love Thee,—I Do Love THEE! If to rejoice in Thy essential majesty and glory; if to feel a vital joy overspread and cheer the heart at each perception of Thy blessedness, at every thought that Thou art God, and that all things are in Thy power; that there is none superior or equal to Thee; be to love Thee,—I Do Love THEE! If comparatively to despise and undervalue all the world contains, which is esteemed great, fair, or good; if earnestly and constantly to desire Thee, Thy favour, Thy acceptance, Thyself, rather than any or all things Thou hast created, be to love Thee,—I Do Love THEE!." Again, she writes;—"Give God the praise for any well-spent day. But I am yet unsatisfied, because I do not enjoy enough of God. I apprehend myself at too great a distance from Him. I would have my soul more closely united to Him by faith and love. I can appeal to His omniscience, that I would love Him above all things. He that made me knows my desires, my expectations, my joys all centre in Him, and that it is He Himself that I desire; it is His favour, it is His acceptance, the communications of His grace, that I earnestly wish for more than anything in the world; and that I have no relish or delight in anything when under apprehensions of His displeasure. I rejoice in His essential glory and blessedness. I rejoice in my relation to Him, that He is MY FATHER, MY LORD, AND MY GOD! I rejoice that He has power

201

over me, and desire to live in subjection to Him; that He condescends to punish me when I transgress His laws, as a father chasteneth the son whom he loveth. I thank Him that He has brought me so far; and will beware of despairing of His mercy for the time which is yet to come, but will give God the glory of His free grace."

Five and twenty years later, amidst the desolations of her widowhood, she describes her spiritual condition in the same calm and confident strain, though not without an expression of regret that she did not long for heaven with far greater intensity. "God is being itself! the I AM! and therefore must necessarily be the Supreme Good! He is so infinitely blessed, that every perception of His blissful presence imparts a vital gladness to the heart. Every degree of approach towards Him is, in the same proportion, a degree of happiness. And I often think, that were He always present to our mind, as we are present to Him, there would be no pain nor sense of misery. I have long since chose Him for my only good, my all; my pleasure; my happiness in this world, as well as in the world to come. And although I have not been so faithful to His grace as I ought to have been; yet I feel my spirit adheres to its choice, and aims daily at cleaving steadfastly unto God. Yet one thing often troubles me, that, notwithstanding I know that while we are present with the body we are absent from the Lord; notwithstanding I have no taste, no relish left for anything the world calls pleasure; yet I do not long to go home as in reason I ought to do. This often shocks me. And as I constantly pray, almost without ceasing, for thee, my son; so I beg you likewise to pray for me, that God would make me better, and take me at the best." Later still, when infirmities became numerous and eternity was fast approaching, she writes of herself in a more depreciatory strain:—"In the most literal sense, I am become a little child, and want continual succour. "As iron sharpeneth iron, so doth the countenance of a man his friend.' I feel much comfort and support from religious conversation when I can obtain it. Formerly I rejoiced in the absence of company, and found, the less I had of creature comforts, the more I had from God. But, alas, I am fallen from that spiritual converse I once enjoyed ! And why is it so? Because I want faith. God is an omnipresent, unchangeable Good, in whom is no variableness, neither shadow of turning. The fault is in myself; and I attribute all mistakes in judgment, and all errors in practice, to want of faith in the blessed Jesus. O my dear Charles, when I consider the dignity of His person, the perfection of His purity, the greatness of His sufferings, but above all, His boundless love, I am astonished and utterly confounded; I am lost in thought. I fall into nothing before Him I O how inexcusable is that person who has knowledge of these things, and yet remains poor and low in faith and love! I speak as one guilty in this matter." Too much stress must not be laid upon the terms in which Mrs Wesley here speaks of her decline from the spiritual converse, which she once enjoyed. They were written in December 1739, only three months after that memorable Sacramental season of which she said, "I knew God for Christ's sake had forgiven me all my sins." This fact shews that she had not really declined in grace. She was within a few days of completing her seventieth year, and though her faculties were clear and bright, as ever, the mind had necessarily lost some of its earlier vigour. No longer capable of those long-sustained contemplations on the Divine glory and kindred themes, in which she had formerly found so much refreshment and blessing, she suspects that she has fallen from that spiritual converse which she then enjoyed. As we trace her religious course we discover no evidences of any decline. The stream of her inner life,—ever deepening, ever widening,-flowed clear and steady from the beginning, and became deepest, calmest, widest as it approached the broad ocean of the eternal future.

These records of Mrs Wesley's spiritual life will probably dissipate the common notion, that, notwithstanding her deep conscientiousness and punctual attention to all religious duties, she did not experience the inward consolations of the Gospel until late in life. The idea no doubt rests upon a passage in John Wesley's Journal. Under the date of September the third, 1739, he says,— "I talked largely with my Mother, who told me that, till a short time since, she had scarce heard such a thing mentioned as the having forgiveness of sins now, or God's Spirit bearing witness with our spirit: much less did she believe that this was the common privilege of all believers. Therefore, said she, 'I never durst ask for it myself." She then stated how she felt this assurance a short time before while receiving the Sacramental cup, and declared that her father enjoyed the same blessing uninterruptedly for forty years. But, as he never preached it to others, she supposed he also looked upon it as the peculiar blessing of a few, and not common to all believers. These obscure views no doubt held back Mrs Wesley from that fulness of conscious joy which she might otherwise have attained; but to fix upon this moment of clearer revelation on a particular spiritual privilege as her conversion and regard her previous religious condition as one of "legal night," without any inward experience of Divine things, is not warranted by the facts of the case. She had long before laid her burden at the foot of the cross. God had long been the Supreme object of her love, and for many years she had walked in all His commandments and ordinances, blameless. "And though," says Doctor Clarke, "she lived in a time when the spiritual privileges of the people of God were not so clearly defined, nor so well understood as they are at present; yet she was not without large communications of the Divine Spirit, heavenly light, and heavenly ardours which often caused her to sit, "like cherub bright, some moments on a throne of love." She had the faith of God's elect; she acknowledged the truth, which is according to godliness. Her spirit and life were conformed to the truth; and she was not, as she could not be, without the favour and approbation of God."

# XIII. RELATION TO METHODISM.

The Wesleys Mother was the mother of Methodism in a religious and moral sense; for, her courage, her submissiveness to authority; the high tone of her mind, its independence, and its selfcontrol; the warmth of her devotional feelings and the practical direction given to them, came up, and were visibly repeated in the character and conduct of her sons. —ISAAC TAYLOR.

METHODISM which, after an existence of a century and a quarter, now numbers so many thousands among its ministry and membership, in every part of the world, arose into being at a most critical period in the religious history of our country. Profligacy and vice everywhere prevailed; and, according to the Essayists, the moral virtues of the nation were at their last gasp. "There is no such thing as religion in England," wrote Montesquieu, who visited this country in 1730 : "if anyone speaks about religion everybody begins to laugh." The Churches of the land resembled, to a great extent, the valley of vision, full of dry bones. "Behold, there were very many in the open valley; and, lo, they were very dry." Prelates of the Establishment and leading ministers among the Dissenting Communities were lamenting that "religion was dying in the world:" that Christianity was openly proclaimed to be nothing more than a cunningly devised fable, and no longer worthy of serious regard or inquiry. "The Anglican Church," says a living writer, "had become an ecclesiastical system, under which the people of England had lapsed into heathenism, or a state hardly to be distinguished from it;" and "Nonconformity was rapidly in course to be found nowhere but in books." The spirit of evangelistic enterprise had died out, and the little experimental religion which remained was mostly confined within the limits of a few godly households." This melancholy spiritual desolation was the result of a series of causes, which had been powerfully operating for three-quarters of a century; and the Methodism which woke up the nation from its deep moral slumber and quickened it into newness of life, was not the hasty creation of a day. During two or three antecedent generations there had been at work powerful influences in the ancestry of its appointed Founders, which, in the light of after-times, look like providential preparations in connexion with the appointed agents, when they should appear on the field of action to fulfil their marvellous mission. "It must not be regarded as a refinement, when it is affirmed, that the special characteristics of religious Communities,—that is to say, those properties that visibly mark such bodies,— do go down to the second, third, and fourth generation, in the instance of families that have walked forth from the enclosure within which they were born and bred. Family peculiarities may have disappeared,—the physical type, perhaps, has been lost; and yet a note of the religious pedigree survives, and re-appears in grandchildren, sons and daughters." Whatever may be thought of this theory as a whole, it certainly has a remarkable application to the case before us. Who can contemplate the history of John Westley of Whitchurch, without being struck with obvious coincidences between many of his principles and courses of action, and those of the illustrious grandson who bore his name?

In a long conversation with the Bishop of Bristol, distinguished by manly sense, unaffected piety, and extensive religious knowledge, he holds that the grand qualifications for the ministry are "gifts and graces;" that he himself was "called to the work of the ministry, though not to the office;" that the inward call of God and "the approval of judicious able Christians, ministers and others," were a sufficient warrant for his preaching, without any formal ordination, either by Prelates or Presbyters; that it was lawful to preach wherever the people invited him to do so; and that the best vindication of his Divine call to the sacred work was the "conversion of several souls to the power of godliness from ignorance and profaneness." These successes attended him in every place where he exercised his gifts,—"at Radipole, Melcombe, Turnwood, Whitchurch, and at sea." "If it please your Lordship," he nobly declares, "to lay down any evidences of godliness agreeing with the Scriptures, and they be not found in those persons intended, I am content to be discharged from my ministry. I will stand or fall by the issue thereof." Here, then, we find an unordained evangelist; a lay Helper; an Itinerant Preacher; and a beautiful pre-shadowing of the principles more extensively embodied in the early Methodist preachers whom Wesley associated with himself in the glorious revival of the eighteenth century. Like the Dorsetshire evangelist, they performed the "work" of the ministry rather than exercised its "office." They went out and preached everywhere; but neither governed the Churches nor administered the Sacraments. Their qualifications were "grace and gifts," rather than extensive erudition or high mental culture. Their authority was the inward call of God, the moving of the Holy Ghost, and the "approval of good and able Christians," without any formal ordination; and the prime test of the Divinity of their mission was "fruit" in the conversion of sinners and the edification of them that believe. "They went forth and preached everywhere, the Lord working with them, and confirming the word with signs following." It is necessary to observe, however, that this initiatory state of things in reference to the status of Wesleyan ministers, has long since passed away. Methodism now claims for her pastorate the call to the "office," as well as to the "work" of the ministry; and for her Societies, all the rights and privileges of a distinct and Scriptural Church of the Lord Jesus Christ.

There is also another link in this ancestral chain, which is not usually adverted to in this connexion. About 1667, under the earnest preaching of one or two London clergymen, several young men were brought "to a very affecting sense of their sins, and began to apply themselves in a very serious way to religious thoughts and purposes." Their ministers advised them to hold weekly meetings among themselves; and rules were drawn up for the better regulation of their assemblies. They were to avoid all controversy, and to converse only on such subjects as conduced to practical holiness. They were to promote schools, and the catechising of "young and ignorant persons in their respective families." They contributed weekly for the relief of the poor, and appointed stewards to receive and distribute their charities. Encouraged by a few dignitaries of the Church, and several clergymen, these Societies multiplied and grew, until in a few years there were forty in London, a considerable number in the provinces, and nine in Ireland.

Now here we have the very germ and pattern of those Societies which John Wesley formed as the basis of the Methodist economy. In his early days their growth had been checked, and only very few of them existed. He did not overlook them, however, but warmly admired and adopted them. Even in Georgia, he advised the more serious of his flock "to form themselves into a little Society, and to meet once or twice a week, in order to reprove, instruct, and exhort one another." And when he returned to London, he was a constant visitor at these little religious assemblies; and in one of them he felt his heart "strangely warmed," and obtained the blessing of conscious pardon. This readiness to look favourably upon what were unquestionably regarded by the Churchmen of his times as unjustifiable irregularities, was only following in his father's steps. The rector of Epworth, High-Churchman as he is commonly represented to be, had published a noble defence of these Religious Societies, in which he boldly pleaded for their formation in every parish. He would undoubtedly have established them among his own parishioners, had his Diocesan given his consent. "Now, if this religious discourse be lawful and commendable where it is accidental, or among a few persons only, I would fain know how it should come to be otherwise, when it is stated and regulated, and among a greater number? Is it any more a conventicle than any other meetings? Is there any law that it offends against? Is it any greater crime to meet and sing psalms together, than to sing profane songs, or waste hours in impertinent chat or drinking? Indeed, one would almost wonder how a design of this nature should come to have any enemies. Nor can I see any reason why good men should be discouraged from joining in it by those hard words,—faction, singularity, and the like,—when all possible care is taken to give no just offence in the management of it. The design of these Societies, as I am satisfied by considering the first founder, and the encouragers of them, and their rules as well as practice, is, by no means to gather Churches out of other Churches; to foment new schisms and divisions; and to make heathens of all the rest of their Christian brethren; which would be as indefensible in itself as dangerous and fatal in its consequences, both to themselves and others. So far are they from this, that they have brought back several to the Church who were divided from it. But their aim is purely and only to promote, in a regular manner, that which is the end of every Christian, the glory of God, included in the welfare and salvation of themselves and their neighbours. And if any rational method could be proposed, besides those they have already pitched upon, to guard against these possible inconveniences, there is no doubt but that they would embrace it. Though, after all, how there can be any possible occasion of schism, any crevice for it to creep in at, where nothing is done but in subordination to the lawful ministry, and by direction from it; and where one of the very bonds of the Society is the frequenting of public prayers and communions; while on the other side, there is no visible private interest to serve, no faction to flatter or humour, I must confess I am not sharp-sighted enough to discern, and dare challenge any instance of a schism anywhere occasioned, in such circumstances, ever since the birth of Christianity." Does not this vigorous apology remind us of those noble defences of the United Societies which, in the early years of Methodism, John Wesley was frequently called upon to make? Had those Societies been in existence at the time, the rector's pen could not more eloquently have pleaded their cause. And when his sons commenced their career of spiritual and philanthropic toil at Oxford, they were cheered on amidst the scorn and contempt of the whole University by their father's countenance and advice. "For my part," he wrote, "on the present view of your actions and designs, my daily prayers are, that God would keep you humble; and then I am sure that if you continue to suffer for righteousness' sake, though it be but in a lower degree, the Spirit of God and of glory shall in some good measure rest upon you. And you cannot but feel such a satisfaction in your own minds as you would not part with for all the world. Be never weary of well-doing; never look back, for you know the prize and the crown are before you; though I can scarce think so meanly of you, as that you should be discouraged with the 'crackling of thorns under a pot.' Be not high-minded, but fear. Preserve an equal temper of mind under whatever treatment you meet with, from a not very just or well natured world. Bear no more sail than is necessary, but steer steady. The less you value yourselves for these unfashionable duties,—as there is no such thing as works of supererogation,-the more all good and wise men will value you, if they see your works are all of a piece; or, which is infinitely more, He by whom actions and intentions are weighed will both accept, esteem, and reward you. I hear my son John has the honour of being styled 'the Father of the Holy Club. If it be so, I am sure I must be the grandfather of it; and I need not say, that I had rather any of my sons should be so dignified and distinguished, than to have the title of 'His Holiness.'" Account for it how we may, these facts clearly prove that "a note of the religious pedigree" survived and reappeared in the rector of Epworth, the representative of the third or fourth generation of the Wesley Family. But is there any indication that this "religious pedigree," so observable in the paternal ancestry, appeared likewise in the Mother of the Founder of Methodism 7 No one can study the life of John Wesley, without observing that maternal influence exerted over him an all but sovereign control. His mental perplexities, his religious doubts and emotions were all eagerly submitted to the judgment and decision of his Mother, who was every way competent to be his religious adviser. And on her part there seems to have been a solicitude for his religious welfare greater, if possible, than that which she felt for any other of her children. His wonderful rescue from the burning pile of the parsonage appears to have impressed her with the thought, that God had delivered him from so great a death for a life of more than common usefulness, and therefore she must meet with corresponding earnestness these additional claims.

There is a precious meditation, written on the evening of 17 May 1711, when John was not quite eight years old, in which this feeling strongly manifests itself. "What shall I render unto the Lord for His mercies? The little unworthy praise that I can offer, is so mean and contemptible an offering, that I am even ashamed to tender it. But, Lord accept it for the sake of Christ, and pardon the deficiency of the sacrifice. I would offer Thee myself, and all that Thou hast given me: and I would resolve, -O give me grace to do it — that the residue of my life shall be all devoted to Thy service. And I do intend to be more particularly careful of the soul of this child, that Thou hast so mercifully provided for, than ever I have been; that I may endeavour to instill into his mind the principles of Thy true religion and virtue. Lord, give me grace to do it sincerely and prudently; and bless my attempts with good success 1" This maternal influence is very discernible in John Wesley's views and movements in after life. When the time arrived for deciding his future course, it was a grave question with him whether he should enter into Holy Orders. He distrusted his motives, and his most serious apprehensions were awakened. As the dread responsibilities rose up before his mind, he quailed at their weight, and hesitated to proceed. With his usual frankness, he consulted his parents. His father, not liking what he calls "a callow clergyman," laid out for him a long course of study, and concluded, "By all this you see I am not for your going over hastily into Orders." The tone of his Mother's reply was very different. "I think the sooner you are a deacon the better, because it may be an inducement to greater application in the study of practical divinity, which, of all other studies, I humbly conceive to be the best for candidates for Orders. . . . . The alteration of your temper has occasioned me much speculation. I, who am apt to be sanguine, hope it may proceed from the operations of God's Holy Spirit, that, by taking off your relish for earthly enjoyments, He may prepare and dispose your mind for a more serious and close application to things of a more sublime and spiritual nature. If it be so, happy are you, if you cherish those dispositions ! And now, in good earnest, resolve to make religion the business of your life; for, after all, that is the one thing that, strictly speaking, is necessary. All things besides are comparatively little to the purposes of life. I heartily wish you would now enter upon a strict examination of yourself, that you may know whether you have a reasonable hope of salvation by Jesus Christ. If you have, the satisfaction of knowing it will abundantly reward your pains. If you have not, you will find a more reasonable occasion for tears than can be met with in a tragedy. This matter demands great consideration by all; but especially by those designed for the ministry; who ought, above

211

all things, to make their own calling and election sure, lest after they have preached to others, they themselves should be cast away." These judicious and weighty counsels were decisive. John Wesley made up his mind to enter the ministry; gave himself earnestly to the study of divinity; and pressed his father to consent to his immediate ordination. What would have been the consequences to the Church and the world had he refused to receive Orders, and spent his life in some other calling? And who can tell how much his decision was influenced by his Mother's wise advice? Had the father's counsels for delay been followed, or not counteracted by the influence and reasoning of his Mother, the Church might never have numbered him among her ministerial sons, nor the world so largely and permanently benefited by his labours.

The same influence had much to do in the formation and settlement of his early theological opinions. When he fairly commenced the study of divinity he made constant references to his Mother, and solicited her explanations. The letters which passed between them in connexion with these important inquiries range over a great variety of topics, and comprehend discussions on some of the most difficult questions in theology. One example, however, must suffice. It is well known that John Wesley was the chief instrument in the revival and extension of the doctrines of an evangelical Arminianism, as opposed in many important points to a rigid Calvinism. In his earlier theological studies, however, he was much perplexed about the vexed question of predestination. He fully communicated his doubts to his Mother, stating that he believed it to be contrary both to reason and Scripture. Mrs Wesley concurred in his views, and expressed her own sentiments in the following passages:— "I have often wondered that men should be so vain as to amuse themselves by searching into the decrees of God, which no human wit can fathom; and do not rather employ their time and powers in working out their salvation, and making their own calling and election sure. Such studies tend more to confound, than inform the understanding; and young people had best let them alone. But since I find you have some scruples concerning our article of predestination. I will tell you my thoughts of the matter; and if they satisfy not, you may

212

desire your father's direction, who is surely better qualified for a casuist than me. The doctrine of predestination, as maintained by rigid Calvinists, is very shocking, and ought utterly to be abhorred, because it charges the most holy God with being the author of sin. And I think you reason very well and justly against it; for it is certainly inconsistent with the justice and goodness of God to lay any man under either a physical or moral necessity of committing sin, and then punish him for doing it. Far be this from the Lord! Shall not the Judge of all the earth do right? I do firmly believe that God from all eternity, hath elected some to everlasting life; but then I humbly conceive that this election is founded in His foreknowledge, according to that in the eighth of Romans:—'Whom He did foreknow, He also did predestinate to be conformed to the image of His Son: moreover, whom He did predestinate, them. He also called; and whom He called, them. He also justified; and whom He justified, them. He also glorified.'" After a brief running exposition of what she regarded as the meaning of this passage, she continues,— "This is the sum of what I believe concerning predestination, which I think is agreeable to the analogy of faith; since it does in no wise derogate from the glory of God's free grace, nor impair the liberty of man. Nor can it with more reason be supposed that the prescience of God is the cause that so many finally perish, than that our knowing the sun will rise to-morrow is the cause of its rising." And once more, she writes:— "I cannot recollect the passages you mention, but believing you do the author, I positively aver that he is extremely in the wrong in that impious, not to say blasphemous assertion, that God by an irresistible decree hath determined any man to be miserable, even in this life. His intentions, as Himself, are holy, and just, and good; and all the miseries incident to men, here or hereafter, spring from themselves." These, in substance, were the same views on this long-controverted question which John Wesley himself adopted and defended. The sermons of the Founder of Methodism are distinguished by simplicity of style, freedom from all unnecessary niceties of distinctions, and directness of appeal; and it is highly probable that his Mother's sound advice largely contributed to these admirable qualities of his preaching. No sooner was he ordained than he sought and

213

received her counsel on this most important subject. "Suffer now a word of advice," she writes. "However curious you may be in searching into the nature, or in distinguishing the properties, of the passions or virtues of human kind, for your own private satisfaction, be very cautious in giving nice distinctions in public assemblies; for it does not answer the true end of preaching, which is to mend men's lives, and not fill their heads with unprofitable speculations. And after all that can be said, every affection of the soul is better known by experience than any description that can be given of it. An honest man will more easily apprehend what is meant by being zealous for God and against sin, when he hears what are the properties and effects of true zeal, than the most accurate definition of its essence." Eight years afterwards she presses upon his attention the depravity of human nature, the absolute necessity of a Divine Mediator, the all-sufficiency of the atonement, the nature of faith, and the agency of the Holy Spirit as the most important subjects on which his preaching should dwell. "Here, surely," she exclaims, "you may give free scope to your spirits; here you may freely use your Christian liberty, and discourse without reserve of the excellency of the knowledge and love of Christ, as His Spirit gives you utterance. What, my son, did the pure and holy Person of the Son of God pass by the fallen angels, who were far superior, of greater dignity, and of a higher order in the scale of existence, and choose to unite Himself to the human nature? And shall we soften, as you call it, these glorious truths? Rather let us speak boldly, without fear. These truths ought to be frequently inculcated, and pressed home upon the consciences of men; and when once men are affected with a sense of redeeming love, that sense will powerfully convince them of the vanity of the world, and make them esteem the honour, wealth, and pleasures of it as dross or dung, so that they may win Christ. As for moral subjects, they are necessary to be discoursed on; but then I humbly conceive we are to speak of moral virtues as Christians, and not like heathens. And if we would indeed do honour to our Saviour, we should take all fitting occasions to make men observe the essence and perfection of the moral virtues taught by Christ and His apostles, far surpassing all that was pretended to by the very

214

best of the heathen philosophers. All their morality was defective in principle and direction; was intended only to regulate the outward actions, but never reached the heart; or, at the highest, it looked no farther than the temporal happiness of mankind. "But moral virtues, evangelised or improved into Christian duties, have partly a view to promote the good of human society here, but chiefly to qualify the observers of them for a much more blessed and more enduring society hereafter." I cannot stay to enlarge on this vast subject; nor, indeed, considering whom I write to, is it needful. Yet one thing I cannot forbear adding, which may carry some weight with his admirers, and that is, the very wise and just reply which Mr Locke made to one that desired him to draw up a system of morals. 'Did the world," said he, 'want a rule, I confess there could be no work so necessary nor so commendable; but the Gospel contains so perfect a body of ethics, that reason may be excused from the inquiry, since she may find man's duty clearer and easier in revelation than in herself.'" When John Wesley became the acknowledged head of the Oxford Methodists, he sent to his Mother an account of their zealous endeavours after personal holiness; their efforts for the spiritual welfare of the prisoners and others; and the manifold sneers and persecutions which they had to endure. She at once countenanced and encouraged him without any complaint about irregularities, or even a mild exhortation to caution. "I heartily join with your small Society in all their pious and charitable actions, which are intended for God's glory; and am glad to hear that Mr Clayton and Mr Hall have met with desired success. May you still, in such good works, go on and prosper ! Though absent in body, I am present with you in spirit; and daily recommend and commit you all to Divine Providence." In May 1738, John Wesley passed through that important crisis of his religious life in which he was delivered from the Spirit of bondage, and received the Spirit of adoption. He soon became anxious to lay the whole case before his Mother, that he might obtain her advice. Within fourteen days of that memorable night at the little Society in Aldersgate Street, he hastened to Salisbury, to bid her farewell before he departed for Germany. During this interview he read a paper containing a clear and succinct account of his own heart-struggles for true spiritual rest. It traced these moral conflicts from the earliest stirrings of religious feeling in his soul, to the hour when the Divine Spirit assured him of his redemption through the blood of Christ, even the forgiveness of sins. As he so deeply valued his Mother's judgment on all questions relating to experimental religion, it was no small satisfaction that "she greatly approved the document which he read, and said she heartily blessed God, who had brought him to so just a way of thinking." It was industriously circulated in the days of early Methodism, that Mrs Wesley "lived long enough to deplore the extravagances of her sons." The same notion still lingers in some quarters; and as it originated in certain circumstances partly connected with the paper to which reference has just been made and bears upon Mrs Wesley's relation to Methodism, this is the proper place for the examination of the entire question. Wesley's own account must first be quoted. "In the morning I came to London; and after receiving the Holy Communion at Islington, I had once more an opportunity of seeing my Mother, whom I had not seen since my return from Germany. I cannot but mention an odd circumstance here. I had read her a paper in June last year, containing a short account of what had passed in my own soul, till within a few days of that time. She greatly approved it, and said, she heartily blessed God, who had brought me to so just a way of thinking. While I was in Germany, a copy of that paper was sent, without my knowledge, to one of my relations. He sent an account of it to my Mother; whom I now found under strange fears concerning me, being convinced, 'by an account taken from one of my own papers, that I had greatly erred from the faith." I could not conceive what paper that should be; but on inquiry, found it was the same I had read her myself. How hard is it to form a true judgment of any person or thing from the account of a prejudiced relater! yea, though he be ever so honest a man : for he who gave this relation was one of unquestionable veracity. And yet by his sincere account of a writing which lay before his eyes, was the truth so totally disguised, that my Mother knew not the paper she had heard from end to end, nor I that I had myself wrote it." The man of "unquestionable veracity," who gave this "sincere account" of the document in

216

question, was none other than Samuel Wesley of Tiverton. And had the writing only been before his eyes, we doubt whether he would have formed so perverted a judgment as to its true meaning. Influences, of which John Wesley at the time was probably ignorant, had been powerfully operating upon his brother's mind. Many-tongued rumour had been exceedingly busy. Only two days before Mrs Wesley heard the paper with so much satisfaction, a violent letter had been forwarded to Samuel, declaring that John had "turned a wild enthusiast, or fanatic;" that it would be a great charity either to "confine or convert him;" that he taught people to expect assurance of pardon through the medium of dreams and extraordinary visions. These accusations, skilfully mixed up with a number of grotesque and spicy anecdotes in perfect keeping, and coming from a personal friend, who had shown great kindness to John and Charles, worked their mischievous intention in the eldest brother's mind. With his thoughts fully prepossessed by these glaring misrepresentations, and having himself a strong prejudice against the doctrine of assured forgiveness, who can wonder that he formed an incorrect judgment of his brother's own statement? There followed a vigorous and somewhat sharp controversy between the brothers on the main point at issue, into which it is not necessary for us to enter. But Samuel also communicated the misrepresentations to his Mother. Her surprise and alarm were naturally excited; and she combated the notions erroneously attributed to her younger sons with great acuteness and moderation. A single interview would have dispelled all her fears. This, however, was probably impossible at the time, and Whitefield seems to have employed himself somewhat successfully in softening, if not entirely removing the erroneous impressions. Writing to John, he says, "Your prayer is heard! This morning I visited your Mother, whose prejudices are entirely removed, and she only longs to be with you in your Societies at London. Arguments from Tiverton, I believe, will now have but little weight. We parted with prayer. Brother Hall rejoiced in spirit, and so, methinks, will you and brother Charles." The impression made upon Mrs Wesley's mind by this interview may be gathered from the following passage in a letter to Samuel, written about a month afterwards:—"You have heard, I suppose, that Mr Whitefield is taking a progress through these parts to make a collection for a house in Georgia for orphans, and such of the natives' children as they will part with to learn our language and religion. He came hither to see me, and we talked about your brothers. I told him I did not like their way of living, wished them in some place of their own, wherein they might regularly preach, &c. He replied, I could not conceive the good they did in London; that the greatest part of our clergy were asleep; and that there never was a greater need of itinerant preachers than now. Upon which a gentleman that came with him, said that my son Charles had converted him, and that my sons spent all their time in doing good. I then asked Mr Whitefield if my sons were not for making some innovations in the Church, which I much feared. He assured me they were so far from it, that they endeavoured all they could to reconcile Dissenters to our Communion; that my son John had baptized five adult Presbyterians in our own way on Saint Paul's-day, and he believed would bring many to our Communion. His stay was short, so that I could not talk with him so much as I desired. He seems to be a very good man, and one who truly desires the salvation of mankind. God grant that the wisdom of the serpent may be joined to the innocence of the dove!" In the same letter she observes, "I have been informed that Mr Hall intends to remove his family to London. He hath taken a house, and I must, if it please God I live, go with them, when I hope to see Charles; and then I can fully speak my sentiments of their new notions, more than I can do by writing." And as soon as she had the coveted opportunity of "fully speaking her sentiments concerning their new notions," she found that their doctrines were none other than the very doctrines which she had herself approved only a few months before. All misunderstanding immediately vanished away. She expressed her devout appreciation of their teaching; attended their ministry; and sanctioned their proceedings by her personal presence in their religious assemblies. The ungenerous charge, therefore, that Mrs Wesley lived long enough to deplore the extravagances of her sons utterly falls to the ground. There is one other case in which the influence of Mrs Wesley over the Founder of Methodism led to very important results. When his soul-converting ministry was excluded from the churches which he so much loved, Wesley felt that necessity was laid upon him to enter every open door, and preach to gathering crowds in the fields and highways; in the "conventicle," the barn, or the market-place. His hope was that the clergy in the various parishes would cheerfully shepherd the sheep which he had fetched from the wilderness. But in this hope he was disappointed. His spiritual children were regarded as enthusiasts, schismatics, heretics; and were often rudely repelled from the Lord's table. Seeing many and increasing Societies springing up in London, Bristol, and other places, he asks, "What was to be done in a case of so extreme necessity?" No clergyman would assist him. Believing himself to be eminently called to the work of an evangelist, he could not remain in any one place: and yet, in London especially, necessary organisations for conserving and extending the work of God were daily growing up. It would not do to leave Classes, Bands, prayer-meetings, and schools without some responsible supervision. The only course open to him was to find one among the converts themselves, of upright heart and sound judgment in the things of God, and desire this more gifted brother to meet his fellow disciples "as often as he could, in order to confirm them, as he was able, in the ways of God, either by reading to them, or by prayer, or by exhortation." Driven by this necessity, he appointed Thomas Maxfield, "a young man of good sense and piety," to watch over the Society in London. He met the Classes and Bands; instructed and reproved as occasion required; read the Scriptures, sometimes offering a little exposition as he went along; and delivered an occasional address. His abilities as a public speaker soon attracted attention, and he ventured at last to take a text and preach a sermon in the usual way. When Wesley heard of this he seriously disapproved it, and hurried to London in no pleasant mood to stop the mouth of this forward and unauthorised young man. When he arrived at the Foundery, his countenance gave indications of more than ordinary concern and displeasure. His Mother inquired the reason of this unusual anxiety. "Thomas Maxfield has turned preacher, I find," was the abrupt reply. Whether any long conference ensued, in which the arguments on both sides were carefully canvassed, we cannot tell; but the judgment of Mrs Wesley was unmistakable. "John," said she, "you know what my sentiments have been. You cannot suspect me of favouring readily anything of this kind. But take care what you do with respect to that young man; for he is as surely called of God to preach as you are. Examine what have been the fruits of his preaching, and hear him yourself." This counsel, too wise to be despised, and coming from one to whose judgment he had paid so much deference in many critical circumstances, and which had never led him astray, Wesley was not the man to disregard. He heard Maxfield preach, and at once expressed his satisfaction. "It is the Lord!" he exclaimed; "let Him do what seemeth Him good. What am I that I should withstand God?" Thus his last scruples about the general employment of unordained preachers, and of those who were not Episcopally inducted into the sacred office, yielded to his Mother's argument, and fell before her calm rebuke. Whether the necessities of the work of God would have compelled Wesley to give his sanction to lay preaching in later years of his successful career, is not a question for discussion in these pages; but it may be accepted as a moral certainty, that the employment of such an agency would not have been tolerated at so early a period but for the clear judgment and parental influence of Mrs Wesley. To her, as an instrument in the Divine hand, are we indebted for an institution which has developed into a regular ministry, second to none on the face of the earth; and which, at the same time, recognises an order of lay preachers by whose Sunday labours the kingdom of Christ is largely extended in the earth. In estimating Mrs Wesley's relation to Methodism, a reference must also be made to those remarkable Sabbath evening proceedings in the Epworth parsonage, described in the last chapter. The services which she there conducted were a beautiful type of some of the main features in the movements of her sons in after years. They were auxiliary to the Church services, and tended to gather a number of people to its communion and worship. They were purely religious, and resulted in great spiritual good. "We meet not," says Mrs Wesley, "on any worldly design. We banish all temporal concerns from our Society. None is suffered to mingle any discourse about them with our reading or singing. We keep close to the business of the day; and as soon as it is over, they all go home." What was this but a glorious Methodist irregularity? Even the very name *Society* is employed to designate the little community. Would proceedings like these exert no influence upon the thinkings and sentiments of John Wesley in after life? He was then an intelligent, thoughtful, and deeply serious boy, nine or ten years old. He mingled, and probably with no common interest, in these extraordinary gatherings. He saw and heard his own Mother read prayers and sermons; and with his sweet youthful voice joined in the evening hymn, which closed the happy Sabbath-worship. Would he ever forget these hallowed seasons? Did they not linger long in his retentive memory? How significant is the reference to them, in connexion with the record of his Mother's death:—"I cannot but further observe, that even she, as well as her father, and grandfather, her husband, and her three sons, had been, in her measure and degree, a preacher of righteousness!" When God made John Wesley the honoured instrument in an extensive revival of religion, how often would these beautiful scenes present themselves to his mind! Who can tell how far many of his prejudices were softened or destroyed by the remembrance of those Sabbath evenings in the home of his youth? How could he be afraid to gather religious assemblies in private dwellings, when his father's house, clergyman as he was, had been so consecrated? How could he refuse to sanction "holy women," burning with love to souls and possessing gifts of usefulness, taking an active part in the Church, when he remembered that his own Mother, whose judgment he so much revered, "had been, in her measure and degree, a preacher of righteousness?" And now, with the details and illustrations of this chapter fresh in his memory, we think it cannot escape the notice and reflection of the reader, that Methodism, in some of its grand principles of economy, its thoroughly evangelical doctrines, and the means by which the former were promulgated and the latter brought into action,— "had its specific, healthy, though slowly-vegetating seeds in the original members of the Wesley Family." But the pre-eminence in this honourable ancestry must undoubtedly be given to HER WHO

221

AROSE A MOTHER IN ISRAEL. Well has it been said that, as we contemplate the religious power which ruled the entire household in the Epworth parsonage, and the godly training which Mrs Wesley gave to her children, we cannot "escape the conclusion, that to the seed then sown in John Wesley's heart we should trace very much of the religious idea that originated the first Methodists in Oxford, and was subsequently elaborated in the United Societies." And when we note her love of order and practical devotion to system which enabled her to manage the complicated affairs of her household so easily and so well, do we not discover the very same qualities in the Founder of Methodism, which enabled him to accomplish so much work and govern a large Christian community, down to the smallest details with such perfect ease? Who can tell how much Christianity and the world, through the instrumentality of Methodism, are indebted to this noble woman? Had her influence, so deservedly great, been exerted in the opposite direction, holding her son back instead of encouraging and guiding him with good discretion, who can imagine the consequences which would have followed?

The name of Susanna Wesley has long been had in reverence among the spiritual children of her sons; and we hope that our loving task, in endeavouring to place on record an honest and truthful impression of her character and influence, will awaken in all the Churches of Methodism earnest gratitude to God for the Mother of the Wesleys; "the warmth of whose devotional feelings and the practical direction given to them, came up, and were visibly repeated in the character and conduct of her sons."

# XIV. SONS AND DAUGHTERS.

Her house
Was order'd well, her children taught the way
Of life, who, rising up in honour, call'd
Her blessed.
-POLLOK.

"I AM obliged to you," writes young Samuel Wesley to his brother John in 1727, "for the beginning of the portrait of our family. How I may judge when I see the whole, though I may guess nearly within myself, I cannot positively affirm to you. There is, I think, not above one particular in all the character which you have drawn at length that needs further explanation." This passage indicates that John Wesley had formed the intention of sketching the character of each member of the Epworth family. Had he completed the task, which he had evidently commenced, and had the document been preserved, the personal history of the individuals forming that interesting circle, as well as their dispositions and habits, would have been free from the obscurity by which so many of them are now surrounded. If, however, all the necessary material were within reach, the limits of a single chapter would not allow any minute details. Yet, as the history of the parents of this interesting family has been somewhat fully related in the previous pages, the following brief sketches of those of Mrs Wesley's children who grew up to maturity, may possibly gratify the reader, and, as a sort of supplement, give a completeness to the volume which it would not otherwise possess. The biographies of the sons have been written at length, and are easily accessible; but concerning some of the daughters, the following records are probably the most ample which have yet been published. Taking them in chronological order, SAMUEL first claims attention. He was born in London, on 10 February 1690. The incidents of his childhood, beyond those already recorded, were few and unimportant. He enjoyed one advantage, if so it may be called, above the rest of the family, in the services of a tutor. "Your old schoolmaster, John Holland, whose kindness you wear on your knuckles," writes his father in characteristic style, "was making homewards about a month or six weeks since, and got within ten or a dozen miles of Epworth, where he fell sick out of rage or despair. He was taken home in a common cart, and has been almost mad ever since. Peter Foster, the Anabaptist preacher, gave him two-pence to buy him some brandy, and thought he was very generous. His mother fell a-cursing God when she saw him. She has just been with me to beg the assistance of the parish for him. What think you of this example?" This poor dissipated man was a young clergyman. His father had given him an expensive education, "in hopes he would live to help his sister and brothers." He was dismissed from thirteen situations "for his wickedness and lewdness." Many times he pawned his gown and clothes in order to gratify his worst passions. He ruined his father, who was committed to Lincoln Castle for debt, without any hope of release, and finally brought himself to the awful end which the rector so graphically describes. How long young Samuel continued under the tuition of this pedagogue, or what benefit he derived from it, is not known. Early in 1704, he was sent to Westminster; and were we writing his biography instead of attempting the briefest summary of his personal history, we should describe his good progress in all knowledge at that ancient and celebrated school; his sore trouble at Bishop Sprat selecting him, "hoarse and purblind" as he was, from among all the pupils "to read him books at night;" and how, after his election to Christ Church, Oxford, he threw himself into the Whistonian controversy on the "Ignatian Epistles," and also by his solid attainments and the productions of his ready pen, became distinguished among the wits and scholars of the University. Then would follow his intimacy with Pope, Addison, Swift, and Prior; his strong love for the wily and clever Atterbury, whom he regarded as the victim of an unrighteous persecution, but whose real character he never divined; and his friendship with Lord Oxford, whose liveried servants fleeced him by their clamorous demands for gratuities, until he was compelled to compound with them for a definite sum "once a month and no more." We should pass in review his return to the old haunts of Westminster, where he remained twenty years as one of the ushers, and was refused the second mastership for his vigorous lampoons upon some of the leading Whigs of the day; his happy marriage with the daughter of John Berry, that good parish priest of Watton; the active part he took in founding the first Infirmary in Westminster,-now Saint George's Hospital, Hyde Park Corner;—his removal to Tiverton, where he proved himself a model teacher of youth, extended the fame of the grammar-school through all the west of England, and lived in great domestic happiness and comparative competency; his deep interest and active liberality in connexion with the formation of the Georgian colony; and his able controversy with his brother John on the doctrine of assurance. For these and other details, reference must be had to the memoirs prefixed to his collected poems. The epitaph on his tomb in Tiverton churchyard describes him as a man of uncommon wit and learning, benevolent temper, simple manners, deservedly esteemed and beloved by all: an excellent preacher, whose best sermon was the constant example of an edifying life; a follower of his blessed Master's example in doing good; of such scrupulous integrity that he declined occasions of advancement in the world through fear of being involved in dangerous compliances, and avoided the usual ways to preferment as studiously as many others seek them. After a life spent in the laborious employment of teaching youth, he resigned his soul to God, in the forty-ninth year of his age. We have no sympathy with this amiable man's High Church principles, which he sometimes pushed to unwarrantable extremes. His intense dislike to everything extemporaneous in public or social worship, led him to scatter, with liberal hand, his keenest sarcasms upon those who, to use his own words in one of his satires, regarded forms of prayer as,— "At best a crutch the weak to aid, A cumbrance to the strong." When his brothers broke through many of the old restraints in order more effectually to minister the Gospel of God to the perishing

225

masses, and promote a great national reformation as well as a glorious revival of religion, he passed some harsh criticisms upon their proceedings, and besought them to return to the old paths. He declared that he would much rather see them picking straws in the University, than preaching in the area of Moorfields. Yet, with him religion had always been a matter of principle. He lashed the libertines of his age, and boldly stood forth to vindicate Christianity against the infidel blasphemies of Hobbes and his followers. Though, like many other divines of his time, he controverted the doctrine of the Holy Spirit's direct attestation to the believer's adoption into the family of God, he had a reverent faith in the doctrines of atonement, justification, and holiness. As he neared the world of un-clouded light, the mist of misapprehension melted away, and several days before he went hence, God had given him a calm and full assurance of his interest in Christ. He gave himself up so thoroughly to his scholastic profession, that a single volume of poems, written as a pleasant recreation rather than a serious employment, is the only remaining fruit of his pen. The volume contains many beautiful hymns, some of which are constantly sung in the public worship of various denominations, and a few lofty meditations upon religious themes. The majority of the compositions, however, belong to the realms of wit and humour. Notwithstanding an occasional coarseness, which offends against the more refined taste of later times, they display the true poetic genius, abounding in vivid fancies and elegant classic allusions. How beautiful and tender is the following epitaph on an infant:— "Beneath, a sleeping infant lies; To earth whose ashes lent More glorious shall hereafter rise, Though not more innocent. When the archangel's trump shall blow, And souls and bodies join,

What crowds will wish their lives below
Had been as short as thine!"

And what can exceed the keen sarcasm of his lines on the erection of a monument to the author of Hudibras, in Westminster Abbey?

"While Butler, needy wretch! was yet alive,
No generous patron would a dinner give;
See him, when starved to death and turn'd to dust,
Presented with a monumental bust!
The Poet's fate is here in emblem shewn,—
He asked for BREAD, and he received a STONE."

We could linger long on the beautiful features displayed in the character of this most amiable man: Notwithstanding our strong love for his brother John, as the Founder of Methodism, and his brother Charles, as the sweet hymnist of our Churches, we believe that, in the fineness of his natural temper, devout filial affection, and brotherly love; in self-denying liberality to his parents and the rest of his family, for whom he sometimes literally emptied his own purse; and in solid scholarly attainments, Samuel was the first of those three noble sons which Susanna Wesley gave to the Church and the world.

All the published sketches of EMILIA, the first of the Wesley daughters, are meagre and incorrect. "The life of such a woman," says Clarke, "must have furnished innumerable anecdotes of the most instructive kind. But, alas! For want of a collector, they have been borne away long since, on the gale that never returns, and buried in the viewless regions of endless oblivion." Happily, we have gathered up a few of the anecdotes, and are enabled to present a more extended and accurate notice of this remarkable woman.

Baptized at South Ormsby in the middle of January 1692, she was probably born in December of the previous year. Her parents bestowed special attention upon her early education; and under her father's tuition, she is reported to have acquired a good knowledge of the classic tongues. When the disastrous fire consumed the parsonage and scattered the household among different families, Emilia had the privilege of being her Mother's only companion for an entire year. She worked hard all day; read some pleasant book at night; and, though she had few diversions and was never suffered to wander abroad, she was contented and happy. She grew up a woman of "outward majesty and grace," in whom "virtue, form, and wit" were combined in "perfect harmony." Her intellectual powers, – "By

227

reason polished, and by arts refined,"—were so strong, well-balanced, and highly-cultivated, that she may be regarded as a thoroughly intellectual and educated woman. She had an exquisite taste for the beautiful, especially in poetry and music. Her brother John—no mean judge on such a subject—pronounced her the best reader of Milton he had ever heard; and Hetty, who devoutly loved her, sang the praises of her personal beauty and mental and moral excellence, in soft and flowing numbers, but with a true sisterly obliviousness of some of the keener qualities of Emilia's nature. Her affections and antipathies were alike intense. Her love for her Mother was strong as death; and she regarded her brother John with a passionate fondness. Though so much younger than herself, she selected him as her "most intimate companion; her counsellor in difficulties," to whom her "heart lay open at all times." Toward her father, her letters exhibit an angriness of disposition and asperity of language, which cannot be justified. There was a sharpness of temper and impatience of opposition that vividly reflect some of the rector's most prominent infirmities. She also possessed his resolute energy, indomitable perseverance, and imperious self-will, combined with a courage, which did honour to her sex. For many years, she nobly took her share of the common family trials, and relieved her Mother of many household cares. But at length, disappointed in love, chafed by straitened circumstances, "provoked at all her relations, and wishing to be out of their sight," her high spirit could brook it no longer. She entered a boarding school at Lincoln, and "readily fell into that way of life," though she "had never so much as seen one before." Well-dressed, with money in her pocket, and respected by all around her, she felt as if she had entered a new world. After five years' hard work and comparative happiness, the "school broke up," and her Mother urged her to return home and take charge of the house at Wroote, the living of which had just been conferred upon her father, in connexion with Epworth. Here she toiled hard for the welfare of the household, and "found her own clothes" until her scant savings were exhausted. But "in this distress," she writes, "we enjoy many comforts. We have no duns, nor any of that tormenting care to provide bread, which we had at Epworth. In short, could I lay aside all thought of the future, and could be content without three things, money, liberty, and clothes,—I might live very comfortably." After three or four years, probably in 1728, Emilia again left home and went to Mrs Taylor's boarding school, at Lincoln." Here, she was visited by her brothers, on their return from Epworth to Oxford, in 1729. Her lively letter to John after their departure gives us the following genuine specimen of boarding school gossip and criticism. "Pray tell Brother Charles, Mrs Taylor gives her service to him, not excluding you; and orders me to tell him that her daughter Peggy has had the toothache ever since he went away. Miss Kitty is by me, and says he is a saucy cur, and she will turn him off because he never went to see her at Gainsborough. Mrs Taylor desires him, the next time he is here, to let his eyelids fall a little lower, which she thinks will become him better than his staring."

By this prim school-mistress she was unkindly treated, and had the hardest possible work to obtain any portion of her small salary. She, therefore, quitted this establishment at Christmas, 1730, and resolved to commence a school at Gainsborough. The project was laid before her brothers, who, after a little hesitation, consented to it, and gave her some trifling help. According to her own account, she had a fairer prospect at Gainsborough than she originally expected: but was "much afraid of being dipped in debt at first. But," she adds, "God's will be done! Troubles of that kind are what I have been used to." In this buoyant spirit, she entered upon her new enterprise. We know not whether this "fairer prospect" was ever realised; but as her Mother found a refuge in her house after her father's death in 1735, she must have remained in this quiet town five or six years. On her first visit to London, Emilia formed an acquaintance with a young gentleman named Leyborne, whom she passionately loved. When anything grieved her, he was always her comforter. When afflictions pressed hard upon her, he was at hand to relieve. She thought "his love sufficient recompense for the loss or absence of all other worldly comforts." Then, "at the end of three years, ill fate, in the shape of a near relation,"—probably her brother Samuel,—"laid the groundwork of my misery, and, joined with my Mother's

229

command and my own indiscretion, broke the correspondence." Her brother Samuel probably knew too much of this young man's real character and thought himself justified in interfering on his sister's behalf. Even Emilia herself afterwards discovered that his affection for her was far from being genuine. Yet, with a true womanly heart, she long cherished a strong regard for this object of her first love, and refused to believe anything disparaging to his character. While at Gainsborough, a medical gentleman paid her some attention. He happened, however, to belong to the Society of Friends; and this led her brother John, to whose opinion she always paid great deference, to argue the impropriety of such an alliance, and entreat her not to receive his addresses. She wavered for a while, and then "chance furnished her with sufficient matter to turn the scale," which her brother had previously brought to an equality. Her lover's Whiggish principles were far more provoking to her than his Quakerism. One morning they discussed the University of Oxford, Lord Clarendon, and the Stuarts, whom she defended with all the energy of her nature. The controversy waxed hot, and lasted about two hours, when they parted in a most unenviable temper. "I was thoroughly provoked at him for contradicting me so violently," she writes; "it being, as you know, my avowed doctrine that an unmarried woman can never be wrong in any conversation with a bachelor." The engagement was broken off, and poor Emilia moralises after the following fashion;—"When, after a variety of ill fortune, I seemed settled here with an excellent physician, . . . a companion and friend to whom I could speak freely at all times, and, must I add too, the most passionate lover, what ails my fortune now? Why, he is a Quaker, and my own brother, for whom I have the tenderest regard, he whom I never willfully disobeyed or grieved, presses it on me as a strict duty to part with this faithful friend, this delightful companion; and I have done it, it is true. But now what is there left in life worth valuing? Truly not much; and if I should comply with my Mother's desire, throw up my business here, and go home, I do not see there could be much in it, since my Creator seems to have decreed me to a state of suffering here, and always deprives me of what I love, or embitters it to me. Who can contend with Omnipotence? No. I will strive no more; no more labour to make myself what they call easy in the world, since it is all striving against the stream, labour in vain, and, in the strictest sense, not only vanity, but vexation of spirit." Finally, after all these interruptions to the courses of her love, when she was approaching her fiftieth year, Emilia was married to Mr Harper, an apothecary at Epworth. Her husband probably did not survive the marriage many years; and in the days of her widowhood, she removed to London. The brother whom she so much loved cared earnestly for both her temporal and spiritual wants. Her last years were spent in the chapel house, West Street, Seven Dials, where she expired about 1771, having nearly arrived at her eightieth year. Her faculties had become feeble, and she had "survived the major part of her incomparable memory:" but her benevolent disposition lived in unabated vigour, and her somewhat warm and petulant temper was much softened and subdued. Though we have no account of her last hours, there are satisfactory indications that, as she advanced in life, real spiritual religion gained a deeper hold upon her heart. For many years, she constantly attended the services at the Foundery, where she derived much spiritual profit. When she removed to West Street, her apartments communicated with the chapel, where she could throw open the sashes and join in the public worship, without leaving her own room. In this comfortable retreat, "in the very bosom of the Church," she finished her course, and, there is every reason to believe, obtained her dismission to the Church of the first-born in heaven.

SUSANNA, the second daughter, also born at South Ormsby, was good-natured, very facetious, and a little romantic, yet distinguished for the "strictest moral correctness." With a beautiful form and lovely countenance, she possessed a mind strong, vivacious, and well refined by education. Her Mother took the greatest pains with her intellectual and moral training. The elaborate exposition of the Apostles' Creed was written for her especial instruction, and concludes with this touching and earnest appeal to the girl of fourteen;—"I cannot tell whether you have ever seriously considered the lost and miserable condition you are in by nature. If you have not, it is

231

high time to begin to do it: and I shall earnestly beseech the Almighty to enlighten your mind, to renew and sanctify you by His Holy Spirit, that you may be His child by adoption here, and an heir of His blessed kingdom hereafter." She lived some time with her uncle Wesley in London; and her wealthy uncle Annesley, gathering his fortune among the merchandise of the Indies, promised to make her some handsome provision. But he changed his mind, and the poor girl's hopes were rudely dashed to the ground. Stung by this unkindness, she committed a rash deed which linked her after-life with untold misery. Her Mother reveals the melancholy sequel in the following passage to this ungenerous relative:—"My second daughter, Sukey, a pretty woman, and worthy a better fate, when by your unkind letters, she perceived that all her hopes in you were frustrated, rashly threw herself upon a man,—if a man he may be called that is little inferior to the apostate angels in wickedness,—that is not only her plague, but a constant affliction to the family."

> Sukey, having known the extreme poverty of her parents' home, married a wealthy man without much thought as to whether she loved him and without her parents' permission. She sincerely believed he was a gentleman farmer of good prospects and considerable wealth. Instead of being a gentleman, he was a coarse, vulgar, immoral man who also abused his wife. She had four children with him, and finally left him. "Pathway to HIS Presence," by B. J. Funk, of the South Georgia United Methodist Conference.

The man of whom this terrible character is given, was Richard Ellison, "a gentleman of good family, who had a respectable establishment;" a coarse, vulgar, immoral man. The rector declared him the "wen" of his family, whose company at the parsonage was not more pleasant to him "than all his physic." He treated his wife with so much harshness, that she well-nigh sank into her grave. "Poor Sukey!" writes her youngest sister, "she is very ill. People think she is going into a consumption. It would be well for her if she was where the wicked cease from troubling, and the weary are at rest." Ellison's conduct at length rendered him intolerable; and when a fire burnt down their dwelling, his wife deserted him altogether. After using all ordinary means to induce her return, he advertised his death in various newspapers. She hurried home to attend his funeral and look after her children; but finding him still alive, she instantly returned to London. Other calamities fell upon this unfortunate man, which completely ruined his temporal circumstances. Through the "neglect of the commissioners of the sewers, who ought to keep the drains open," all his meadow land was under water more than two years, and he could get no compensation. All his cows and all his horses, save one, died off; and he had "very little left to subsist on." In his extremity, he applied to the brother of his injured wife. John Wesley, ever forgiving and benevolent, even to the evil and the unthankful, induced his friend, Ebenezer Blackwell, to "place the name of Richard Ellison among those who were to have a share of the money disposed of by Mr Butterfield," declaring that "the smallest relief could never be more seasonable." It is generally believed that the separation between Ellison and his wife was final. But as he subsequently removed to London and became a reformed man, it is possible that conjugal harmony was restored. Concerning the time and circumstances of his much-injured wife's departure to that rest she had so much reason to desire, we have no information. It probably took place in London or Bristol; where, surrounded by the spiritual advices and prayers of her brothers and the Methodist people, there is every reason to hope that she died in peace. And is it not refreshing to find the following beautiful notice of the final hour of her poor prodigal husband? "Yesterday evening," writes Charles Wesley on the eleventh of April 1760, "I buried my brother Ellison. Sister Macdonald, whom he was always very fond of, prayed by him in his last moments. He told her he was not afraid to die, and believed God, for Christ's sake, had forgiven him. I felt a most solemn awe overwhelming me, while I committed his body to the earth. He is gone to increase my father's joy in Paradise; who often said every one of his children would be saved, for God had given them all to his prayers. God grant I may not be the single exception!"

MARY, the third grown-up daughter, born in 1696, just before the family left South Ormsby, was a deeply interesting character. From an injury received in infancy, probably through the carelessness of her nurse, she grew up deformed and little of stature. This exposed her to unseemly merriment from the vulgar when she walked abroad. But she bore the trial without resentment or complaint. How touching is her own allusion to this infirmity when comforting an afflicted friend "I think I may say, I have lived in a state of affliction ever since I was born, being the ridicule of mankind and the reproach of my family; yet I dare not think God deals hardly with me. And though He has set His mark upon me, I still hope my punishment won't be greater than I am able to bear. Since I am sensible God is no respecter of persons, I trust I shall be happier in the next life than if I enjoyed all the advantages of this." There was, however, a merciful compensation for this deformity, in exquisitely beautiful features, which formed "a fair and legible index to a mind and disposition almost angelic." Her sister Hetty writes in raptures about her "jetty eyes;" her "brow serene, benignant, clear;" the "taintless whiteness of her skin," and "the roseate beauties of her lip and cheek." Her even temper and obliging manners made her the favourite of the whole family. Hetty regarded her as one of the most exalted of human beings. Her brothers constantly spoke of her with tenderest affection; and, notwithstanding her deformity, Providence provided for her a meet companion. A poor boy, who displayed considerable aptitude for learning, was brought under the notice of Mary's father. Transferred from the charity school to the study in the parsonage, he was duly installed as the rector's amanuensis. Four years he was employed in transcribing the Latin Dissertations on the Book of Job, and adorning them with "maps and figures as well as he could by the light of nature." These creations of the "ingenious artist" are roughly denounced as "the first efforts of an untutored boy;" the "most execrable that could be conceived; the worst that ever saw the sun." During this period of literary drudgery, however, the boy had the golden opportunity of receiving instruction from the rector in the higher branches of learning. Fitted for the University, he was placed under the tuition of John Wesley at Oxford. "If he goes on as he has begun," wrote his tutor, "I dare take upon me to say, that, by the time he has been here four or five years, there will not be such an one, of his standing, in Lincoln College, perhaps not in the University of Oxford." He became "a valuable person, of uncommon brightness, learning, piety, and indefatigable industry; possessing a very happy memory, especially for languages, and a judgment and intelligence not inferior; always loyal to the King, zealous for the Church, and friendly to our Dissenting brethren. And for the truth of this character," adds his admiring patron, "I will be accountable to God and man."

This was John Whitelamb, or as Mrs Wesley playfully calls him, "poor starveling Johnny." Obtaining orders, he returned to Epworth and became the rector's curate. His proposal of marriage to Mary Wesley was approved by the family, and they were married in 1733, the bride being in her thirty-seventh year, and her husband several years younger. Whitelamb, educated by the charity of the Wesleys, was also dependent upon them for his clerical outfit. "John Whitelamb," writes Wesley to his brother Samuel, "wants a new gown much, and I am not rich enough to buy him one at present. If you are willing, my twenty shillings,—that were,—should go towards that. I will add ten to them, and let it lie till I have tried my interest with my friends to make up the price of a new one." His wife, of course, brought him no rich dower. The marriage, however, was the result of purest affection on both sides; and "better is little with the fear of the Lord, than great treasure, and trouble therewith. Better is a dinner of herbs where love is, than a stalled ox and hatred therewith." The rector resolved to do his utmost to make some provision for them. "Though I can give but little more with her," he writes, "yet I would gladly give them a little glebe land at Wroote, where I am sure they will not want springs of water. But they love the place, though I can get nobody else to reside at it." In compliance with his earnest request, the Lord Chancellor transferred the living to Whitelamb. The "low levels" where it was situated, were frequently overflowed from the surrounding dykes. The fruits of the hard husbandry of the parishioners were destroyed, and distress and desolation covered the entire neighbourhood. The

235

income, though now considerable, was barely fifty pounds a-year. This, however, Mary's father promised to supplement by an annual gift of twenty pounds. In good heart and hope they took possession of the parsonage, and prepared themselves for a life of useful toil among their rustic flock. But, alas, how transitory is all mere earthly good! Within one short year, the destroyer smote down the mother and her infant child. They were buried in the same grave, November the first, 1734; but no monumental tomb, or even humble stone, marks the place of their sepulture." A brass plate, fastened to the south wall, inside the ancient church, bears the following inscription — "Near this place lieth the remains of Samuel Smyth, son of Barnett and Frances Smyth, late Rector of Panton, Lincolnshire; departed the fourth of October, 1765; aged fifty-five. ALSO, MARY WHITELAMB, WIFE OF THE LATE RECTOR OF WROOTE." This is the only intimation we can discover as to the precise locality of her grave, which, it would seem, is within the church.

Hetty composed the following touching epitaph, which, though it has never been engraven on stone, deserves to be quoted at length:—

"If highest worth, in beauty's bloom,
   Exempted mortals from the tomb,
 We had not, round this sacred bier,
   Mourn'd the sweet babe and mother here,
 Where innocence from harm is blest,
 And the meek sufferer is at rest !
   Fierce pangs she bore without complaint,
 Till Heaven relieved the finish'd saint.
 If savage bosoms felt her woe,—
 Who lived and died without a foe,—
 How should I mourn, or how commend
 My tenderest, dearest, firmest friend?
   Most pious, meek, resign'd, and chaste,
 With every social virtue graced !
   If, reader, thou would'st prove and know
 The ease she found not here below;

Her bright example points the way
To perfect bliss and endless day."

There was great lamentation for Mary's departure. Her three brothers honoured her memory and expressed their grief at her loss. "When you write again," says Charles to Samuel, "we should be much obliged to you for your elegy upon sister Molly. My brother preaches her funeral sermon when he gets thither, and will still leave matter enough for a copy of verses. I should be glad to follow him either way; but cannot say which I shall be soonest qualified for." The funeral sermon was preached and the elegy most likely written, though we have not been able to discover it.

Whitelamb's grief for her loss was so distressing that he determined to haste away from the scenes which so constantly reminded him of her. He offered himself to accompany the Wesleys to Georgia, but for some reason not known his desire was not realised. He settled down in his parish, and remained rector of his native village more than thirty years. When John Wesley was an outcast from many of the churches, Whitelamb freely offered him the use of his, and also attended the open-air services in Epworth churchyard, when Wesley preached on his father's tomb. "The sight of you," he wrote, "moves me strangely. My heart overflows with gratitude. I feel in a higher degree all that tenderness and yearning of bowels with which I am affected towards every branch of Mr Wesley's family. I cannot refrain from tears when I reflect;—This is the man who at Oxford was more than a father to me; this is he whom I have heard expound, or dispute publicly, or preach at Saint Mary's, with such applause; and—O that I should ever add '-whom I have lately heard preach at Epworth on his father's tombstone." He was a man of retired habits, fond of solitude, and punctual in the discharge of his parochial duties. On his way to church one Sabbath morning in the summer of 1769, he was suddenly seized with his fatal sickness, which soon ended his life. The memory of his kindly bearing was long cherished by his surviving parishioners; but all intercourse between him and the Wesleys had ceased long before his death. For some years he wandered from the simplicity of Christ, and seems to have been

237

all but a Deist. There are, however, reasons to "hope that his former principles regained their influence and ascendancy; and that he died in the faith of our Lord Jesus Christ." The next, and by far the most gifted of Mrs Wesley's daughters, is MEHETABEL, or Hetty, to whose poetical compositions frequent allusion has already been made. The incidents of her life, with a careful analysis of her mental powers, a full estimate of her highly poetic genius, and a complete collection of her poems, would form a volume of no ordinary interest and value. She was the first of the Wesleys born at Epworth, probably toward the close of 1697. Her childhood was distinguished by a gaiety and merry-heartedness, which gave her parents some concern, and occasionally led her into sportive inadvertences, which offended against the rules of the household. There was a development of intellectual power, ready wit, and poetic genius beyond her years. So ready was she in the acquisition of knowledge that, it is said, she read the Greek Testament with comparative ease when she was only eight years old. Her father delighted to have her as his companion and assistant in the study, where she followed her more learned pursuits under his immediate direction. Of beautiful features, graceful form, and attractive demeanour, she had many suitors during her girlish years; "but they were generally of the airy and thoughtless class, and ill-suited to make her either happy or useful in matrimonial life." And yet, had she accepted the most unpromising of them all, her married life, which forms a tale of unmitigated sadness, would probably have been far happier than it was. In April, 1725, "a gentleman in the profession of the law," who met Hetty at Kelstein, near Louth, requested her father's consent to their marriage. The rector frankly told him that, "being a perfect stranger, he must enquire of his character." Finding that "he was not so good as he ought to be, either in estate or morals," he refused his consent; and the events which followed brought some of the heaviest sorrows into the Epworth parsonage. The conduct of Hetty was the reverse of blameless; and evidence in our possession shews that her father was justified in calling the man who sought her hand "an unprincipled lawyer." Hetty left her home, and was married,—probably about the close of the same year, to John Wright, a plumber and glazier in London.

The rector has been censured for urging this marriage upon his daughter; but our information leads us to doubt whether he knew anything of Wright until after the marriage. It is said that Hetty's uncle gave her five hundred pounds, with which her husband commenced business on his own account." This account is drawn from documents of unquestionable authority, for which I am indebted to Mr G. J. Stevenson of London. Wright, as may be supposed, was an uneducated man, utterly unsuited to be the life-companion of the refined and accomplished Hetty. At the time of the marriage he was probably sober and industrious; but he subsequently abandoned himself to habits of intemperance, and association with low and vulgar companions. He was hard-working in business, but spent the greater part of his nights in public-houses, leaving his affectionate wife to watch through the weary hours for his return. She deeply felt this neglect, and remonstrated with him in tender and touching strains:—

"For though thine absence I lament
When half the lonely night is spent:
Yet when the watch or early morn
Has brought me hopes of thy return,
I oft have wiped these watchful eyes,
Conceal'd my cares, and curb'd my sighs,
'In spite of grief, to let thee see
I wore an endless smile for thee."

All her efforts failed to reclaim her husband from his evil ways. Her health gave way under her complicated trials; and all traces of former beauty, "except a lively piercing eye," vanished from her once handsome countenance. Her children all died young, killed, as she declared, by the white-lead connected with her husband's business. Shut out from all congenial society, she sank into a deep melancholy. She sought consolation in the strains of her tuneful lyre, and poured forth her sorrows in verse perfect in the soft flow of its rhythm, yet so tender and affecting that it can scarcely be read without tears. How inimitable for its pathos and highly-polished numbers, is the following address to her dying infant, dictated from her trembling lips a day or two after her confinement:—

239

"Tender softness! infant mild!
Perfect, purest, brightest child!
Transient lustre! beauteous clay !
Smiling wonder of a day !
Ere the last convulsive start
Rend thy unresisting heart;
Ere the long-enduring swoon
Weigh thy precious eye-lids down;
Ah, regard a mother's moan,
Anguish deeper than thy own :
Fairest eyes! whose dawning light
Late with rapture blest my sight,
Ere your orbs extinguish'd be,
Bend their trembling beams on me !
Drooping sweetness! verdant flower !
Blooming, withering in an hour !
Ere thy gentle breast sustains
Latest, fiercest, mortal pains,
Hear a suppliant! let me be
Partner in thy destiny!
That whene'er the fatal cloud
Must thy radiant temples shroud;
When deadly damps, impending now,
Shall hover round thy destined brow,
Diffusive may their influence be,
And with the BLOSSOM blast the TREE."

Amid her many trials, and through the kindly instruction
and intercourse of her brothers, Hetty was brought to look for
her true consolation in the enjoyment of experimental religion.
She sought and found Him who is the Comforter of the
sorrowful. She was for some time restrained from an open
profession of her spiritual attainments by a fear that she would
relapse into her former state; and when that fear was removed,
she tells us, "I was taxed with insincerity and hypocrisy
whenever I opened my mouth in favour of religion, or owned
how great things God had done for me. This discouraged me
utterly, and prevented me making my change so public as my

folly and vanity had formerly been. But now my health is gone, I cannot be easy without declaring that I have long desired to know one thing,-Jesus Christ and Him crucified; and this desire prevails above all others. And though I am cut off from all human help or ministry, I am not without assistance. Though I have no spiritual friend, nor ever had one yet, except perhaps once in a year or two, when I have seen one of my brothers, or some other religious persons by stealth; yet, no thanks to me, I am enabled to seek Him still, and to be satisfied with nothing less than God, in whose presence I affirm this truth. I dare not desire health; only patience, resignation, and the spirit of a healthful mind. I have been so long weak, that I know not how long my trial may last; but I have a firm persuasion and blessed hope, though no full assurance, that, in the country I am going to, I shall not sing 'Hallelujah!' and "Holy, holy, holy l' without company, as I have done in this. Dear brother, I am unable to speak or write on these things; I only speak my plain thoughts. Adieu !" During the following year, 1744, she went to Bristol, where she profited much by the ministry of her brothers and the conversation of many Christian friends. The restraints imposed upon her religious liberty by her husband were removed after her return to London. She became a Methodist, and no longer needed to seek religious communion by stealth. Her brothers were more frequent visitors at her house, and she was strengthened and comforted in her weakness and sorrow. To one who visited her not long before her departure, she said, "I have long ardently wished for death, because, you know, we Methodists always die in a transport of joy." But this expected "transport of joy." did not gladden her last hour. "I prayed by my sister Wright," says her brother Charles, "a gracious, tender, trembling soul; a bruised reed, which the Lord will not break." "I found my sister Wright very near the haven; yet still in darkness, doubts, and fears, against hope believing in hope." A few minutes before four o'clock in the afternoon of March 21, 1750, while London was in consternation from a succession of earthquake-shocks, "her spirit was set at liberty. I had sweet fellowship with her," continues Charles, "in explaining at the chapel those solemn words, "Thy sun shall no more go down, neither shall thy moon withdraw itself; for the Lord shall be

241

thine everlasting light, and the days of thy mourning shall be ended. All present seemed partakers both of my sorrow and my joy." And five days afterwards, he writes, "I followed her to her quiet grave, and wept with them that weep." In what part of the great city may that "quiet grave" be found? Does any stone mark the spot, and bear a memorial of one so lovely and pleasant in her life? To these questions we have obtained no answer; but Hetty's own epitaph upon herself, written under her deepest sorrows and before her heart was filled with the peace and joy of faith, deserves recording:—

"Destined while living to sustain
 An equal share of grief and pain:
All various ills of human race
Within this breast had once a place.
Without complaint, she learn'd to bear
A living death, a long despair;
Till, hard oppress'd by adverse fate,
Overcharged, she sunk beneath the weight;
And to this peaceful tomb retired,
So much esteem'd, so long desired!
The painful mortal conflicts o'er:
A broken heart can bleed no more."

Her husband, bad as he was, felt her loss very acutely. "Last Monday," writes Charles Wesley, "I followed our happy sister to her grave. Her husband is inconsolable, not knowing Jesus Christ. I was much affected by his saying, with tears, he hoped I should not forsake him now my sister was dead." He lived some years after her death; and married a second time; but the facts of his subsequent history are unknown. There is, however, a most affecting record of some of this poor man's last hours. "He is struck down by the dead-palsy," says Charles Wesley in one of his letters; "longed, above all things, for my coming; rejoiced and wept to see me. His stubborn heart was much softened by the approach of death. Now he is a poor sinner indeed, full of horror and self-condemnation, yet not without hope of mercy —I prayed again with my poor penitent; and left him a little easier and composed.—A messenger called

242

me, between one and two, to my brother. He told me he was dying; that his feet were dead already; was perfectly sensible; told me, before his wife, how he had settled his affairs,—not enough to her advantage, I think;— expressed a good hope and earnest desire for one, one only thing; wished for the voice of a trumpet, to warn all mankind not to walk in the paths wherein he had walked; made me witness of his reconciliation with his wife; and said, he expected to die at four or five. I spoke comfortably to him of Jesus, our Atonement, our Peace, our Hope; prayed with free access, as we did last night in the Society; saw no symptoms of immediate death, yet would not lessen his apprehensions of it.—I preached at five to a numerous congregation, and prayed with confidence for a Christless, dying sinner." This is the last glimpse we have of Hetty Wesley's husband. Is it possible that, after all his wanderings in sin, he has joined her whom he so deeply wronged, in that better life where all is harmony, happiness, and love? There is scarcely any information about ANNE, the fifth daughter of Mrs Wesley. She was born sometime in 1702; but there is not a single hint about her personal appearance, or the character of her mind. The only glimpses we have of her girlhood are in connexion with the movements of old Jeffery, and have already come under notice. Writing to her brother John in September 1724, Emilia says, "Sister Nancy, I believe, will marry John Lambert,"—an anticipation very soon fulfilled. Lambert was a land-surveyor; an intelligent and well-read man; and in all probability the marriage with Anne Wesley was in every way suitable. He took great pains to collect all the publications of his father-in-law, and illustrated them with many notes. The harmony of their married life was uninterrupted. After a few years' residence in the neighbourhood of Epworth, they removed to Hatfield, in Hertfordshire, where Charles Wesley visited them twice in the summer of 1737. "After spending some time at Hatfield," he writes, August the seventeenth, "I set out with my brother Lambert for London. At Epping he went back full of good resolutions." These "good resolutions" were not very lasting. Lambert was in danger of intemperance, and was easily led astray by this besetment. "This evening," says Charles Wesley,

243

in November, 1738, "my brothers Lambert and Wright visited me. The latter has corrupted the former, after all the pains I have taken with him, and brought him back to drinking. I was full, yet could not speak; prayed for meekness, and then set before him the things he had done in the Devil's name, toward reconverting a soul to him. He left us abruptly. I encouraged poor John Lambert to turn again unto God." We hope these exhortations were not lost. When he next met with Lambert and his wife, Charles had spent a remarkable day. Before six in the morning, he was in Newgate, praying with several unhappy men whose hour had come. He went with them to the gallows, where "none shewed any natural terror of death; no fear, no crying, no tears." Exactly at twelve, "they were turned off," and the ardent evangelist, who had been the means of saving their souls from death, returned home full of confidence in their final happiness. "That hour under the gallows," he exclaims, "was the most blessed hour of my life." Arriving at his humble lodgings in Little Britain, he says, "We renewed our triumph. I found my brother and sister Lambert there, and preached to them the Gospel of forgiveness, which they received without opposition." This is the last record of Anne Wesley and her husband. We would fain hope that they received from the heart those holy truths, which their zealous brother delivered unto them.

But what shall we say of JOHN, the next in order of this remarkable family; a man of whom even Macaulay affirms that he was the instrument of "a most remarkable moral revolution; whose eloquence and logical acuteness might have rendered him eminent in literature; whose genius for government was not inferior to that of Richelieu, and who, whatever his errors may have been, devoted all his powers, in defiance of obloquy and derision, to what he sincerely considered the highest good of his species?"

All the world is familiar with the fame of JOHN WESLEY, the Founder of Methodism. He was born on 17 June 1703, and several notices of his personal history have already passed under the reader's eye. Resolved, "to be more particularly careful of the soul of a child whom God had so mercifully provided for" by his wonderful deliverance from the burning parsonage, his Mother paid special attention to his early religious training. Her care was recompensed in the seriousness of his deportment; and he was permitted to receive the Lord's Supper when only eight years old. He went to the Charter-house in 1714, "where he was noticed for his diligence, and progress in learning; endured a good deal of unwelcome persecution from the older boys; and preserved his health by observing his father's command to run three times round the grounds every day. He cherished a lasting affection for this venerable school, and regularly visited it once a year to the end of his life. Elected to Christ Church, Oxford, at the close of his seventeenth year, he pursued his studies with great advantage. His natural temper was "gay and sprightly, with a turn for wit and humour;" and he soon "appeared the very sensible and acute collegian; a young fellow of the finest classical taste, and of the most liberal and manly sentiments." When elected to the Fellowship of Lincoln College, he was "acknowledged by all parties to be a man of talents, and an excellent critic in the learned languages." His skill in logic "was universally known and admired;" and he was chosen Greek Lecturer and Moderator of the Classes only a few months after gaining his Fellowship. But he soon became known as a man of more than ordinary religious strictness. "Blessed with such activity as to be always gaining ground, and such steadiness that he lost none," he gathered around him a little band of young men whose hearts the Lord had touched, and who recognised him as their head. There was "something of authority in his countenance; yet he never assumed anything above his companions." They visited the prisons and conversed with the wretched inmates, among whom they had prayers twice a week, a sermon on Sunday, and the Sacrament once a month. They visited poor families, gave them money, admonished them of their vices, and examined their children. They established a school, John Wesley paying the mistress, and clothing most of the children out of his own pocket. They also taught "the children in the workhouse, and read to the old people as they did to the prisoners." Amidst all these activities, one of his companions tells us he could say much of John Wesley's "private piety; how it was nourished by a continual recourse to God, and preserved by a strict watchfulness in beating down

245

pride, and reducing the craftiness and impetuosity of nature to a child-like simplicity, and, in a good degree, crowned with Divine love and victory over the whole set of earthly passions. He thought prayer to be more his business than anything else; and I have seen him come out of his closet with a serenity of countenance that was next to shining: it discovered what he had been doing."

We can only refer in the shortest possible way to his further toils and successes at Oxford; his mission to Georgia, with its manifold trials and disappointments; his intercourse and controversies with the Moravians; the blessed change in his religious experience, which laid the foundation of his subsequent extensive usefulness; the formation of the Methodist Societies, and the manner in which, under his fostering care and skilful government, they grew up into beautiful and flourishing Churches; the violent persecutions which he endured from brutal mobs; his extraordinary itinerant journeyings, in which he travelled on horseback nearly five thousand miles a year, and preached a thousand sermons, for fifty-two years in succession; and his marvellous industry, which enabled him, amidst all these rapid movements, to conduct extensive correspondence, deal with cases of conscience, write or abridge two hundred volumes, keep himself abreast of the literature of the times, maintain his classical studies, and manage the whole concerns of a complicated and wide-spread Church organisation;"—declaring, meanwhile, that he had no time to be in a hurry; that he never felt low-spirited for a quarter of an hour in his life, or lost a night's sleep until his seventieth year; and that ten thousand cares sat as lightly upon his mind as ten thousand hairs upon his head. With similar brevity must be named his genial temper, warm but not fiery, and "radiant with religious joyfulness;" his clear and strong intellect; his playful humour and sparkling wit; his unselfish benevolence, bounded only by the length of his purse; the wondrous power of his preaching, under which thousands wept and prayed in crowded meeting-houses, on bleak mountain sides, or in open market-places: his genuine philanthropy and patriotism; his intelligent and ardent piety; his noble catholicity of spirit; and his unrivalled conversational

246

powers, which charmed the most cultivated minds of his day, made him the ever-welcome guest of humbler households, and the choicest companion of little children. "John Howard blessed his loving words, and under their inspiration went forth to his prison journeys with greater heart than ever. Bishop Lowth sat at his feet, and hoped he might be found there in another world: and Alexander Knox kindled into raptures as he recalled the fine old man with a child's heart and a seraphic face, realising his own idea of angelic goodness." "Wesley and his Times," by the Rev. W. M. Punshon. He pursued his apostolic toils until 2 March 1791, when, having served his generation by the will of God, he passed to his reward, leaving a reformed nation and a flourishing Church— numbering more than a hundred and fifty thousand members, five hundred and fifty ministers, and thousands of local preachers—as his best and most enduring monument. "I consider him," wrote Southey to Wilberforce, "as the most influential mind of the last century; the man who will have produced the greatest effects centuries, or perhaps millenniums hence, if the present race of men should continue so long." The leaven of his labours is still working in the world. During the seventy-two years since his death, hundreds of thousands have been converted and translated to heaven through the instrumentality of the Community which he formed; and at the present moment there are not less than three millions of Methodists, associated with the parent Society and its various offshoots, who reverence his memory and rejoice in their connexion with his name. Between John Wesley and his sister

MARTHA, who next claims our attention, there was a very remarkable resemblance. Their stature, form, and countenance were so much alike, that Doctor Clarke, who knew them both well, declared had they been dressed in similar attire he could not have distinguished the one from the other. Like her brother, she also reflected deeply on every subject, controlled every appetite and passion with rigid exactness, and felt herself answerable to her reason for everything she did. Even their handwriting was so much alike that the one might be easily mistaken for the other. Their mutual affection was exceedingly strong. Patty's love for her brother seemed to be innate, rather than acquired. When a helpless infant, "afflicted and moaning with pain, the sight of this beloved brother immediately calmed and cheered her, causing her to forget her sufferings." She was distinguished for deep thoughtfulness, grave deportment, and an evenness of temper, which nothing could ruffle. By all kinds of witty mischief, her more lively companions sought to disturb her gravity and excite her temper; but she opposed all their jests and playful tricks with solid arguments. When her abhorrence of satire, which the rest of the children had at ready command, provoked its attacks in many a stinging epigram, she calmly reasoned about its moral evils, and always contended that ridicule never cured any vice. Her Mother entering the nursery one day, and finding it a scene of noise and frolic during play hours, pleasantly observed,—"You will all be more serious one day." Patty, calm amidst the tempest, looked up from her retired corner, and said, "Shall I be more serious, Mother?"—an appeal which instantly drew forth a negative response. She regarded herself as the only one of the family who was destitute of wit; and her brother Charles used to say, "Sister Patty was always too wise to be witty." She grew up a thoroughly intellectual and accomplished woman. With a clear perception and considerable logical power, was combined an incomparable memory, which became a repository of the most striking events in the history of the past; and she could also repeat the greater part of the best English poets with perfect accuracy. She delighted in literary conversation, theological discussion, and argumentation on moral and metaphysical questions, in which she displayed great acuteness and the results of careful and extensive reading. Even Doctor Johnson valued her conversation, which in many instances supplied the absence of books; and he frequently invited her to Bolt-court that he might enjoy the pleasure of her society. She had, however, a natural horror of all melancholy topics. Persons who could delight to see or hear details of misery that they could not relieve, or descriptions of cruelty, which they could not punish, she regarded as destitute of all real feeling. She hardly ever spoke of death. "It was heaven, the society of the blessed, and the deliverance of the happy spirit from this tabernacle of clay, on which she delighted to dwell, rather than on the pang of separation, of which she always expressed considerable fear." She objected strongly to those expressions in one of her brother's hymns, which represent a corpse as having a "lovely appearance" and being one of the fairest earthly sights. She could not bear to look upon a dead body, because, she said, "it was beholding sin sitting upon his throne." All her movements were deliberate and steady. There was an innate dignity and grace in her eye, her step, her speech; yet all this was blended with so much gentleness and good nature that it excited uniform reverence and respect. There was a philosophic calmness that never forsook her, even in the hour of danger to life and limb. Her charity was large and always ready for every case of distress. Her brother Charles used to say, "It is in vain to give Pat anything to add to her own comforts, for she always gives it away to some person poorer than herself." Yet with all poor Martha's fine and noble qualities, in some of which she so much resembles her Mother, her married life was more unhappy than even that of any of her sisters. While residing with her uncle in London, a young gentleman named Hall, one of John Wesley's pupils at Oxford, solicited her hand. He was a man of agreeable manners, good education, competent means, and appeared to be deeply religious. She accepted his proposals, and he solemnly betrothed her to himself, without the knowledge of her relatives. When, however, he visited Epworth in company with her brothers, he became enamoured of her younger sister, won her affections, and promised her marriage. But no sooner was he back in London than he made arrangements to fulfil his pledge to Martha. The family, ignorant of any prior engagement with the elder sister, were astonished at this shameful conduct. Hall endeavoured to justify himself by some wild talk about visions and revelations of the Divine will. The marriage took place, and for some years the young clergyman and his wife lived happily together. Their house afforded an agreeable home to Mrs Wesley during many months of her widowhood, and they treated her with the greatest kindness.

But once began to change, his downward course was swift and awful. He became a quietist, disregarding the appointed ordinances of religion; a practical antinomian; a deist, if not an atheist; and, finally, polygamist, and illustrated his creed by his practice. The heart sickens at the records of his fearful immoralities, and we will not inflict upon ourselves or our readers the pain of a circumstantial detail. He lived on in his career of crime—often away from his wife and family months, and even years together—until the end drew near. "I came" to Bristol, says John Wesley, "just time enough, not to see, but to bury, poor Mr Hall, my brother-in-law, who died on Wednesday morning, January the sixth, 1776, I trust in peace; for God had given him deep repentance. Such another monument of Divine mercy, considering how low he had fallen, and from what heights of holiness, I have not seen, no, not in seventy years. I had designed to have visited him in the morning; but he did not stay for my coming. It is enough if, after all his wanderings, we meet again in Abraham's bosom." The heavy sorrows incident to the faithful wife of such a man, Mrs Hall bore with exemplary patience and fortitude. Believing that the Scriptures forbade her to dispute the authority of her husband, she submitted without a murmur to the most grievous wrongs, declaring that she "acted as a Christian, not as a woman." Certainly, nothing but religion could have sustained her under provocations so great. Like her Mother, she kept an occasional diary, in which she recorded her spiritual experience; and one or two passages will shew the real source of her strength, and the genuineness of her piety. "I have dedicated myself anew to Thee, O my God," she writes in 1734. "I have given Thee my soul and body. O claim me for Thine own! O let none take me again out of Thine hand. I have resolved to make my conversation more useful, at least to endeavour it; to avoid all fierceness, and uncharitable truths. I have resolved, likewise, to spend some time in meditating on what I read." Again, in 1740, when she seems to have understood more clearly the way of a sinner's acceptance with God, she observes:—"How many resolutions have I made, and how poorly kept them; which was indeed no wonder, for I knew not that Thou, O my Saviour, wouldst justify the ungodly Oh, blessed love that nothing but misery and vileness should recommend us to Thy mercy! With all my soul, I believe and embrace this blessed truth. I come vile and ungodly, pleading nothing but the promise; but Thou hast died that I might live forever! Amen 'Lord, I believe; help Thou my unbelief!'" Four years later there is the following passage, which contains evident allusion to the crisis in her spiritual history indicated in the last quotation:—"Of what infinite importance it is for every Christian to be continually watching; praying against a Laodicean state. What infinite mercy has the blessed Saviour shewn to me! How gently has He called me, when I slumbered and slept! It is now about four years since I had such a sense of the remission of sins as delivered me from all fear. I believed, in a little measure, on the Lord Jesus. He gave me to believe that because He lived, I should live also. He came that His sheep might have life, and that they might have it more abundantly. Since I received this blessed sense first, I never had any painful fear of my state; nor yet any doubt that I had deceived myself, except for a few moments, even though * never believed my testimony; never, that I know of, in any degree strengthened my hands in God. Yet notwithstanding this great goodness of my blessed Redeemer, I insensibly grew lukewarm. I did not earnestly cry for the second gift, as I had for the first. But He that had begun His work would not leave it unfinished. All love, all glory be unto Thee, O my blessed Redeemer, forever. Amen. Hallelujah! Near a year ago, I was one evening retired into my chamber, with a design to spend some time in private prayer; but before I kneeled down, all at once, without a thought of mine, I had a full, clear sense that the Lamb of God had made an atonement for me; that He had made full satisfaction for my sins; so that, were He that moment to appear to judgment, I could stand before Him. I saw, I felt,—for I know not any better words to use, that the justice of the Almighty Father was satisfied, and that I could even appeal to it! For I could say, 'There is my Surety He hath paid my whole debt!' Hallelujah!" In the possession of this blessed experience, she lived to the end of life. Though she had such a natural aversion to conversing on melancholy subjects, she spake of her own death with the utmost serenity. A little before her removal she called her niece to the bedside and said,—"I have now a sensation that convinces me my departure is near. The heart-strings seem gently, but entirely loosened." When asked if she had any pain, she replied, "No; but a new feeling." Just before she closed her

251

eyes, she pressed the hand of her niece with tenderest affection, and said,—"I have the assurance which I have long prayed for. Shout!" The next moment all was still. Her happy soul passed to its rest on 12 July 1791, in the eighty-fifth year of her age. She was the last survivor of the Epworth family. She died four months and nine days after her brother John; and her remains are interred in the same tomb. They "were lovely and pleasant in their lives, and in their death they were not divided." It cannot be expected that we should attempt anything more than the briefest notice of Charles, Mrs Wesley's youngest son, and the Hymnist of the Methodist Churches. Born prematurely on 18 December 1708, the utmost care was required to preserve him alive. After passing through the same home-training as his brothers, he went to Westminster, where he was lively and somewhat daring, but not inattentive to his studies. At the age of eighteen, he was elected a scholar of Christ Church, Oxford. For some time he was careless about his spiritual interests; but at length an important change came. Writing to his brother John, he says,—"It is owing, in a great measure, to somebody's prayers,—my Mother's most likely,—that I am come to think as I do: for I cannot tell myself how or when I woke out of my lethargy, only that it was not long after you went away." The change soon manifested itself in a weekly attendance at the Lord's Supper; a stricter course of conduct; and the commencement of zealous efforts to do good, which brought upon himself and his companions no small persecution, and won for them the title of Methodists.

For the details relating to his mission and complicated trials in Georgia; the joyous reception of conscious salvation on the twenty-first of May, 1738; his earnest efforts to bring his friends into the enjoyment of the same grace; the itinerant journeys which he took in preaching the Gospel; the success of his ministry in the conversion of souls; his marriage and happy domestic life; and various other important facts in his history,– recourse must be had to his biographies and his own journals. For ten years before his death he was very infirm. Early in 1788, he was almost entirely confined to the house, and the time drew near that he must die. "He had no transports of joy, but solid hope, and unshaken confidence in Christ, which kept his mind in perfect peace." Two days before his departure, after an interval of silence, he called his wife to the bed-side, and dictated the following lines,—his last contribution to that rich heritage of sacred verse which he has left as a priceless legacy to the Church and the world:—

"In age and feebleness extreme,
Who shall a helpless worm redeem?
Jesus, my only hope Thou art,
Strength of my failing flesh and heart.
O, could I catch one smile from Thee,
And drop into eternity!"

Nature's powers were now exhausted, and on March 29, 1788, "the wheels of weary life at last stood still." He was buried in the Marylebone churchyard, where a beautiful monument, erected at the expense of the Wesleyan Conference, covers his grave.

Long as the English language remains, and true spiritual religion continues to be enjoyed, the name of Charles Wesley will be fragrant among the Churches of the Lord Jesus Christ. His noble hymns, numbering several thousands, give expression to all the heights and depths of feeling proper to the spiritual life. Christian experience,—through all the gradations of doubt, fear, desire, faith, and hope, to all the transports of perfect love in the very beams of the beatific vision, Christian experience furnishes him with everlasting and inexhaustible themes, which he has illustrated with an affluence of diction and splendour of colouring rarely, if ever, surpassed. He has invested these themes with a power of truth and pathos which endears them to the imagination and affections; which makes feeling conviction, and carries the understanding captive by the decisions of the heart. These sacred lyrics have been translated into many languages of the earth, and are heard wherever Christian congregations assemble for worship. They are "sung now,"—says the author of "The Christian Life in Song,"— "in

253

collieries and copper-mines. How many has their heavenly music strengthened to meet death in the dark coal-pits! On how many dying hearts have they come back, as from a mother's lips, on the battlefield! On how many deathbeds have they been chanted by trembling voices, and listened to with joy unspeakable. How many have they supplied with prayer and praise, from the first thrill of spiritual fear to the last rapture of heavenly hope! They echo along the Cornish moors as the corpse of the tin-miner is borne to his last resting place. They cheer with heavenly messages the hard bondage of slavery. They have been the first words of thanksgiving on the lips of the liberated Negroes. They have given courage to brave men, and patience to suffering women. They have been a liturgy engraven on the hearts of the poor. They have borne the name of Jesus far and wide, and have helped to write it in countless hearts."

We must now direct attention to the last of this family group.

KEZIA, Mrs Wesley's youngest child, was born some time in March 1710. Probably through the influence of her eldest sister, then the head teacher in the establishment, she obtained a situation in a Lincoln boarding school, when she was about eighteen. Half pupil and half assistant, she boarded free and received instruction in some branches of learning as remuneration for her services. In 1730, she left "for want of money" to procure the clothes necessary for her position. Yet, like many other people, she contrived to find the means for imitating her venerable sire's bad habit of taking snuff, from which Charles bribed her to abstain, at least for a time. "Pray desire brother Charles," she writes, "to bring Prior, the second part, when he comes; or send it, according to promise, for leaving off snuff till next May; or else I shall think myself at liberty to take as soon as I please."

The natural shyness of her disposition made her shrink from company and from strangers. Her mind was painfully anxious for improvement; but a feeble constitution and almost uninterrupted illness rendered her incapable of close mental application. At Lincoln, where she had better health and more time for study, she was destitute of books. Nelson's "Manual of

Devotion," and "The Whole Duty of Man," formed her entire library, "without so much as one book in history or poetry." Her brother John, who took great interest in her, did his best to supply this deficiency, and many times gave her suitable advice. Moving along the path of life under the constant impression that she would die young, her mind was ever meditating upon her latter end. "There is no danger," she writes, "of any one's being fit for death too soon, it being a sufficient work for a whole life. Certainly, I shall not think any pains too great to use that will be any help to me in so great a work: and it would be less excusable for me to be unprepared than others; because it always was and is my persuasion that I shall die young. I am at present fearful of death; but I hope it will please God to make me willing and ready to die, before He calls me out of the world.

"None know what death is but the dead;
Therefore we all by nature dying dread,
As a strange doubtful path
we know not how to tread.'"

These feelings, in connexion with a less sanguine temperament, probably caused that indifference to all things earthly that formed so remarkable a feature in her character. When her friends pressed her to marry, and her favourite brother urged her to accept the attentions of one who had his mind drawn towards her, she replied,— "If I were inclined to enter into the holy estate of matrimony, I can't say but the man you are acquainted with might be worthy of love.

"But to a soul, whose marble form
None of the melting passions warm,"

All his good qualities would appear lighter than vanity itself. It is my humble opinion I shall live the life of a nun, for which reason I would not give one single farthing to see him this minute." When what was considered an eligible offer presented itself, she also observes, "I am entirely of your opinion that we ought to endeavour after perfect resignation; and I have learned to practise this duty in one particular, which

255

I think is of the greatest importance in life, namely, marriage. I am as indifferent as it is lawful for any person to be, whether I change my state or not; because I think a single life is the more excellent way; and there are also several reasons why I rather desire to continue as I am. One is, because I desire to be entirely disengaged from the world: but the chief is, I am so well apprised of the great duty a wife owes to her husband, that I think it is impossible she should ever discharge it as she ought. But I can scarce say I have the liberty of choosing; for my relations are continually soliciting me to marry. I shall endeavour to be as resigned and cheerful as possible to whatever God is pleased to ordain for me." And when the perfidious Hall, concerning whose offer this very paragraph was written, so basely deserted her after gaining her consent, her "perfect resignation," tested to the severest possible degree, enabled her to bear the blow with meek and unruffled fortitude. She freely forgave him the wrong, and even resided for some time with him and her sister after their marriage. We cannot accurately trace her subsequent movements. Her brother Samuel offered her a home at Tiverton, if John would pay for her board; but the offer was not accepted. After leaving the Halls at Wootton, she lived for a time among friends in London, and probably also with the venerable clergyman of Bexley, who, according to Charles, "agreed to board my sister Kezzy." She was supported by the kindness and liberality of her brothers, until her death in the spring of 1741.

From her childhood, Kezzy was particularly attentive to the duties of religion, and her disposition was eminently serious. But it was not until she came under the evangelical preaching of her brothers, that she experienced the inward and abounding joy arising from a knowledge of personal acceptance with God. Charles paid special attention to her spiritual condition, and the record of some of their interviews is deeply impressive. "Calling accidentally in the evening at my sister Kezia's room, she fell upon my neck, and in a flood of tears begged me to pray for her. Seeing her so softened, I did not know but this might be her time, and sat down. She anticipated me, by saying she had felt here what she never felt before, and believed now there was such a thing as the new creature. She was full of earnest wishes for Divine love; owned there was a depth in religion she had never fathomed; that she was not, but longed to be, converted; would give up all to obtain the love of God; renewed her request with great vehemence that I would pray for her; often repeating, "I am weak, I am exceeding weak!' I prayed over her, and blessed God from my heart; then used Pascal's prayer for conversion, with which she was much affected, and begged me to write it out for her." While he read "Law's account of Redemption, she was greatly moved, full of tears and sighs, and eagerness for more." She continued in the same temper; "convinced that all her misery had proceeded from her not loving God;" continually calling upon her friends to pray with her; "still pressing forward;" and receiving the Lord's Supper almost daily from the hands of her brother. Alas, Charles Wesley himself was not fully instructed on the doctrine of simple trust in the atonement of Christ, as the only effectual cure for those terrible conflicts and sorrows through which his amiable and penitent sister was now passing! He had been the means of producing in her heart a terrible "conscience of sin;" but he knew not the plain and simple method of deliverance. A few months afterwards, he was taught the way of the Lord more perfectly, and out of the fulness of his own experience, he "spoke fully and plainly to Kezzy." She regarded his doctrine of salvation by faith only, as enthusiastic and contrary to her experience. "My sister would not give up her pretensions to faith; told me, half angry, 'Well, you will know in the next world, whether I have faith or no!" I asked her," continues Charles, "'Will you, then, discharge me, in the sight of God, from speaking to you again? If you will, I promise never more to open my mouth till we meet in eternity." She burst into tears, fell on my neck, and melted me into fervent prayer for her."

The struggle ended in a full recognition of the doctrine of faith, and the reception of a conscious deliverance from the sins which had so much distressed her. The time and surrounding circumstances of her triumph, as well as her subsequent religious experience, are hidden from our view. But the record of her last moments, noticed in an earlier chapter, speaks of her readiness for another and a higher rest. "Yesterday," writes her brother Charles on the ninth of March, 1741, "sister Kezzy died in the Lord Jesus. He finished His work and cut it short in mercy."

In concluding these brief sketches of the sons and daughters of the Wesley Family, we are tempted to ask, —What might these children have become without the counsel and example, the care, instruction, and piety of their parents? Had Mrs Wesley and her husband, like many other heads of families, remained destitute of religion, who can imagine the all but inevitable consequences to their family and the world? In all probability their children would have grown up ignorant of experimental godliness; and though some of them might have risen to eminence in learning and worldly station, they could never have benefited the human race to any great extent; and their name, like that of many other respectable households of their day, would soon have been written in the dust. But now, is not that name more widely known and heartily reverenced than the name of any other human being? And since the days of Abraham and Sarah, and Joseph and Mary of Nazareth, has there ever been a family to which the human race is more deeply indebted? It is a solemn truth and well deserves the attention of those whom it concerns, that parental influence cannot be ignored. For good or for evil, it is ever working; and, to a large extent, it forms the character, and shapes the destiny of the children. Subtle and imperceptible it may be; but it is not the less potent or real. "As from the eyes of some individuals and the tongues of others, there issues an evil influence; as between the vital spirits of friends and relatives there is a cognation, and they refresh each other like social plants; so in parents and children, there is so great a society of nature and manners, of blessing and cursing, that an evil parent cannot perish in a single death; neither can holy and consistent parents eat their meal of blessing alone; but they make the room shine like the fire of a holy sacrifice." <sup>Jeremy Taylor</sup> And that sacred flame shall not go out when the years of their own pilgrimage are ended. The children who gathered around it in the days of their fathers, and caught their first religious glow from its Heaven-kindled heat, shall guard and feed it in generations to come; and children's children shall walk in its light and rejoice in its genial warmth. A good man, though poor as Lazarus himself, leaves a priceless patrimony to his children. For "the mercy of the Lord is from everlasting to everlasting upon them that fear Him, and His righteousness unto children's children; to such as keep His covenant, and to those that remember His commandments to do them." O, then, let the light of parental piety be like the domestic lamp placed on the lamp-stand, that it may give light to all who are in the house. Then will the blessed promise be fulfilled;—"I will pour water upon him that is thirsty, and floods upon the dry ground; I will pour My Spirit upon thy seed, and My blessing upon thine offspring; and they shall spring up as among the grass, as willows by the water-courses. One shall say, I am the Lord's; and another shall call himself by the name of Jacob; and another shall subscribe with his hand unto the Lord, and surname himself by the name of Israel."